Media matters

Critical Thinking in the Information Age

INSTRUCTOR GUIDE

CNN® Turner Le@rning™

VISIT US ON THE INTERNET
www.swep.com
www.thomsonlearning.com

South-Western EDUCATIONAL PUBLISHING
Thomson Learning™

Australia • Canada • Denmark • Japan • Mexico • New Zealand • Phillipines
Puerto Rico • Singapore • South Africa • Spain • United Kingdom • United States

South-Western Educational Publishing is a division of Thomson Learning.
Thomson Learning is a trademark used herein under license.

ISBN: 0-538-68777-0

1 2 3 4 5 6 7 8 9 0 WV 05 04 03 02 01 00 99

Printed in the United States of America

Electronic Media Limited Warranty

South-Western Educational Publishing ("South-Western") extends the following warranty to only the original customer:

Warranty Coverage

This warranty covers the media on which the South-Western software/data are recorded. This limited warranty does not extend to the information contained on the media and in the accompanying book materials (the "Software/data"). The media product is warranted against malfunction due to defective materials or construction. This warranty is void if the media product is damaged by accident or unreasonable use, neglect, installation, improper service, or other causes not arising out of defects in material or construction.

Warranty Duration

The media product is warranted for a period of three months from the date of the original purchase by the customer.

Warranty Disclaimers

The following should be read and understood before purchasing and/or using the media:

a. Any implied warranties that arise out of this sale are limited in duration to the above three-month period. South-Western will not be liable for loss of use of the media or other incidental or consequential costs, expenses, or damages incurred by you, the consumer, or any other user. Furthermore, South-Western will not be liable for any claim of any kind whatsoever by any other party against the user of the Software/data.

b. South-Western does not warrant that the Software/data and the media will be free from error or will meet the specific requirements of the consumer. You, the consumer, assume complete responsibility for any decisions made or actions taken based on information obtained using the Software/data.

c. Any statements made concerning the utility of the Software/data are not to be construed as expressed or implied warranties.

d. SOUTH-WESTERN MAKES NO WARRANTY, EITHER EXPRESSED OR IMPLIED, INCLUDING BUT NOT LIMITED TO ANY IMPLIED WARRANTY OR MERCHANTABILITY AND FITNESS FOR A PARTICULAR PURPOSE, REGARDING THE SOFTWARE/DATA AND MAKES ALL SOFTWARE/ DATA AVAILABLE SOLELY ON AN "AS IS" BASIS.

e. In no event will South-Western be liable to anyone for special collateral, incidental, or consequential damages in connection with or arising out of the purchase or use of the Software/data. The sole and exclusive liability of South-Western, regardless of the form of action, will not exceed the purchase price of the media.

f. Some states do not allow the exclusion or limitation of implied warranties or consequential damages, so the above limitations or exclusions may not apply to you in those states.

Further Disclaimers of Warranty

South-Western will extend no warranty where the software is used on a machine other than that designated on the software package.

Media Replacement

Provided that you, the customer, have satisfactorily completed and returned a copy of the License Agreement, South-Western will replace, during the warranty period, any defective media at no charge. At South-Western's option, the defective media must be returned, postage prepaid, along with proof of purchase date. Please contact South-Western at the address shown below for return instructions before returning any defective media.

South-Western Educational Publishing
Media Services
5101 Madison Road
Cincinnati, OH 45227

Legal Remedies

This warranty gives you specific legal rights, and you may also have other rights that vary from state to state.

Technical Support Hotline

The Technical Support Hotline (800/543-0453) is available to help you with any technical problems you may be having with this media product.

If you identify a problem, please check your hardware to make sure it is working properly. If the hardware is functioning correctly, call the number given. Please have the following information and materials with you when calling the hotline:

- program or template diskette
- text
- instructor's manual
- list of any error messages
- students' printouts
- description of the problem
- computer type and model
- computer's memory configuration
- version number of operating system
- name and version number of commercial software (if applicable)

Please do not permit your students access to the hotline number. If you want to order software, call (800) 354-9706. If you need product information, call (800) 824-5179.

Foreword

In an age when traditional media such as television and radio are being supplemented and even displaced by the Internet and other new media, students must develop a similarly new and sophisticated form of literacy: media literacy. We hope that MEDIA MATTERS helps students acquire that sophistication and the healthy skepticism that accompanies it. This multiple media project builds on our belief that understanding grows through two complimentary processes: deconstruction, whereby students break a product down into its parts, and construction, whereby students actively build products of their own. By tearing down and building up, they learn that media products are human products that bring with them a producer's point of view. In forming their own opinions, students learn to seek multiple perspectives and to differentiate truth from opinion and fact from exaggeration.

As one of the world's largest media companies, Time Warner has partnered with South-Western/Thomson Learning to develop MEDIA MATTERS because we believe that students must become educated consumers of media. They live in a world profoundly influenced by messages from the media, messages which flow from every television, radio, and computer, from the packaging in stores, and from the sides of buses. Even math textbooks feature consumer products in their word problems. In these last few generations, media have truly reached the masses, and they touch no one more profoundly than our youth. It is critical that, as a society, we understand the extent of this impact, and as educators, we work with students to help them grasp it.

We believe that a course on media literacy must provide students with a variety of different media—to explore, to critique, and to debate. At Time Warner we are uniquely suited to provide these examples. Our company's products embrace all forms of media, and we are exploring new ones all the time. The Time Warner brands used in this guide range from CNN (including CNN Interactive and CNN Radio), to TNT, to the Turner Entertainment Library, and from World Championship Wrestling (WCW) and Cartoon Network, to *Teen People*, New Line Cinema, and Warner Brothers Nashville. We are justifiably proud of our brands, yet we realize that as producers of the very media we have asked students to deconstruct, you may find us suspect in our endeavor. We believe this product speaks for itself. Produced by educators—both within Turner Learning, the educational division of Turner Broadcasting, and within the broader educational community—the content has been reviewed, developed, and approved by some of the leading experts in media literacy.

We put forth MEDIA MATTERS in order to start a variety of conversations: conversations about the reliability of media, the effect of media on violence, the future impact of media conglomerates—even about the possible conflicts in our nation between our First Amendment rights and our dreams of a better society. The media continually permeate our lives in new ways, and every day the terms "freedom of speech" and "freedom of the press" present us with more and more difficult choices.

The materials in this kit provide a springboard for critical thought and analysis of these issues. It is our sincere intent that the media literacy skills your students learn here help them become informed and active citizens in our democratic society. We believe that by examining the character of advertising, entertainment, docudrama, documentary, and news, students will become more critical viewers, capable of more interesting and informed arguments, well on the road to becoming better global citizens.

Instructor Guide Table of Contents

Introduction vi

"Skills and Strategies for Media Education" by Elizabeth Thoman, Founder, Center for Media Literacy IG-xii

Media Literacy Resources IG-xvi

Text of Learner Guide

Introduction

Introduction to MEDIA MATTERS: Critical Thinking in the Information Age

Overview and Rationale

The average U.S. citizen watches over 1,000 hours of television every year. This number is astonishing, yet it doesn't even take into account other forms of media exposure, such as radio, magazines, CDs, Web sites, advertising, billboards, bumper stickers, clothing labels, and other formats. These individuals need an opportunity to consider critically the many media messages that command their daily attention. *Media Matters* offers a challenging and enjoyable opportunity to interpret and evaluate these messages in order to make responsible decisions about viewing habits and consumer choices.

Of course, there are many ways to interpret media. In literature classes we give students strategies and tools by which to analyze and evaluate literature, and we teach them that literary works can be open to multiple interpretations. Likewise, learners need tools for interpreting the messages of the media, and to learn that although interpretations may differ, the goal is to think critically about the messages.

When learners understand the workings of a particular medium, they are empowered because they can question and evaluate it. They can still enjoy the medium's entertaining aspects even as they recognize its conventions, and in their critical distance they can better determine whether or not they agree with the message that the medium is presenting. The skills that they learn will help them to become more successful consumers and citizens.

Today's careers are also dependent on an understanding of information formats beyond print. Professionals need to work with and interpret computer software and videos as well as print reports. They are often responsible for multiple medium presentations. Not only must students learn how to analyze media productions, but also they must learn how to create them. International media education expert Chris Worsnop says, "Media education is not about teaching kids how to watch TV, but about using the media to help kids make sense of the world around them, and to help them be better learners themselves." Media cover the world of information and in so doing, they can be used in conjunction with communications, business, and even health education and training. Students and professionals will become better interpreters of information through the study of media.

What Is Media Literacy?

With our ever-expanding modes of communication, literacy has moved far beyond the ability to read and write competently. It has expanded to become "the ability to access, analyze, evaluate, and communicate information in a variety of formats, including print and nonprint" (*Telemedium*, "An Introduction to Media Literacy," Vol. 41, No. 2). Elizabeth Thoman, Executive Director for the Center for Media Literacy, states that "Media literacy provides the framework for better understanding the historical, economic, political, and cultural influences on media systems and messages as a foundation for informed advocacy and rational action for change—whether personal, local, national, or global." Because mass media products are an integral part of daily life, it is essential that students learn to recognize them, evaluate them, and determine their relative worth in their own lives.

The beauty of the media literacy/higher-order thinking skills combination is that students can learn important critical thinking skills by exploring media to which they are already drawn: popular music, blockbuster films, top-rated television shows, popular magazines, etc. In their work, they will be actively comparing and contrasting contemporary and time-honored media samples, problem solving, generalizing, experimenting, and creating. Media education is a high-interest means to introduce the more difficult, but essential skills involved in higher-order thinking.

Media literacy is not a particular body of knowledge. It is, instead, a set of skills, a process that one can continue to refine, just as one can build up a greater ability for reading comprehension and analysis. The point is not to memorize facts about the media; it is knowing how to ask questions about media messages. Thus, most of the questions in the student chapters do not have right or wrong answers. With media literacy, the important step is simply to question: What is the message? Is it valid? Why do I think so (or not think so)? Is it representative of real life? What is its main purpose? And so on.

Fulfilling Communications and Workplace Standards

Media Matters: Critical Thinking in the Information Age has carefully followed available state and national guidelines for media literacy by including methods of discovery and investigation, deconstruction, media recognition, comparison and contrast, analysis, interpretation, evaluation, and production of a variety of media formats and technologies. Participants will explore essential questions as a class and in small groups. In the process they will gain the skills necessary to go beyond the specific examples in order to generalize and apply their knowledge to other media experiences they encounter.

- The 1996 published *Standards for the English Language Arts* includes as its sixth standard that "students apply knowledge of language structure, language conventions, media techniques, figurative language, and genre to create, critique, and discuss print and nonprint texts."
- Texas standards state the importance of analyzing "relationships, ideas, and cultures as represented in various media," distinguishing "the purposes of various media forms such as informative texts, entertaining texts, and advertisements," and "deconstruct[ing] media to get the main idea of the message's content."
- The Secretary's Commission on Achieving Necessary Skills (SCANS) (U.S. Department of Labor, 1992) lists acquiring, interpreting, and evaluating information; and using/applying technology in the SCANS competencies required for solid job performance.

Extensive Coverage of Media Topics

All of the lessons in *Media Matters* were created with active learning in mind. Students learn by doing, both analyzing media products and building new media messages of their own. The exercises are designed to accommodate heterogeneous groupings and allow participants to capitalize on their individual learning styles and strengths.

- **Lesson 1** deals directly with the question, "Why study the media?" and shows how media education can enhance the enjoyment of media messages.
- **Lessons 2 and 3** introduce the strategies of media deconstruction and construction while exploring interesting media formats: cartoons, speeches, and docudrama.
- **Lesson 4** discusses the stereotyping that can be found in many types of media, using a teen beauty pageant as an example.
- **Lessons 5 through 13** each focus on a particular medium or genre that is especially influential in today's society:
    - news
    - entertainment in television and film
    - advertisements
    - talk shows
    - documentaries
    - radio
    - music
    - magazines
    - the World Wide Web
- **Lesson 14** challenges students to use the skills they have gained to make responsible media choices and to speak out when they suspect unfair media practices.

Flexible Lesson Design for Active Learning

Each lesson contains the same main categories to enhance organization for the instructor and student. These components are:

- **What's Ahead?** – a quick introduction to the subject of the chapter, with a few main points that will be explored further within the chapter.
- **Did You Know?** – interesting facts and statistics to further interest students in the chapter.
- **Key Terms** – media vocabulary that students will encounter in the chapter.
- **Get Started** – key information about the topic of the chapter that students need to know or question in order to complete the activities that follow.
- **Break It Down** – an activity that helps students analyze the components of a media message.
- **Sum It Up** – an evaluation of the media message and the activity.
- **Put It Together** – students create their own media messages.
- **Take It Further** – additional activities and projects for classes with extensive time to study media.

Break It Down is the main deconstruction activity of the chapter. In media literacy, deconstruction means to recognize or analyze the parts and techniques that make up a media product. These parts and techniques are examined to understand their importance to the whole production. For instance, one might notice that an extreme close-up shot placed extra emphasis on a character who previously seemed to be of minor importance.

Sum It Up gives students a chance to evaluate the media product that they deconstructed. At times, they are also asked to evaluate the worth of the activity itself. They can look over the work they have done in deconstructing a media message and consider the importance of such a skill.

Put It Together is the counterpart of a deconstruction activity. To be truly media literate, students must not only be able to understand and interpret existing media messages, but also be able to create media messages of their own. These skills also empower students to use media effectively to communicate messages that they believe are important. According to Dr. Renee Hobbs, Director for the Harvard Institute on Media Education, "There's no better way to truly understand the power of television than to create your own messages and explore the way in which images and sounds can be creatively manipulated. When young people create their own messages on video, they truly become empowered in the sense of being able to control their own environment and make a difference in the lives of others."

Special Features

Each lesson includes feature boxes drawn from the following topics:

- **Then and Now** – introduces elements of history (of the media or great historical media productions, such as *Gone With the Wind*) and compares them to their contemporary counterparts.
- **In the Spotlight** – gives students opportunities to explore careers in the media through interviews with media professionals, such as film editors, writers, and radio producers.
- **Production Notes** – creates a close-up look at tools used to evaluate media, Nielsen ratings, Web searches, and words of master media makers.
- **Ethics in Action** – explores ethical questions in the industry, such as propaganda and censorship.
- **World Views** – explores messages and issues in media production from international perspectives.

Many features include optional activities, and others include information that is likely to generate lively class discussions.

Take It Further activities and projects are suggestions for classes that have time to investigate the chapter topics more fully. However, they can also be substituted for the **Break It Down** or **Put It Together** activities in many instances.

Scheduling *Media Matters*

Each of the fourteen lessons is independent and can be used as a short unit or in conjunction with the other lessons for a more complete program. As a result, *Media Matters* can be used by a wide variety of instructors, from those who can include only a few sections into their core subject syllabus to those teaching a semester course of media education. Depending on the time, equipment, and skills of the students, instructors can incorporate and evaluate the exercises accordingly. Many require the use of video equipment. But even if your learning environment does not provide access to such equipment, it is not necessary to forego the exercises. Much can be gained by creating storyboards and writing scripts or production proposals.

In the activity-related sections, multiple options are given for exercises and projects. Instructors can pick and choose the activities and features that best suit their learners, environment, and available time.

If you are limited in time, consider ways to cut down on the time required by modifying the activities. For example, if an exercise asks students to watch a genre of show for a week, you can ask them to watch one the evening before their next class and report on it immediately. You can ask students to watch short pieces of shows rather than whole shows. The lessons are designed to allow you to select complete activities within a class period rather than carrying activities into homework when you are limited by time.

Multimedia Support Materials

A special feature of the *Media Matters* module is the large variety of excellent media examples included on video, DVD, and CD.

Please preview all media examples to be sure they are appropriate for your learners, available equipment, and course schedule.

The videotapes, DVD, and audio CD contain media examples that will bring the text to life and provide material for high-interest class discussions and debates. Classic examples from the Kennedy/Nixon debates, *Gone With the Wind*, and Martin Luther King's *I Have a Dream* are mixed with current topics and media presentations such as John Glenn's return to space, recent nuclear tests, and Faith Hill's *This Kiss* music video. Students will analyze the aim and audience of a new popular magazine and consider reasons why pro wrestling is consistently among the top ten rated television programs. See p. vi for a complete listing of the media examples and running times.

The Readings & Resources (R&R) Disk contains additional, supplemental readings along with media worksheets that can be duplicated for each lesson. See p. vii for a complete listing of the files on this disk.

Unique Features of DVD

- easy to use—audio, video, and data can be accessed easily and with great flexibility, with remote-control, mouse, or bar code scanner
- nearly indestructible
- fast and unlimited access—a user can display any segment within seconds
- special effects for enhancement of a presentation—freeze frame, slow motion, fast motion
- compact storage space—DVDs are compact, yet hold a large amount of information

A Media Matters Web site (http://www.mediamatters.swep.com) contains additional topics and activities for each lesson plus links to a variety of pertinent Web sites.

The Instructor Guide offers detailed teaching suggestions and guidelines on which media examples to use with each lesson. Graphic icons in the margins will also direct readers to go to:

- video/DVD presentations
- audio examples
- Readings & Resources disk
- Web pages

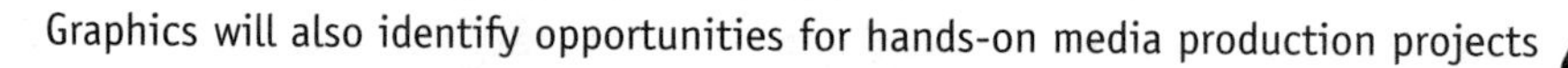

Graphics will also identify opportunities for hands-on media production projects and group projects and collaborations

.

Projects to Portfolios: Opportunities for Assessment

While assessing a student video or recording is not as clear-cut as, say, determining the correctness of a spelling quiz, there are certainly ways to make a fair and authentic assessment in media work.

Participants can keep portfolios (though if their work includes video presentations, a typical paper portfolio may not serve them completely). Worksheets included in each chapter may be turned in for the instructor's review, then put into the portfolio. Class participation and collaboration in exercises are also important components for assessments. Finally, an objective test bank is included with this module.

Canadian media educator Chris Worsnop has contributed greatly to the field of assessing media work. According to him, all communication shares five similar characteristics: ideas/content, organization, effective use of media language, voice/audience, and technical competence. Each of these five characteristics can be further broken down. In the area of ideas and content, for instance, one should find a controlling main idea, supporting details, and development of the information.

Media Matters Components

Learner Guide	*ISBN: 0-538-68776-2*
Set of 15 Guides	*ISBN: 0-538-69292-8*
Resource Package	*ISBN: 0-538-68784-3*
Instructor Guide	*ISBN: 0-538-68777-0*
Video Tape 1	*ISBN: 0-538-68779-7*
Video Tape 2	*ISBN: 0-538-68780-8*
DVD Video	*ISBN: 0-538-69232-4*
Readings and Resources CD	*ISBN: 0-538-68781-9*
Audio CD	*ISBN: 0-538-68778-9*
Test Bank	*ISBN: 0-538-68782-7*
Web Site	*www.mediamatters.swep.com*

From here, one can apply descriptions to how well a student accomplishes each task in the form of rubrics. Fairly standard descriptors involve the use of a 1–5 scale, with "5" indicating that a student has exceeded expectations; "4," usually meets expectations and occasionally exceeds them; "3," usually meets expectations; "2," inconsistently meets them; and "1," does not meet expectations. Tasks and rubrics can be charted as follows:

	Ideas & Content	Organization	Effective Use of Media Language	Voice/ Audience	Technical Competence
Level 5					
Level 4					
Level 3					
Level 2					
Level 1					

Below is an example by Worsnop of how to apply the scale in a particular circumstance:

ASSESSMENT SCALE FOR RESPONSE TO MEDIA

LEVEL 5
The student integrates personal feelings, experiences, hopes, fears, reflections or beliefs with the text. The personal response is rooted in the text, a clear understanding of the whole text and its subtext(s), and makes connections to other texts.

LEVEL 4
The student connects personal feelings, experiences, hopes, fears, reflections or beliefs with the text. The personal response refers to the text, conveys a sense of understanding of the text and partial understanding of its subtext.

LEVEL 3
The student explores personal feelings, experiences, hopes, fears, reflections or beliefs making only a superficial connection to the text.

LEVEL 2
The student retells or paraphrases the text or identifies devices in isolation making only a superficial reference to personal feelings or experiences.

LEVEL 1
The student response shows little or no interaction with or commitment to the text. The personal response may be weak, unconnected to the text or absent.

(Permission to use above materials granted by Chris Worsnop)

Worsnop's book *Assessing Media Work* is highly recommended for more specific information on setting up descriptive expectations and assessing them using charts and scales (available from Wright Communications, 2400 Dundas Street West, Unit 6, Suite 107, Mississauga, Ontario L5K 2R8; see more information at http://www.media-awareness.ca/eng/speakers/cw/medwrk.htm).

Skills and Strategies for Media Education

A pioneering media literacy leader outlines the core principles and key components of this new educational agenda.

By Elizabeth Thoman
Founder, Center for Media Literacy

In the 1990 movie *Avalon*, Barry Levinson's film portrait of an immigrant family before and after World War II, the delivery of the family's first TV set is portrayed as a significant milestone. Three generations of Krichinskys squeeze together in front of their tiny new television set and stare vacantly at a black and white test pattern. "Just wait," one of the children says, "something will happen."

And it did. Throughout the '60s and '70s, television grew from a diversion in the living room into a national obsession. From moon landings to *Leave It to Beaver*, a president's assassination to Mr. Clean, media images moved from the background to the foreground of our daily lives.

From the clock radio that wakes us up in the morning until we fall asleep watching the late night talk show, we are exposed to hundreds, even thousands of images and ideas not only from television but now also from newspaper headlines, magazine covers, movies, websites, photos, video games and billboards. Some are calling today's young people, *screenagers*.[i]

Until recently, few questioned the increasing dominance of media in our lives. Those who did were inclined to focus on content issues like the amount of sex and violence in television and movies. Some advocated censorship, while others simply urged families to turn the TV off. But the fact is, though you can turn off the set, unless you move to a mountaintop, you cannot escape today's media culture. Media no longer just influence our culture. They *are* our culture.

Elizabeth Thoman is Founder and President of the Center for Media Literacy, (www.medialit.org) *a Los Angeles-based national organization that develops model training programs and publishes and distributes media literacy teaching materials for use with children, youth, families and community groups. A former English teacher-turned-journalist, she is one of the pioneering leaders of the media literacy movement in the United States.*

Media's pivotal role in our global culture is why media censorship will never work. What's needed, instead, is a major rethinking of media's role in all of our lives—a rethinking that recognizes the paradigm shift from a print culture to an image culture that has been evolving for the past 150 years since the invention of photography and the ability to separate an object or a likeness from a particular time and place—and still remain real, visible and permanent.[ii]

For 500 years, we have valued the ability to read print in order to participate fully as informed citizens and educated adults in society. Today the family, the school and all community institutions, including the medical and health community, share the responsibility of preparing young people for living in a world of powerful images, words and sounds.[iii] Call it "media literacy."

What is media literacy?

Just what it sounds like—the ability to interpret and create personal meaning from the hundreds, even thousands of verbal and visual symbols we take in everyday through television, radio, computers, newspapers and magazines, and of course advertising. It's the ability to choose and select, the ability to challenge and question, the ability to *be conscious* about what's going on around you and not be passive—and therefore, vulnerable.

Media researchers now say that television and mass media have become so ingrained in our cultural milieu that we should no longer view the task of media education as providing "protection" against unwanted messages. Our goal must be to help people become competent, critical and *literate* in all media forms so that they control the interpretation of what they see or hear rather than letting the interpretation control them. Len Masterman, author of *Teaching the Media*, calls it "critical autonomy."[iv]

Other definitions point out that media literacy is not so much a finite body of knowledge but rather a skill, a process, a *way of thinking* that, like reading comprehension, is always evolving. To become media literate is not to memorize facts or statistics about the media, but rather *to raise the right questions* about what you are watching, reading or listening to.[v]

At the heart of media literacy is the *principle of inquiry*.

Learning What to Look For

What do kids (and adults, too) need to know about the media?

Over the years, media educators have identified five ideas that everyone should know about media messages, whether the message comes packaged as a TV sitcom, a computer game, a music video, a magazine ad or a movie in the theatre.[vi]

> **"We must prepare young people for living in a world of powerful images, words and sounds."**
>
> UNESCO, 1982

1. Media messages are "constructed."

Whether we are watching the nightly news or passing a billboard on the street, the media message we experience was written by someone (or probably several people), pictures were taken and a creative designer put it all together. But this is more than a physical process. What happens is that whatever is "constructed" by just a few people then becomes "the way it is" for the rest of us. But as the audience, we don't get to see or hear the words, pictures or arrangements that were rejected. We only see, hear or read what was accepted.

Helping people understand how media is put together—and what was left out—as well as how the media shape what we know and understand about the world we live in is an important way of helping them navigate their lives in a global and technological society.

2. Media messages are constructed using a creative language with its own rules.

Each form of communication—whether newspapers, TV game shows or horror movies—has its own creative language: scary music heightens fear, camera close-ups convey intimacy, big headlines signal significance. Understanding the grammar, syntax and metaphor system of media language increases our appreciation and enjoyment of media experiences, as well as helps us to be less susceptible to manipulation. One of the best ways to understand how media is put together is to do just that—make your own personal video, create a website for your Scout troop, develop an ad campaign to alert kids to the dangers of smoking.

3. Different people experience the same media message differently.

Because of each individual's age, upbringing and education, no two people see the same movie or hear the same song on the radio. Even parents and children do not see the same TV show! This concept turns the tables on the idea of TV viewers as just passive "couch potatoes." We may not be conscious of it but each of us, even toddlers, are constantly trying to "make sense" of what we see, hear or read. The more questions we can ask about what we are experiencing around us, the more alert we can be about accepting or rejecting messages. Research indicates that, over time, children of all ages can learn age-appropriate skills that give them a new set of glasses with which they can "read" their media culture.[vii]

4. Media are primarily businesses driven by a profit motive.

Newspapers lay out their pages with ads first; the space remaining is devoted to news. Likewise, we all know that commercials are part and parcel of most TV watching. What many people do not know is that what's really being sold through television is not only the advertised products to the audience—but also the audience to the advertisers! The *real* purpose of programs we watch on commercial TV, whether news or entertainment, is not just to entertain us but rather to create an audience (and put them in a receptive mood) so that the network or local station can sell *time* to sponsors to advertise their products in commercials. Every second counts! Indeed sponsors pay for the time based on the number of people the station predicts will be watching. The sponsors also *target* their advertising message to specific kinds of viewers—for example, women 20-35 who have the ability to spend money on the advertised products or children 2-7 who influence their parent's spending.

Maybe it's not the way we'd like it to be—but, in truth, most media are provided to us, as researcher George Gerbner says, by private, global corporations with something to *sell* rather than by the family, church, school or even one's native country, with something to *tell*.[viii]

5. Media have embedded values and points of view.

Media, because they are constructed, carry a subtext of who and what is important—at least to the person or persons creating the construction. Media are also storytellers (even commercials tell a quick and simple story), and stories require characters and settings and a plot that has a beginning, a middle and an end. The choice of a character's age, gender or race mixed in with the lifestyles, attitudes and behaviors that are portrayed, the selection of a setting (urban? rural? affluent? poor?), and the actions and re-actions in the plot are just some of the ways that values become "embedded" in a TV show, a movie or an ad. It is important to learn how to "read" all kinds of media messages in order to discover the points of view that are embedded in them. Only then can we judge whether to accept or reject these messages as we negotiate our way each day through our mediated environment.

"At the heart of media literacy is the principle of inquiry."

Learning What to Ask

From these concepts flow a series of five basic questions[ix] that can be asked about any media message. Note that each one could open up many layers of deeper questions:

1. Who created this message and why are they sending it?
2. What techniques are being used to attract my attention?
3. What lifestyles, values and points of view are represented in the message?
4. How might different people understand this message differently from me?
5. What is omitted from this message?

Usually the questioning process is applied to a specific media "text"—that is, an identifiable production or publication, or a part of one: an episode of *Mighty Morphin Power Rangers*, an ad for Pepsi, an issue of *Seventeen* magazine, a billboard for Budweiser beer, photos and articles about a bank robbery on the front page of a newspaper, the SuperBowl telecast.

Sometimes a media "text" can involve multiple formats. A new animated Disney film, for example, involves not only a blockbuster movie released in thousands of theatres but also a whole campaign of advertising and merchandising—character dolls and toys, clothes, lunchboxes, etc.—as well as a website, storybooks, games and perhaps eventually, a ride at one of the Disney theme parks.

Uncovering the many levels of meaning in a media message and the multiple answers to every question is what makes media education so engaging for kids and so enlightening for adults.

How to Question the Media

The process for examining media texts will be different depending on the setting—school classroom, afterschool program, summer camp, church youth group, a family at home—as well as the age and educational level of the participants. Several approaches, from the basic to the more complex, are possible:

- ***Core Questioning***

To be a functioning adult in a mediated society, one needs to be able to distinguish between different media forms and know how to ask the basic questions and core concepts cited above. Although most adults today learned through literature classes to distinguish a poem from an essay, it's amazing how many people do not understand the difference between a daily newspaper and a supermarket tabloid.

Increasingly as information about national and world events is delivered to the public instantaneously via television and the Internet, individuals will need to know how to verify information themselves, how to check sources and how to compare and contrast different versions of the same information in order to detect bias or political "spin" control.

Basic core questioning about the media can start as early as three or four: make a game of "spot the commercial" to help children learn to distinguish between entertainment or news programs and the commercial messages that support them. Parents can also use children's picture books to help kids understand the storytelling power of images.[x] As children grow and become able to distinguish the world of fantasy from the real world they live in, they can begin to explore how media are put together by turning the sound off during a cartoon and noting the difference it makes, or creating their own cereal box to demonstrate how advertisers package products to entice us to buy.

- ***Close analysis***

Media experiences go by so quickly that there is no time for thoughtful reflection on what is being said, how it grabs our attention and what meanings we may be taking from it. Too often our senses are bombarded for hours at a time with carefully crafted images, sounds and ideas that flow in and out of our minds, many at an unconscious or subliminal level.

While getting "caught up" in a storytelling experience has been the essence of entertainment since our ancestors told tales around the fire, the relentless pace of entertainment media today requires that at least once in awhile, we should stop and look, really look, at how a media message is put together and the many meanings that can derive from it. The method for this is called "close analysis." Use the following process on your own or better yet, with your family or a group of students.

The first step is to isolate a particular media message to examine. Commercials are often good choices because they are short and tightly packed with powerful words and images, music and sounds. Find a commercial to analyze by recording not the programs but *just the commercials* during an hour or two of TV watching! Play the tape and look for a commercial that is particularly interesting. Replay it several times. First, write down everything you can about the visuals—lighting, camera angles, how the pictures are edited together. Then turn the picture off and listen to the sound track. Write down all the words that are spoken. Who says them? What kind of music is used? Does it change in the course of the commercial? How? Are there other sounds? What is their purpose?

Once you become familiar with the surface level you'll then begin to notice more and more of what the commercial is really "saying" underneath the surface: values expressed and unexpressed; lifestyles endorsed or rejected; points of view proposed or assumed. Write down your insights along with what's left out of the message and how different people might react differently to it. Finally, reflect on whether you will accept or reject the message of this media "text," and why.

While no one has the time to subject every media message to this kind of analysis, it takes only two or three experiences with close analysis to give us the insight to "see" through other media messages in the future. It's like having a new set of glasses that brings the whole media world into focus.

- ***Action Learning (The Empowerment Spiral)***

Teachers and group facilitators have the challenge of organizing media education activities with groups of children, young people or adults. Although collections of media literacy curricula have been published in recent years (and are available through organizations such as the Center for Media Literacy), each teacher and leader needs to develop his/her own set of guidelines around which to organize classes and group meetings.

The Action Learning model has proven to be an excellent one for uncorking a spiral of inquiry that leads to increased comprehension, greater critical thinking and ability to make informed judgments. It also offers an opportunity for groups to organize for action and advocacy, especially in relation to the social impact of media in our lives and our culture—to *do something* about issues like violence in the media, stereotyping of women and minorities, the trivialization of news and the decline of an informed electorate.

Action Learning, based on the work of Brazilian educator Paolo Freire, can be summarized as a four-step "empowerment" process: *Awareness, Analysis, Reflection and Action.*[xi]

In the *Awareness step*, the group participates in some activity (e.g., counting the number of violent incidents in a children's cartoon or imitating various stances of the female models in fashion ads and magazines) that leads to the insight: "Oh! I never thought of that before." Awareness activities provide the "ah-ha" moments that unlock a spiral of critical inquiry and exploration that is the foundation of media literacy pedagogy.

The next step, *Analysis*, provides time for the group to figure out "how" an issue came to be. Core questioning and close analysis are two techniques used in this step to better understand the complexity of the selected

Three Steps to Success

How to Organize an Effective Media Literacy Program

"Media Literacy" is an overall term that incorporates three interrelated approaches leading to the *media empowerment* of citizens of all ages:

The first approach is simply becoming aware of the importance of **balancing or managing one's media "diet,"** that is, helping children and families make healthy choices and manage the amount of time spent with television, videos, electronic games, films and various print media forms.

The second approach is teaching specific skills of **critical viewing**—learning to analyze and question *what* is "on the screen," *how* it is constructed and *what* may have been left out. Skills of critical viewing are best learned though inquiry-based classes or interactive group activities as well as from *creating and producing one's own media messages.*

The third approach—**social, political and economic analysis**—goes "behind the screen" to explore deeper issues of *who* produces the media we experience—and *for what purpose?* What is the *impact of media* in our culture and how do we approach issues such as media violence, racial stereotyping and consumerism?

Through inquiry, discussion and action projects, both adults and young people look at how each of us (and all of us together in society) take and make meaning from our media experiences and how the mass media drive our global consumer economy. This approach also can set the stage for various *media advocacy efforts* to challenge or redress public policies or corporate practices.

Although television and electronic media may seem to present the most compelling reasons for promoting media education in contemporary society, the principles and practices of media literacy are applicable to all media from television to T-shirts, from billboards to the Internet.

Elizabeth Thoman
Center for Media Literacy

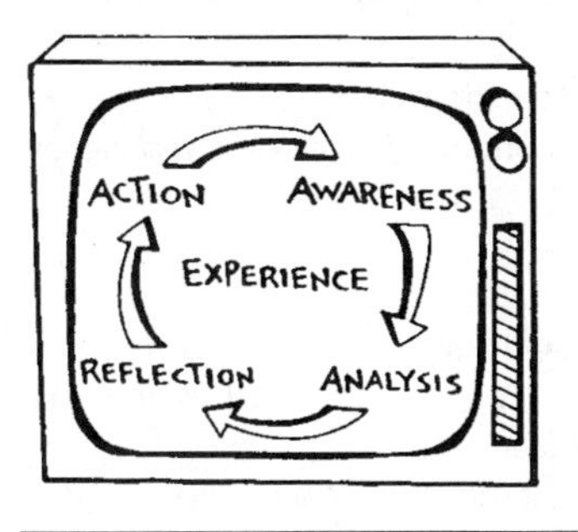

"Let's turn the one-way system of commercial media into a two-way process of discussion, reflection and action with each other and with the media themselves."

media topic. Production experiences could also help the group understand "how" and "what" happens in the exchange between a media producer and the audience.

It's important that analysis go deeper than just trying to identify some "meaning" in an ad, a song or an episode of a sitcom. Indeed, try to avoid "why" questions at all. They only lead to speculation, personal interpretation and circular debate which can stop the critical process of inquiry, exploration and discovery. Instead ask "how" and "what": *How* does the camera angle make us feel about the product being advertised? *What* difference would it make if the car in the ad were blue instead of red? *What* do we know about a character from her dress, make-up and jewelry? *How* does the music contribute to the mood of the story being told? The power of media literacy lies in figuring out how the *construction* of any media product influences and contributes to the meaning we make of it.

In the *Reflection* step, the group looks deeper to ask "So what?" or "What *ought* we to do?" Depending on the group, they may want to also consider philosophical or religious tenets, ethical values or democratic principles that are accepted as guides for individual and collective decision making. Is it right to download a map from the Internet and put it into a report without crediting the source? Does the First Amendment protect advertising? How about the advertising of dangerous products, like cigarettes? Contrast the behaviors described in the Sermon on the Mount ("Blessed are the poor in spirit. . . ") with the behaviors portrayed in a popular sitcom or a collection of advertisements.

When the forever fighting Ninja Turtles were at the peak of popularity, one young father allowed his two elementary age boys to watch the show *only* if they would imagine a fifth turtle named "Ninja Gandhi." After every episode the children had to explore with him how the nonviolent Ninja could have solved the conflict presented in the show.

Finally the *Action* step gives participants an opportunity to formulate constructive action ideas. It's important to remember that action doesn't have to be life-changing or earth-shattering. Indeed the most long-lasting actions are often activities that symbolize or ritualize increased internal awareness.

- After discovering and reflecting on the amount of violence they saw in one week of children's cartoons, one second grade class wrote a "Declaration of Independence" from violence on TV. Each child signed his/her name just like the Founding Fathers and they posted their declaration on the bulletin board in the school lobby for all to read.
- A group of teens in a church youth group put out their own 'zine to share with friends their exploration of popular music and movies.
- One young couple, concerned that their two-year-old was beginning to watch TV all the time, designated a special "blankie" to put over the TV set after viewing selected shows so that the television could take a nap, too.
- Another mom with two pre-teen girls, decided to start a family media journal in a large scrapbook with everyone adding comments about the TV shows they watched and the movies they went to see as a family.

Window of Opportunity

Today's media environment offers a window of opportunity for the introduction of media education not only in schools but throughout society. Already over 50% of the viewing audience has discovered other alternatives to network broadcasting. Over 80% of homes have VCRs and one in four people use the Internet at least weekly.[xii] Leisure time is on the rise and "quality of life" issues are a major concern for young families and the social system (schools, churches, health care, governments) that serves them.

More critically, concern around issues such as alcohol and tobacco abuse, body image and eating disorders, teen sexual behavior and the proliferation of violence have prompted teachers, parents and caregivers to examine the role that media messages play in shaping the cultural environment in which our children are growing up.

Educating young people to select their media choices, teaching people of all ages to evaluate media's underlying values and, in general, promoting a media "consciousness" is the challenge for educators, activists and service providers who recognize that for our society to flourish into the next century, we must turn the closed, one way system of commercial mass media into a two-way process of discussion, reflection and action with each other and with the media themselves.

References:

[i] Rushkoff, Douglas, *Playing the Future: How Kids' Culture Can Teach Us to Thrive in an Age of Chaos.*, 1996

[ii] From the work of Stewart Ewen, especially *All Consuming Images: Politics of Style in Contemporary Culture*, 1988.

[iii] From the Final Report, UNESCO International Symposium on Education of the Public in the Use of Mass Media, Grunwald, 1982.

[iv] Masterman, Len, *Teaching the Media*, 1989, chapter 2.

[v] From the mission statement of *Media&Values* magazine, a publication of the Center for Media Literacy, Elizabeth Thoman, executive editor.

[vi] Adapted from media education documents from England and Canada and first published in the U.S. by Jay Davis as "Five Important Ideas to Teach Your Kids about TV," *Media&Values* #52/53; Fall, 1990.

[vii] Hobbs, Renée, *Tuning in to Media: Literacy for the Information Age*, 1995 video, distributed by the Center for Media Literacy.

[viii] Gerbner, George, "Television Violence and the Art of Asking the Wrong Question," in *The World & I: A Chronicle of Our Changing Era*, July, 1994.

[ix] Thanks to Renée Hobbs for her work in articulating these core questions through her training and teaching.

[x] For ideas and suggestions see Considine, Haley and Lacy, *Imagine That!: Developing Critical Thinking and Critical Viewing Through Children's Literature*, 1994 Teacher Ideas Press.

[xi] *From Awareness to Action: Media Literacy for the '90s*, Center for Media Literacy, 1990.

[xii] *USA Today*, December 12, 1997.

Media Literacy Resources

[Unless otherwise noted, resources below are available from either the Center for Media Literacy (*) or the Media Education Foundation (**). These organizations' contact information is listed below.]

Books and Print Publications

Biagi, Shirley. *Media Impact,* Fourth edition. Wadsworth Publishing Co., 1999. *Text giving not only historical information on the media, but also a grasp of the interrelations between media and economic, social, political, and cultural forces.*

* Chen, Milton. *The Smart Parent's Guide to Kid's TV*. KQED Books, 1990. *Managing children's viewing and using TV to create positive family communication.*
* Considine, David and Gail E. Haley. *Visual Messages: Integrating Imagery into Instruction*. Second edition. Libraries Unlimited, 1999. *A guide to critical thinking and critical viewing skills.*
* Douglas, Susan J. *Where the Girls Are*. Henry Holt, 1996. *Four decades revealing mixed messages conveyed to girls and women through the media.*
* *Images That Injure*. Praeger, 1996. *Explores the subtle ways that images become stereotypes.*

Jawitz, William. *Understanding Mass Media,* Fifth edition. National Textbook Company, 1995. *A high-school text exploring mass media genres.*

* McLuhan, Marshall and Quentin Fiore. *The Medium Is the Massage*. Hardwired, 1967. *A media classic.*
* Pungente, John and Martin O'Malley. *More Than Meets the Eye: Watching Television Watching Us. A surprising, insightful, and entertaining guide to critical viewing by acclaimed media education experts.*

Rosenthal, Alan. *Writing Docudrama: Dramatizing Reality for Film and TV*. Focal Press, 1995.

* Summers, Sue Lockwood. *Media Alert! 200 Activities to Create Media-Savvy Kids*. Hi Willow Research & Publishing, 1997. *Fifty learning units for four different age groups.*
* Tyner, Kathleen. *Literacy in a Digital World: Teaching and Learning in the Age of Information*. Erlbaum, 1998. *Traces the history of literacy and its role in education.*
* Worsnop, Chris. *Assessing Media Work*. Wright Communications, 1996 (Tel. 905-823-8230). *A valuable resource giving teachers concrete guidelines by which to assess seemingly subjective projects.*

Worsnop, Chris. *Screening Images: Ideas for Media Education*. Wright Communications, 1994. *Explores theories and pedagogy of media literacy while providing practical tips and techniques.*

Computer Software

Understanding Media. New Mexico Media Literacy Project (www.nmmlp.org)

* *How to Make Your Movie,* Electronic Vision, 1997. *Lets future filmmakers explore and master the fundamental techniques of film production.*

Videos

* Anderson, Neil and Pungente, John J., SJ. *Scanning Television*. Canada: Harcourt Brace & Co., 1997. *40 short video segments on media issues. With leader's guide.*

**Buy Me That!* HBO and Consumer Reports. *Video series on advertising strategies.*

* *Is Seeing Believing?* Freedom Forum Newseum, 1997. *Video exploring the impact of digital alteration on news photography and media images.*

** *The Myth of Liberal Education,* featuring Noam Chomsky and Edward Herman. *Presents the idea that the news media are subordinated to corporate and conservative interests.*

** *Slim Hopes: Advertising and the Obsession with Thinness,* featuring Jean Kilbourne. *An in-depth analysis of how female bodies are depicted in advertising.*

* *Signal to Noise: Life with Television*. ITVS, 1996. *Three 60-minute videos on all aspects of TV culture.*

Think for Yourself: Media Literacy for the Millennium. NMSA and Quality Work Environments Inc. (1-800-528-NMSA).

* *Tuning in to Media: Literacy for the Information Age,* Renée Hobbs. Media Literacy Outreach, 1994. *An introduction to the fundamentals of media literacy by the field's leading proponents.*

Web Sites

Cable in the Classroom (www.cableducation.ca/)
Center for Media Education (www.cme.org)
Center for Media Literacy (www.medialit.org)
C. Worsnop Media Literacy Site (www.media-awareness.ca/eng/speakers/cw/WORSNOP.htm)
CNN (www.cnn.com)
Court TV Home (www.courttv.com)
Directory of International Media Literacy Organizations (http://interact.uoregon.edu/MediaLit/FA/MLDirectory)
Just Think Foundation (http://www.justthink.org/newindex.asp)
Library of American Broadcasting (www.lib.umd.edu/UMCP/LAB)
Media Literacy Clearinghouse (http://129.252.124.240:81/medialit/default.htm)
Media Literacy Online Project (http://interact.uoregon.edu/MediaLit/HomePage)
Media Matters Text Site (http://mediamatters.swep.com)
National Academy of Television Arts and Sciences, "Creating Critical Viewers On-Line" (www.criticalviewing.com)
New Mexico Media Literacy Project (www.nmmlp.org)
Old-Time Radio (www.otr.com/comedy.html)
Turner Entertainment Group (www.turner.com)

***** ***Available from the Center for Media Literacy, 4727 Wilshire Blvd., Ste. 403, Los Angeles, 90010, 800-226-9494* (www.medialit.org)**

****** ***Available from Media Education Foundation* (http://www.mediaed.org/)**

Media matters

Critical Thinking in the Information Age

CNN®

Turner Le@rning™

VISIT US ON THE INTERNET
www.swep.com
www.thomsonlearning.com

Australia • Canada • Denmark • Japan • Mexico • New Zealand • Phillipines
Puerto Rico • Singapore • South Africa • Spain • United Kingdom • United States

South-Western Educational Publishing is a division of Thomson Learning.
Thomson Learning is a trademark used herein under license.

ISBN: 0-538-68776-2

1 2 3 4 5 6 7 8 9 0 WV 05 04 03 02 01 00 99

Printed in the United States of America

Welcome to Media Matters

The Power of the Media

With *Media Matters*, you will learn to think critically by interacting with a wide variety of media messages. You will get to examine what the media is, why it is important, the power it holds, how stories are constructed, and how and why the media should be interpreted. You will analyze the kinds of media messages you see and hear *every day*—even those you think of as entertainment! In these lessons, you'll find challenging opportunities to:

- analyze television shows.
- evaluate advertisements.
- determine target audiences for magazines.
- learn the film techniques used to create particular effects.
- study the news media.
- consider song lyrics and music videos.
- evaluate Web sites.
- study popular programs like cartoons, talk shows, and professional wrestling.

You'll also learn how to create your own media projects! The media are powerful, and the more you know about them, the better equipped you will be to both interpret media messages and to create messages of your own.

Think It Through

You may not find the phrase "critical thinking" in a dictionary, but if you look at each word separately, you can figure out the importance of this term. While we often use the word "critical" to mean fault finding, it also applies to a careful analysis and evaluation of something. To think critically goes beyond memorization to analysis, assessment, and evaluation. In your study of the media, you will engage the processes of comparison, contrast, problem solving, generalizing, experimenting, and creating. These are all skills that apply not only to understanding media, but also to learning and processing information that is a part of your daily life.

The Information Age

You have probably heard today referred to as the "Information Age." With the advent of the Internet, an overwhelming amount of information is at everyone's fingertips. You may have had the experience of typing a key word into a search engine as you do research for a school project, only to

have the engine bring you 795,619 possible sites to check! Not only the Web, but also radio stations, billboards, clothes labels, talk shows, posters, buttons, and a myriad of media formats bombard us with information constantly. With so much available, it is helpful and important to know how to judge the value of the information we encounter every day. *Media Matters* will make you think critically about things that are relevant to your survival in the information age.

As you read and complete the exercises in *Media Matters*, you will learn valuable skills and lessons in media literacy by analyzing

- the purposes of media messages.
- the difference between seeing and hearing messages.
- the effects and techniques used in television, film, and radio.
- the jargon of the media world.
- the differences in news reports.
- the types of careers in the media industry.
- the problem of deception in advertising.
- the development of the World Wide Web.
- and much, much more!

The Lessons

The lessons in *Media Matters: Critical Thinking in the Information Age* feature a bold graphic design and are presented in an easy-to-follow organization:

- **What's Ahead?**—a quick introduction to the subject of the lesson
- **Did You Know?**—interesting facts and statistics
- **Key Terms**—media vocabulary used in the lesson
- **Get Started**—key information about the topic that will be needed to complete the activities
- **Break It Down**—the main activity of the lesson, usually involving a close analysis or examination of a media example
- **Sum It Up**—an opportunity to evaluate the media examples and projects
- **Put It All Together**—an opportunity to create media products and use media effectively to communicate messages
- **Take It Further**—additional opportunities to analyze and create media and investigate the lesson topic more fully

The Features

The lessons also include high-interest features with optional activities and information to spark lively class discussions.

- **Then and Now**—introduces elements of history and compares past media to the present
- **Career Profiles**—looks at a variety of careers in the media
- **Production Notes**—explains production techniques used in different media
- **Ethics in Action**—explores ethical questions in the industry
- **World Views**—presents international perspectives on media issues

The Media Resources

Media Matters includes a wide variety of current media examples to enhance the lessons—including over 100 minutes in video clips! These examples have been compiled from well-respected sources such as CNN, Time Warner, *People* magazine, the Cartoon Network, Turner Broadcasting, Inc., and the Ad Council, as well as historical examples from the past. The following graphic icons in the text identify the use of media examples and projects:

An activity that uses a video clip from the videotape or DVD video.

An activity that uses an audio recording from the CD.

An activity that uses one of the readings or worksheets on the Readings & Resources disk.

An activity that offers an opportunity to do research on the Internet.

An activity that provides an opportunity to use media production techniques.

An activity or project that provides an opportunity to work as a group.

Videotape and DVD Resources

Tape 1:

Clip #1.	Cartoon Network's *Dexter's Laboratory* episode (6:45)
Clip #2.	Martin Luther King, Jr., "I Have a Dream" (16:25)
Clips #3–9.	TNT Original: *The Day Lincoln Was Shot* excerpts (12:55)
Clips #10–11.	TNT Original: *Cold War* excerpts (3:50)
Clip #12.	CNN/Miss Universe: *Crowning of Miss Teen USA* (0:36)
Clip #13.	CNN Profile: *Miss Teen USA, Charlotte Lopez* (2:38)
Clip #14.	CNN: *Russian Fashion* (3:48)
Clips #15–16.	CNN Newsroom clips on India and Pakistan (7:42)
Clip #17.	National Archive: *Duck and Cover* (1:06)

Tape 2:

Clip #18.	WCW Thunder: *World Championship Wrestling* (5:17)
Clip #19.	Warner Brothers: *Gone With the Wind* excerpt (0:25)
Clip #20.	CNN: *Youth and Advertising* (1:08)
Clip #21.	Ad Council Public Service Announcement (0:20)
Clip #22.	CNN *Talk Back Live* with John Glenn (7:11)
Clip #23.	New Line Cinema: *Hoop Dreams* excerpt (2:06)
Clip #24.	CNN: *Media Circus: Talk Back Radio* (5:09)
Clip #25.	CBS News: *Nixon-Kennedy Debate* (2:17)
Clip #26.	Warner Brothers Nashville: Faith Hill's "This Kiss" music video (0:45)
Clip #27.	Turner Learning: *America Links Up* (2:16)
Clip #28.	CNN *Inside Politics* with Oliver North and Jesse Jackson (8:28)
Clip #29.	Student Production: "Fences: Death of the Land" (10:03)

*Note: All clips appear on the *Media Matters* DVD.

Audio CD Resources

(Running Time: 25:00)

Track #1.	Martin Luther King, Jr., "I Have a Dream"
Track #2.	TNT Original: *Cold War* excerpts from soundtrack
Track #3.	Ad Council Public Service Announcements
Track #4.	CNN Radio
Track #5.	CBS News: *Nixon-Kennedy Debate*
Track #6.	Warner Brothers Nashville: Faith Hill's "This Kiss"

Readings & Resources Disk

File name	Contents
Alert	Lesson 1 Worksheet
Cartoons	Lesson 1 Worksheet
Twain	"Two Views of the River" by Mark Twain
Dream	Lesson 2 Worksheet
Logic	Lesson 2 Worksheet
King	"I Have a Dream" by Martin Luther King, Jr.
FilmTech	Lesson 3 Worksheet
Johnson	Interview with Writer/Director, Mark Steven Johnson
Celebs	Lesson 4 Worksheet
Stereo	Lesson 4 Worksheet
News1	Lesson 5 Worksheet
News2	Lesson 5 Worksheet
Council	Articles on nuclear testing in India and Pakistan
Talks	Articles on nuclear testing in India and Pakistan
Threat	Articles on nuclear testing in India and Pakistan
Hypoc	Articles on nuclear testing in India and Pakistan
India	Articles on nuclear testing in India and Pakistan
HaysCode	Motion Picture Production Code of 1930
Entertain	Lesson 6 Worksheet
Wrestling	Lesson 6 Worksheet
PrintAds	Lesson 7 Worksheet
TVComm	Lesson 7 Worksheet
AdAppeal	Advertising Appeals and Techniques
Closeup	Lesson 8 Worksheet
TalkShow	Lesson 8 Worksheet
ShowHost	Articles by and about popular talk show hosts
Document	Lesson 9 Worksheet
Docudrama	Lesson 9 Worksheet
Radio	Lesson 10 Worksheet
Kosovo	*CNN Interactive* article on Kosovo conflict
WhyRadio	Articles on the popularity of radio
Music	Lesson 11 Worksheet
Survey	Lesson 11 Worksheet
ThisKiss	Lyrics to "This Kiss" by Faith Hill
MagCov	Lesson 12 Worksheet
MagArt	Lesson 12 Worksheet
Forster	Interview with Magazine Writer, Barbara Forster
Reason	"A Reason to Live" by Margaret Nelson from *Teen People*
Websites	Lesson 13 Worksheet
Influence	Lesson 14 Worksheet
Responsibility	Lesson 14 Worksheet

Internet activities for each lesson can be found at www.mediamatters.swep.com.

Credits

Media Matters Writers

Rita Anderson
English Teacher
Eagan High School
Eagan, MN
Virtual High School
(http://vhs.concord.org)

Michael Bergen
Communication Arts Teacher
East Appleton High School
Appleton, WI

Barbara Forster
Freelance Writer
Boston, MA

Christopher Gegen
Technology Specialist
Gwinnett County Public Schools
Lawrenceville, GA

Holly Littlefield
Teaching Faculty
University of Minnesota
Minneapolis, MN

Beverly June Lum
Educational Curriculum Specialist
(Hawai'i Department of Education,
Waianae High School, Campbell
High School)
Honolulu, Hawai'i

J. Lynn McBrien
President
The Learning Toolbox
(www.tltoolbox.com)
Conyers, GA

Marcia Nehemiah
Media Teacher
West Morris Central High School
Chester, NJ

Sue Lockwood Summers
Director, MEDIA ALERT!
Library Media Specialist
Westgate Elementary School,
Jefferson County Schools
Lakewood, CO

Fran Trampiets
National Media Literacy Trainer
& Adjunct Faculty
School of Education
University of Dayton
Dayton, OH

Writer for Lesson 2

Kathleen Tyner
Consultant
Media Analysis & Practice
San Francisco, California

Turner Learning Staff

Senior Editor and Project Manager
J. Lynn McBrien
President, The Learning Toolbox
(www.tltoolbox.com)
Conyers, GA

Executive Producer
Lucy Levy

Senior Producer
Audrey Schewe

Video Producer
Jennifer Ware

Copyeditor
Andrew McMurry for Merrill-Hall New Media

South-Western Staff

Vice-President/Director of Publishing
Peter McBride

Team Leader
Eve Lewis

Project Manager
Laurie Wendell

Editor
Alan Biondi

Production Coordinator
Patricia Matthews Boies

Manufacturing Coordinator
Kathy Hampton

Marketing Manager
Mark Linton

Marketing Coordinator
Tricia Allen

The publisher is grateful for the suggestions and contributions of the following reviewers:

Michael Bergen
Communication Arts Teacher
East Appleton High School
Appleton, WI

James Brooks
English Department Chair
Chaminade-Julienne High School
Kettering, OH

Nicole Hochholzer
English/Communications Teacher
Kaukauna High School
Kaukauna, WI

Steven Schoen
Language and Literature Division
Mt. Hood Community College
Gresham, OR

Fran Trampiets
National Media Literacy Trainer
& Adjunct Faculty
School of Education
University of Dayton
Dayton, OH

Contents

Lesson 1
But I Just Want to Relax!
An Introduction to Media Literacy

What's Ahead?

Goal: This lesson is intended to motivate students to study the media. While they are likely to think of media mainly in terms of entertainment or relaxation, they will learn that a critical understanding of media will not only produce healthy skepticism, it will enrich their enjoyment too.

Disciplines: The contents in this lesson pertain to language arts, history, and business.

Objective: Upon completing this lesson, students will be able to:

- Define key media terms associated with media education.
- Realize that media is carefully constructed, and just like other creations, it has a purpose.
- Realize that the sum of their unique experiences cause them to interpret media messages in individual ways.
- Use reflection and analysis to discover the values and messages intrinsic to the media they view.

Ask students to brainstorm about their favorite ways to relax. Question them to get them to be specific. Look at how many of those answers are media dependent (even answers such as "I go to the mall" will be connected to many types of media: designer labels, sale papers, logos on clothes and at restaurant chains within the mall, etc.)

LESSON 1

But I Just Want to Relax

What's Ahead?

In this text you are being asked to bring the microscope to some favorite forms of relaxation: TV shows, movies, magazines, music, and radio. It may not make sense to you to study media that you enjoy during your leisure time, but suspend your judgment for a moment, and consider this: The subject of this course is something you *like*. If you fall within average statistics, you probably spend more time watching television than you do attending classes. For this course, your homework will have you doing more of what you enjoy the most—paying attention to the media.

Additionally, while you may not have spent time studying the media, you can be sure that media makers have spent plenty of time and money studying you. Why? Most media companies are for-profit businesses, and to be successful they need to produce media that you will watch, listen to, and read. In this course you will learn more about how they do this, and you will learn how to examine media to determine what you like and dislike about the messages.

Main Points to Ponder

- *All media are constructed.* They have a purpose and are carefully designed to evoke a particular response in their audience. The main purposes of media are to inform, entertain, persuade, and sell.

MEDIA MATTE

Discuss the bullet points:

- What purposes could media have? (Ask for examples of informative, persuasive, and entertainment media.) Review points of view studied in literature classes to help students realize the variety of perspectives media can have (first person observer or participant, third person omniscient, limited omniscient, and objective). Ask the class for examples of these points of view from favorite TV shows, movies, or cartoons.
- To help students understand the third bullet, choose a movie that most of them have seen. Ask for their reactions to the movie. They will see how much their opinions differ.

Because media constructions have a purpose, they necessarily contain a particular point of view. The audience must first determine the message, and then decide whether or not they agree with it.

Media messages are received differently by different individuals. Because everyone brings his or her own set of experiences and values to interpreting media messages, individuals' conclusions will differ. The meanings they find may also differ from the original intent of the writers and directors.

Did You Know?

The average U.S. citizen watches 1,000 hours of television every year.

In 1991, three out of four U.S. households owned a VCR.

In 1993, demand began for a "V-chip" to block out violent television.

A dozen nations banned or restricted satellite dishes in 1994.

Key Ideas

Consumer - a person who buys or uses goods or services; one who buys or devotes time to media products.

Ethics - the study of standards of conduct and moral judgment. One shows ethical behavior by acting according to socially acceptable and moral standards.

Mass Media - communications media capable of reaching a large number of people at the same time, such as newspapers, radio, television, Internet.

Media Literacy - the ability to access, analyze, interpret, evaluate, and create many kinds of media.

Medium - (plural, media) the mode by which something is communicated; for example, radio, television, the Internet.

Target Audience - the audience that the writers and producers have in mind when creating and distributing media messages.

Ask students to consider why they react to the movie the way they do. See if they can make connections between the movie and their own lives—likes, dislikes, beliefs, etc.

Did You Know?

Ask students if they are surprised by the statistics in the section. You might discuss what the implications of these statistics are.

Materials

This lesson uses:

- "Maternal Combat" from Cartoon Network's *Dexter's Laboratory* (Video clip #1 - 6:45)
- Mark Twain's "Two Views of the River" (File name *Twain* on Readings & Resources Disk)
- Alert to the Media Worksheet (File name *Alert* on R&R Disk)
- Cartoons Worksheet (File name *Cartoons* on R&R disk)

Key Ideas

Make sure students understand the differences between similar items in the **Key Ideas** box. Ask how they usually hear the term "literacy" being used. In general, it refers to people who can read and write, but more than that, a literate person is one who understands what he or she reads and who is capable of writing effective prose. Someone who is media literate, therefore, is capable of understanding the various types of media and analyzing them for meaning. Additionally, media literate people can create their own media messages, though they may not have the equipment to create elaborate productions.

Get Started

While this lesson focuses on the pervasiveness of television, students are encouraged to begin recognizing how constantly they are immersed in media. To help students see the need for media education and for active involvement with the media, use the following questions for discussion. You may want to discuss them prior to having students complete the worksheet **Deconstructing the Media: Alert to the Media.** The media journal is likely to demonstrate to students that they pay more attention to the media than they think they do.

Get Started

While the term "media" encompasses a large array of communication vehicles—print, radio, billboards, CDs, Web pages, and so forth—there is little doubt that the most influential of today's media, at least in the United States, is television. About 90 million homes in the United States include at least one TV, more than have a telephone.

Ever since television first became popular, critics have argued that the inactive nature of viewing television, even educational programming, has robbed children of hours of experiential, active learning so essential to their development. At its worst, television is seen to deliver beliefs and messages, including violent and unhealthy ones, that young children often watch without adult supervision or the ability to analyze and evaluate.

At its best, television can transport its viewers to worlds of information and experiences that they may otherwise never know. Public television brings audiences into the Kennedy Center for world-class dramatic performances. Travel documentaries transport viewers to exotic islands and adventure safaris. Networks and cable channels provide up-to-the-minute world news reports that were unimaginable throughout most of the history of humankind.

Whether television (or any other form of mass media) subverts its audience, as many critics suggest, or is used to serve the audience is largely determined not by the industry, but by the audience itself. People who are aware of media techniques and purposes can gain the most by enjoying and learning from media while maintaining a healthy dose of skepticism about what they see, read, and hear. Anyone can become an active respondent to media by simply taking the time to think about the messages. What are the purposes of the media in your environment? What do you like about the media messages you view? What portion of them do you want to evaluate and even reject?

Tower of Televisions

Courtesy: PhotoDisc/Nick Koudis

2 MEDIA MATTERS

1. How much time do you devote to your favorite pastimes? How much of it is active? Passive? Do you think this matters? Why or why not? How much time do you think you spend watching TV on a daily basis?
2. Does homework gets in the way of the time you would spend watching TV? Which do you think is more valuable, and why?
3. Do you admire the characters in your favorite shows? Do you want to be like them? Why or why not? Do you agree with the messages that are implied in your favorite shows?
4. What television ads come to mind? Why? Do you buy (or want to buy) the products whose ads you best remember?
5. Do you like music for its lyrics or its instrumentals? Do you know the words to your favorite songs? Do you like the words? Do you agree with them?
6. What was the last movie you saw at the cinema? Why did you go to see it? Did you like it? Why or why not?
7. Do you subscribe to or regularly purchase magazines? Which ones, and why? Do you read the ads as well as the articles? Do you ever go buy items you see advertised? What details about the ads persuade you?
8. What types or categories of media do you avoid? Why?
9. Do you have particular media sources that you consciously watch, read, or listen to in order to be informed about the world? What are they, and why do you choose them?

Additionally, discuss their feelings about positive and negative aspects of television. Do they believe that TV affects the thoughts and actions of its viewers?

Break It Down

Cartoons may be the ultimate in media relaxation and escape. They show up in many media formats: newspapers, magazines, television, movies, and online. Cartoons even have their own cable channel: the Cartoon Network. While some cartoons have secondary purposes (such as satire and social criticism found in political cartoons), most are constructed with a simple purpose in mind: to make us laugh, to entertain. Think of some cartoons you watched as a child. Why did you watch them? What did you like about them? Do you watch any now? Do they differ from those you watched as a child? In what ways?

Video Clip #1

Cartoon Network's *Dexter's Laboratory*

"Maternal Combat"

For this exercise, you will view the television cartoon "Maternal Combat" from the series *Dexter's Laboratory*. As you watch, pay attention to what you enjoy and what makes you laugh. Notice, too, what, if anything, makes you uncomfortable or what you find offensive. Determine the purpose, point of view, and your own reactions to the clip. Answer the questions on the worksheet **Deconstructing the Media: Cartoons** (p. 7). Discuss your reactions in class.

Cartoon Network's *Dexter's Laboratory*

THEN AND NOW

Changing Cartoon Characters

How they've changed! Cartoon characters, that is. Have you ever viewed a vintage cartoon character and compared it to a version of the same character from the 70s or 80s? Mickey Mouse is a classic example. Over his lengthy cartoon existence, there have been many changes in Mickey's appearance, voice, his antics, and the way he relates to other familiar characters.

Full-length cartoon films have changed dramatically as well. The oldest were created by Walt Disney Studios, and they include *Snow White, Sleeping Beauty,* and *Fantasia.* You probably are familiar with these feature films. Think of ways in which they contrast to modern animated features such as *Pocahontas, Mulan,* and *A Bug's Life.* How do these changes in cartoons written primarily for young viewers reflect our changing society? What might they be "teaching" their audience?

Break It Down

Students may initially think cartoons require little analysis. But as they examine "Maternal Combat" (**Video Clip #1**), they will discover that, while it is entertaining, this cartoon contains examples of violence and sexism.

The exaggerations and stereotypes in cartoons are less subtle than the complex messages found in programs aimed at mature audiences. Students will be able to identify the ways *Dexter's Laboratory* uses a mad scientist boy and his simple but savvy sister Dee Dee to poke fun at sibling and family relationships. For example, the scene in which an entire house is destroyed with robot controls will provide them with better material for practicing media analysis than a realistic-looking scene from a police series.

Consider the differences between this comic scene and the typical action scene. You might ask, "What makes this scene funny and the police one sad?" (Possible answer: the exaggeration of the cartoon versus the more plausible scene in the police story). Ask further, "While we may laugh at the scenes of violence in the Dexter cartoon because they are unrealistic, how might the intended audience of young viewers be affected?"

Students might bring up some of the controversial cartoons, such as *South Park, Beavis and Butthead,* and *The Simpsons.* Try to steer students away from a simple discussion of the relative "coolness" of such cartoons and toward a more thoughtful application of the analytical techniques they have just learned. Also bring up for discussion the full-length classics, such as *Snow White* and *Bambi,* and newer ones, such as *Aladdin* and *Tarzan.*

THEN AND NOW

As students discuss cartoons from past eras and from today, they may note many of these differences: Changes in costume; different facial appearances; changes in the voices of characters (especially note how old cartoons signal gender with husky male voices, such as those of Popeye and Brutus, and very high-pitched female voices for characters such as Minnie Mouse and Olive Oil); changing roles for males and females; more sophisticated animation in recent cartoons; different levels of violence (Elmer's modest shooting at Bugs versus GI Joe's blasting away of whole buildings).

Sum It Up

Based on their analysis, students should come up with a list of criteria for evaluating a media clip. They may include criteria such as how well the content serves its purpose and how appropriate the content is for its intended audience.

As the students discuss their answers to the evaluation, use their responses to review the key concepts in this lesson about media construction, purpose, point of view, and audience reaction.

1. Students are likely to discover that they saw details in "Maternal Combat" that they would have passed over if they were not consciously examining it. Examples might include the comments about mother's work, the build of the robots, and the parody of the video game, "Mortal Kombat."
2. Their thinking about cartoons may now be broader, recognizing just how much goes into creating the complete piece. Details could include the sound effects, characterization, and the particular devices used to create laughter (exaggeration, violence overdone to the point of being ridiculous, and the humor of a father oblivious to destruction, capable of greeting two robots as "Honey").
3. Answers will probably be mixed. Students are asked to reflect on the effect of analyzing something that they might normally watch without thinking about it. You might want to hand out to students "Two Views of the River" by Mark Twain (**File name *Twain* on the Reading and Resources disk**) in which Twain records his different feelings about the river before and after acquiring his river pilot expertise. His emotions, too, are mixed.

Sum It Up

Now that you have analyzed "Maternal Combat," evaluate it with the fo lowing questions:

- How well does it achieve its purpose?
- How appropriate is it for its intended audience?
- How much of its content can you enjoy or consider acceptable?
- How much do you dislike or consider unacceptable?

Now that you have taken apart a media sample, ask yourself the follow questions:

1. Did you learn anything about cartoons in general that you did not know before? What?
2. Did what you learn cause you to think about the medium different In what ways?
3. Did your study of the cartoon spoil your enjoyment of the cartoon Explain.

ETHICS IN ACTION

Violence in Programming

George Gerbner, Dean Emeritus of the Annenberg School for Communication and founder of the Cultural Indicators Project, which scientifically analyzed the impact of television on society and the lives of citizens, contends that the quantity of violence on television encourages viewers to believe that violence is normal. The media present the world as more violent than it is. The more television people watch, the more they see the world as a dangerous place in need of strict law-and-order measures such as capital punishment, increased building of prisons, and stricter punishment for offenders according to Gerbner.

Is it ethical to include violent scenes in young children's programming? What about movies targeted at young adults, such as *Scream* and *The Faculty*? Why do you think violence is there to begin with? Can you think of content alternatives that would attract an audience?

Name some movies or programs (or other media, such as magazines, Web sites, radio stations, and "junk mail") that you feel uphold high ethical standards. How do you define such standards? Do you think the general public would concur with your definition? Do you like these media? Why or why not?

Hold a debate in class in w half of the class argues in favor allowing any content to be place media and the other half argues media organizations ought to be ther regulated by the governmen self-regulated to uphold high mo and ethical standards. After ten utes, switch sides. When you hav had the chance to argue both sid discuss what it felt like to defen both sides. Did you learn from it which side do you really stand?

ETHICS IN ACTION

Violence in Programming. A major reason that scenes of violence are in films is because they sell. Students should consider the role of business and economics in the decisions to include this violent content. Why does violence sell? Violent scenes can be informative (in *Schindler's List*) or largely entertaining (in *The Mask of Zorro,* in which the good guys win and the sword fighting scenes add excitement and enjoyment). In the debate, students are likely to bring up the issues of free speech, self-regulation, and censorship.

'ut It Together

elop your own idea for a high-interest program that is appropriate for eneral audience. Write a cartoon or work with a story you know. You work alone or in groups. Consider carefully the main points you have died in this chapter: media construction, purpose, point of view, and ience. What must you include to best get across your message? How you make it engaging and keep the attention of your audience?

at basic elements of media construction may be most important to your creation: staging and props, casting (the appearance and/or personal- of your actors or cartoon characters), background sounds, music? De- be the most important aspects of your show. You may need to write a ple pages of script, describe personalities, gather music or sound sam- , and draw or cut out examples of your characters. Present your pro- and be prepared to answer questions about your choices.

'ake It Further

Be an active watcher of your favorite TV show. What is its purpose? How does the show convey its meaning? From what point of w is the show told? Do you relate to any of the characters? In what s? What changes would you make to the show?

Create your own idea for a new TV series or major motion picture. What is its purpose? What ideas will it communicate, and how? are the main characters, and what are their backgrounds, interests, beliefs? Where and when does the story take place? How will you ad- tise your new production to its target audience?

Research and write an essay on the topic of violence in the media. Make the paper persuasive by taking a side: Do you agree or agree that violence in the media has serious implications? Support your ition with statistics, experts' opinions, and true stories.

SSON 1: BUT I JUST WANT TO RELAX! 5

Put It Together

Students need to learn not only how to analyze a media sample, but also how to create their own media messages. The **Put It Together** exercises throughout the book are project-based media constructions that enable students to creatively use the information they learned in the **Break It Down** and **Sum It Up** sections.

Help students brainstorm ways to present their projects to the class. The artists, for example, may want to create sketches using overhead pens on clear plastic sheets so that the cartoons can be seen easily by the class.

Help students become involved with questions by getting students to go beyond "I like it." Ask "Why do you like it? What is appropriate about the choices? Why are they made? Do they make the product more or less appropriate for its target audience?"

Take It Further

These extension activities are suggested for classes that have time to study media education in depth, over several days.

1. This exercise allows students more opportunities to be critical viewers of media while enjoying a favorite program. It also helps them to separate the fantasy world of the show from their own reality.
2. This activity is similar to the **Put it Together** exercise, but it allows students more freedom in their choice of subject matter. Challenge them to create a show that would both entertain and educate.
3. Help students brainstorm where they can go to research their favorite stars: the Internet, magazines, newspapers, books, TV shows about entertainment. Have them consider: are certain types of media more likely to provide me with information than others? (If they are researching popular contemporary stars, the Web and magazines are better sources than traditional research materials such as books and encyclopedias.) Ask them to question the reliability of their sources by checking several sources. Is the information they find consistent?

Alert to the Media

1. Look for students to mention radio, TV, newspapers, ads, mail, or magazines. Chances are that they often have media in the background but are not always paying direct attention to the media.
2. Each answer should include a variety of media examples.
3. Try to think of incidents in which students have referred to TV programs or commercials, music, magazines, etc. as examples.
4. Help students to brainstorm by asking them how much they talk about favorite shows, stars, musicians, etc.
5. Answers will vary considerably. You might also ask whether the amount of time is their decision, or whether it is controlled by someone else in their home.
6. Studies indicate that some students actually study more effectively with background noise. This experiment will help students to discover the best circumstances for their study time.
7. It is likely that at least some students have chosen TV over an outing on some occasion.
8. This question is designed to help students separate what is popular to watch from what really reflects their own values.
9. Answers will vary. Check to see whether the activities chosen are, indeed, media free.
10. Students should notice differences in advertising between their favorites and media they would not normally choose to see, read, or hear.

WORKSHEET

Alert to the Media

File: Alert

Learn just how much time you devote to media every day and how much impact this has on you. Keep a media journal for one week. Include the following information in the journal.

1. What media are part of your morning routine? How much direct attention do you give to the media? If none, or very little, can you still remember details from what you heard, read, or saw?

2. On your way to your first class, how many media messages do you see and/or hear, and what are they? (These can include billboards, clothing labels, jingles sung by other students, radio, vending machines, bumper stickers, buttons.)

3. How often do students refer to media during the course of discussions in other classes? Specifically, what types of media do they discuss or use to argue a point?

4. How often do you converse with your friends about TV shows, movies, or advertisements?

5. How many hours do you devote to homework? How much time do you spend watching TV or movies?

6. One day, study with absolutely no additional media as "background noise." Observe whether or not you are more focused and faster at completing your work with or without background media. Record your observations about differences.

7. Do you ever decline to participate in an activity in order to watch a TV show? Write about it.

8. What messages are media delivering to you? How do you feel about these messages?

9. Do at least one activity during the week that is completely media free. Describe the activity, your reactions to it, and how difficult it was to come up with such an activity.

10. For a minimum of 30 minutes, watch or listen to media that you would not ordinarily choose. It might be a news show, a documentary, a classical or public service radio station, a special-interest magazine, or newspaper. Describe the experience. Also notice the sponsors/advertisers. Do they differ from those that you see in programming you usually listen to or watch?

WORKSHEET

Deconstructing the Media

Cartoons

File: Cartoons

After viewing "Maternal Combat," answer the following questions:

1. What is the purpose of the cartoon? Do you think it achieves its purpose? Why or why not?

2. Who is the target audience for the program? How do you know? What material is included to appeal to a broader audience?

3. Is the action appropriate for its intended audience? Why or why not?

4. Describe some of the best creative scenes or techniques used in the clip.

5. Why do you think that cartoons are popular?

6. Should the public be concerned about scenes of violence and sexism in children's cartoons? Why or why not?

SSON 1: BUT I JUST WANT TO RELAX! 7

Cartoons

1. The ultimate purpose of the cartoon is humorous entertainment. It is also a satire on female stereotypes and technology. Whether or not it achieves its purpose is largely a matter of individual taste, but look for students to justify their responses.
2. The target is primarily older children. The characterizations and comic situations can be used as proof. Satirical elements that require an audience to have background on other topics, such as characterizations of mothers, and media, especially "Mortal Kombat," broaden the appeal to an older, more informed audience.
3. Some are likely to object to the violence and the destruction of the home as inappropriate for children.
4. Answers will vary, depending on taste. Some are likely to enjoy the creativity in the baked pie scene; others will like the satirical allusion to "Mortal Kombat."
5. Responses may include humorous and creative elements.
6. Answers will vary. Many are likely to express concern about sexism and violence in children's cartoons because of correlations between media use of these topics and violent, sexist behaviors in children.

Lesson 2 Tools of the Trade: *Learning to Analyze the Media*

What's Ahead?

Goals: The "Tools of the Trade" lesson offers practice in the media analysis technique of "deconstruction." Similar to the explication of literary texts, deconstruction is presented in this lesson as a way to probe the meaning and significance of electronic media. The lesson takes students through the deconstruction of image, print and televised media using Dr. Martin Luther King's speech, *I Have a Dream*. The goal is to extend students' understanding of literacy to include a wider range of electronic media. Additionally, it presents the main elements of argumentation and persuasion. These will be found in many media messages that students study throughout the text.

Disciplines: The contents of the lesson pertain to language arts, history, technology, and the arts. A **Take It Further** exercise relates to science.

LESSON 2

Tools of the Trade

What's Ahead?

We usually associate literacy with the ability to read books. But we now use many other media for learning, entertainment, and the expression of our ideas. In addition to traditional print media, our ideas find expression in radio, television, and the Internet. We refer to the ability to understand and use all of these forms of expression as *media literacy*.

You may know about literacy tools such as pen and paper, video cameras, and computers, but the most important literacy tool is your own active mind. When thinking is combined with speaking, listening, viewing, and doing, you will find that media literacy can enhance the way you experience the world. In this lesson you will learn to ask the questions that will help you get the most out of media.

Main Points to Ponder

- The form of media contributes to meaning. For instance, an audience may interpret the same event as heard on the radio or seen on television differently.
- Historical contexts contribute to meaning. Over time, events may be viewed and interpreted differently. As contexts shift, so do the meanings of media messages.
- Media analysis and production work together. To be media literate, one must be able to analyze media products and create new ones.

8 MEDIA MATTE

Objectives: Upon completing this lesson, students will be able to:

- Understand the relationship between print and electronic literacy.
- Deconstruct media in a variety of forms by using media terms associated with production.
- Compare the way that different media forms influence the presentation of content.
- Understand that the historical contexts of media messages are important.
- Use critical questions to investigate the meaning of media messages.
- Identify elements of argumentation and persuasion.

Scholars disagree on the exact definition of literacy. They generally agree that it is an important "social event," but balk at overgeneralized, sweeping definitions. If asked to define the term "literacy," most students will probably think of the traditional meaning, e.g., the reading and writing of print. Ask students to talk about why literacy is an important skill. Make a list of literacy tools that

Did You Know?

American Sign Language consists entirely of hand and arm movements and is the primary means of communication used by the hearing impaired in North America.

Closed captioning was required as a feature of every TV set manufactured in the U.S. after 1980. Originally used by hard-of-hearing or deaf individuals, captioning is now used by others to learn to read, to learn English, or to watch more than one show at once.

In the 1950s, Marshall McLuhan foresaw the ability to videotape movies and replay them on TV sets long before it was technically possible. He called the technology *television platters.* *(Source: P. Marchand.* Marshall McLuhan: The Medium and the Messenger. *[Boston, Ticknor and Fields, 1989], 101)*

Key Ideas

Aesthetics-the study of art, its creative sources, forms, and effects.

Context-the complete situation or background of an event or production.

Deconstruction-in media literacy, recognizing or revealing the parts and techniques that make up the media product. An example might be to notice that a shot in a movie was a special effect rather than a "natural" shot or to notice that there is a cut in a chase scene just before the hero jumps off the cliff into a chasm of raging water.

Figurative Language-words used not in their usual or literal sense; words used symbolically to go beyond literal meaning, such as "The tired tree dropped its leaves." Similes and metaphors are examples of figurative language.

Genre-the French word for *kind* or *type;* it refers to the category of the medium. For example, the medium of television contains genres such as advertising, news, sports, and soap operas, and the medium of film contains genres such as comedy, adventure, and drama.

people use to communicate their thoughts (e.g., pen, pencil, books, computers, speech, video cameras, printing presses, etc.). If possible, divide the list into reading tools and writing tools. For example, a book might be a reading tool, but a computer can be both. Ask each student to prioritize a list of the top three media they use most. Tabulate students' responses to see how the various media rank in order of importance for the class as a whole. Then discuss what importance these literacy tools have to society. This will illuminate students' preconceptions about literacy.

Materials

This lesson uses:

- Martin Luther King, Jr.: *I Have a Dream* (Video clip #2 - 16:25)
- Text of "I Have a Dream" (File name *King* on R&R disk)
- "I Have a Dream" Audio CD Track #1
- "I Have a Dream" Worksheet (File name *Dream* on R&R disk)
- Logical Argumentation Worksheet (File name *Logic* on R&R disk)

Did You Know?

The facts given here refer not only to modern technology but also to important historical breakthroughs in the history of media and communications. Talk about how things like Braille, Morse code, and sign language are important media.

Key Ideas

"Deconstruction" is a term that represents a key concept in media literacy. As all media messages are creations, or "constructions," one must be able to take apart, or "deconstruct," the whole into its various parts to understand fully their effects and the ways in which they work together. As students progress through their workbooks, they will learn more about the pieces of media construction: language, sound, camera techniques, target audiences, financial impact, genre, stereotypes, etc. The more they work with these elements, the more carefully they will come to view and interpret the media that surround them, and they will be more likely to make mature and sophisticated media choices.

Get Started

The concepts in this section help students to think about ways in which they can go beyond simply understanding the surface content of any given medium. The concepts represent a broad summary of tested curriculum content from international media educators. The ideas are intended to serve as underlying principles for teaching about media. Ask students to work in small groups to write down a specific example for each concept to share with the class.

The form of media contributes to meaning. Students will have an opportunity to reflect on the uniqueness of various media as they experience Martin Luther King's *I Have a Dream* speech in print, audio, and televised formats. Some media messages will not work equally well in different media. For instance, a food pyramid would be difficult to explain without the benefit of a graphic. It would not lend itself to a radio presentation. Students may have distinct preferences about content and the medium chosen to represent it. To demonstrate this, ask how many students will watch a televised sport, but not listen to it on the radio. Who prefers it on the radio? Are there any that prefer to get their sports information from the newspaper?

Historical contexts contribute to meaning. Rarely do we respond to anything in isolation. We interpret what we receive in light of our culture, current trends and fashions, social views, contemporary beliefs. It may be very hard, if not impossible, for students to respond to King's speech in the way it was received during the civil rights movement. Adults who lived through the sixties feel it was a monumental decade, but today's students may find it less inspiring. All the same, we can gain more understanding of a media piece when we make the attempt to discover the social backgrounds of the time in which it was created.

Media analysis and production work together to promote literacy. Deconstruction is essential work in understanding the media, but it is only half of the work. Just as we instructors learn more about our subject matter when we must teach it, students learn more when they must create their own media messages. Having to actually work with the elements they observe in media examples will increase their awareness, memory, and competence with the techniques.

Get Started

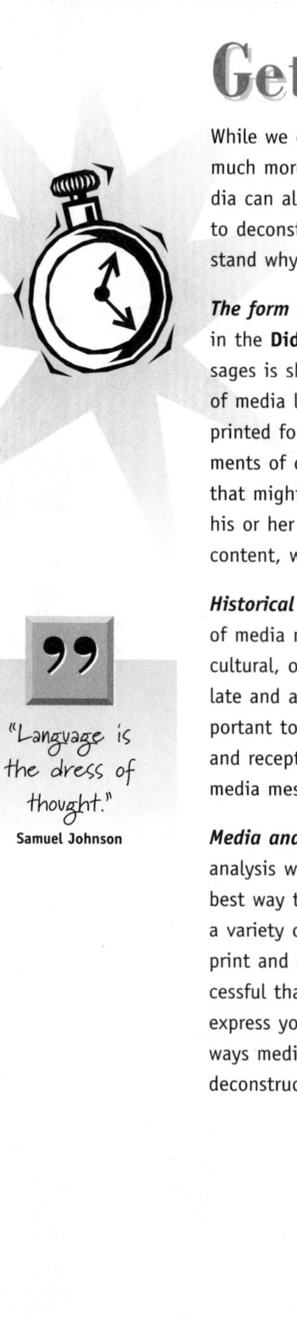

While we often associate mass media only with entertainment, they do much more than keep audiences amused. As you learned in Lesson 1, media can also inform and persuade. To understand how, you must be able to deconstruct media. The following key points will help you better understand why and how to do this.

The form of media contributes to meaning. Marshall McLuhan (mentioned in the **Did You Know?** section) believed that the content of media messages is shaped by the form of each medium. For example, televised forms of media lend themselves to short and concise treatments of issues, while printed forms of media often provide more detailed and complex treatments of content. But print media cannot give readers the understanding that might be gained from seeing a video or listening to a speaker deliver his or her words. By knowing how the form of each medium can influence content, we can use a variety of media to their best advantage.

Historical contexts contribute to meaning. The production and reception of media messages depend upon the prevailing economic, political, social, cultural, or historical conditions of the time. While it is necessary to isolate and analyze the form and content of media messages, it is also important to recognize the historical factors in play during their production and reception. These underlying factors contribute to the meaning of a media message and can be referred to as *contexts.*

Media analysis and production work together to promote literacy. Media analysis works with media production like reading works with writing. The best way to find your own voice is to practice making your own media in a variety of forms. These forms include speech and movement, as well as print and electronic media. Some of your productions will be more successful than others, but it is important to experiment and try new ways to express yourself clearly. In the process, you will learn more about the ways media are constructed. Constructing your own media will help you to deconstruct media created by others.

A Deconstruction Toolbox: *Asking Key Questions about Media Content, Form, and Contexts*

Questions are the tools for thinking critically about media. A good question may not even have one correct answer. Facts are important, but it is also important to speculate about possible answers to media questions and then to follow up with more research to back up your ideas.

Following are sample questions that you can ask every time you want to think about media. Try to think of other questions that you might want to ask as you deconstruct media.

Form - includes such elements as the genre within the medium; media technologies (video, print, digital); the "look" or style of media (composition, special effects, graphics, overall aesthetic, etc.); and, especially in the case of digital media, the ability to navigate or use the information easily.

1. What genre is it?
2. What technology is used?
3. What aesthetic choices did the producer make to convey the message?
4. How do form and content work together?
5. How would you create the message differently?

Content - the message intended by the producer or writer.

1. What is the basic story line?
2. Who produced the media message?
3. Who owns the content?
4. Who is the audience?
5. How is the subject represented?
6. How would you present the message differently?

Contexts - larger historical, economic, cultural, or social factors that influence a media message.

1. Why was the media message produced?
2. What larger factors influenced the media message's form and content?
3. How much did it cost to produce the media message?
4. What were some barriers to production of the media message?
5. How did audiences receive this message in the context of its time?
6. How would audiences receive the message now?

PRODUCTION NOTES

A Deconstruction Toolbox: Asking Key Questions about Media Form, Content, and Contexts. The Deconstruction Toolbox offers the kinds of questions that can be used to investigate a wide range of media. The purpose of asking these questions is not to find "correct" answers, but to practice the process of questioning media with students. One good way to introduce the Deconstruction Toolbox is to choose a media text that you know well, such as a textbook chapter or video clip, and practice asking questions about it using the Form, Content, and Context questions. Then students will be ready to use the questions provided in this lesson.

Break It Down

The *I Have a Dream* speech is a popular topic for a classroom lesson, and students may have read the speech before. Here they will be given the opportunity to take a fresh look at the speech in order to consider its effects as presented in various media formats.

An underlying purpose of the *I Have a Dream* activity is to provide an opportunity for students to practice the deconstruction of different media forms. Students will be asked to deconstruct the text of *I Have a Dream* and then to compare and contrast it with their analysis of the speech in audio and televised forms. (The text is on the R&R disk in file name *King*.) In the process they should learn to identify the basic rhetorical structures of the speech: main points, supporting arguments, and conclusions. In addition, they will have an opportunity to explore Dr. King's uses of metaphor and allusion in the speech. Finally, the speech will lead them to the greater themes and contexts of the Civil Rights Movement of the 1960s.

Using the **Deconstructing the Media: *I Have a Dream*** worksheet, students will take time to first listen, then carefully read the text of the speech and answer some questions. Ask students to share their worksheet responses with the class. Review the Deconstruction Toolbox by asking those critical questions about the text of Martin Luther King, Jr.'s speech.

Listen to the speech **(Audio CD Track #1)**. Watch the televised version of Dr. King's speech with the class **(Video Clip #2)**. Rewind the tape and point out examples of camera techniques in the first few scenes of the video clip. In the next lesson, students will explore camera usage and vocabulary in more depth, but they can still note the differences between times when the camera does a close-up on King and times when the crowd is the subject of the lens. Ask them to consider the effect of going from King to the crowd. How does this affect the audience?

King's speech is frequently anthologized in college readers as an excellent example of an argument that appeals to the emotions. An example of an historical document often anthologized as a logical argument is *The Declaration of Independence,* in which specific acts of England are listed as objections and as reasons for cutting the ties with the British Empire. Students can use that (found on the Web at http://www.law.indiana.edu/uslawdocs/declaration.html) or a more contemporary logical argument for **Deconstructing the Media: Logical Argumentation.**

Break It Down

The Deconstruction Toolbox can be used to examine one of the most famous speeches in the history of the United States. On August 28, 1963, the Reverend Martin Luther King, Jr. delivered a speech from the steps of the Lincoln Memorial to a crowd of more than 200,000 people. Dr. King's speech has come to be known as the *I Have a Dream* speech. The context of this speech is the Civil Rights movement of the 1960s. What do you know about this period and about Dr. King? See how much you can find out by reviewing the appropriate sections of a history book, an encyclopedia, or the Web or by talking to people who were teens or adults during this time period.

Martin Luther King, Jr.

Martin Luther King, Jr. License granted by Intellectual Properties Management, Atlanta, Georgia, as exclusive licensor of the King Estate

Martin Luther King, Jr.: "I Have a Dream"

This lesson will begin by focusing on the concept of media form. You will compare the speech in written, spoken, and televised formats. Pay close attention to the different media elements that are used: text, sound, and visuals.

Listen to the speech as delivered by Dr. King. Pay attention to how Dr. King speaks—his use of volume, emphasis, pauses, and rhythm. After listening, read Dr. King's speech and reflect upon your reaction to the written version of the speech. Words are powerful, and Dr. King, chose each word carefully for his *I Have a Dream* speech. Using the worksheet **Deconstructing the Media: *I Have a Dream*** (p. 15 and 16), read and reflect on the words of his speech (answer questions 1–7). The worksheet also asks you to analyze the contents of the speech as you look at the language Dr. King chooses to address his audience. Discuss your answers in class.

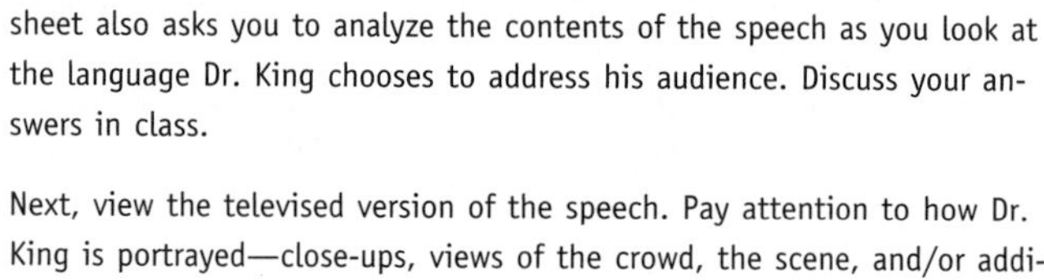

Next, view the televised version of the speech. Pay attention to how Dr. King is portrayed—close-ups, views of the crowd, the scene, and/or additional sounds that you might not have noticed on the audio version. Answer the remaining questions on your worksheet.

Video clip #2

um It Up

npare all three versions and expand your knowledge by using the Destruction Toolbox to analyze Dr. King's *I Have a Dream* speech in
th. How do they differ? What does the audio version do best? The
tten version? The televised version? Which do you prefer and why?

"I look to the day when people will not be judged by the color of their skin, but by the content of their character."

Martin Luther King, Jr.

ut It Together

nk of an issue about which you feel very strongly. Write a persuasive
ech in which you use some of the techniques you discovered when you
lyzed Dr. King's speech. Practice delivering the speech, then tape it on
assette or have another student videotape you giving the speech. Break
o groups of four or five so that all the students in your group can read
l hear or see your tape. Discuss how the message is received differently
the different media. Determine each medium's strengths and weak-
sses.

ETHICS IN ACTION

e Power of Language

THICS There are two principal types of persuasion: an appeal to one's reason so called "logical argumenta-n"), and an appeal to one's emo-ns (sometimes called "emotional umentation"). Logical arguments presentations in which a state-nt or belief is supported using ical, rational appeals to the in-ect such as facts, statistics, ex-t opinions, or research. Emo-nal persuasion uses figurative guage and illustrations that evoke an emotional response in the audience. The tools of an emotional argument include metaphors, allusions, hyperbole, and repetition.

Figurative language, while not literally factual, can be used to clarify facts and strengthen the resolve of the audience. America had not literally "defaulted on this promissory note," but Dr. King's words eloquently capture decades of actual racial injustice. Find other examples in Dr. King's speech in which his words are not literally true but do accurately represent realities and create strong visual images that move the audience. Why do you think Dr. King relies heavily on figurative language?

Think of media messages that use language in persuasive but nonliteral ways. How do they affect you? Do you usually take the time to interpret the rhetoric in order to determine the truth behind the words?

Sum It Up

Use the Toolbox to deconstruct the televised version of the *I Have a Dream* speech. Pay particular attention to the context of the production. As you ask questions, check for understanding, and make a list on the board of those questions that prove difficult for students. Assign students to provide factual material for those questions either by going to the library, their textbooks, or the Internet, or by interviewing a relative or neighbor with first-hand knowledge of the era.

Put It Together

This construction activity asks students to create their own speech, based on the techniques they have learned analyzing the *I Have a Dream* speech. They will have to create their own persuasive language and come up with logical arguments to sway their audience.

Be sure that students understand the importance of having a clear and focused premise to support. If their point is too broad, they will not be able to support it sufficiently with just three main arguments. Go over the logical fallacies (located in the Web-based information for this lesson) to help students avoid faulty logic.

ETHICS IN ACTION

The Power of Language. The power of persuasive language can be very effective in motivating an audience to positive action, but it can also be used to manipulate an audience. George Orwell points this out effectively in his important essay, "Politics and the English Language" (excerpted on the Web at http://home.earthlink.net/~chalquist/orwell.html). In general, emotional language is most effective with an audience that already agrees with the argument but that may need to be motivated to action. Skeptical audiences are more likely to be convinced by logical arguments that use plain language, clear facts, and authoritative statements as proof.

For an activity, you can have students choose a newspaper editorial and analyze it for emotional language. Have them consider which audience might respond to the editorial and who might be offended by it.

Take It Further

The first activity asks students to consider different media formats in deconstructing a science news topic. You could also ask them to construct their own news presentation about the topic using the information they gathered while investigating the subject in various media formats.

Exercise #2 has students using comparison and contrast to analyze media formats. The third activity is perhaps the most inventive, as students need to role-play in order to consider the role of historical or social contexts.

Take It Further

1. Choose a scientific or medical topic that interests you. Collect articles or document news coverage about the story from at least three of the following sources: (a) the Internet; (b) the local newspaper; (c) a large, national newspaper; (d) a magazine; (e) television. Use the Deconstruction Toolbox to analyze what you have learned. Then track the topic for two or three weeks to see how coverage of the story changes over time. Do you see differences in the coverage between the various sources? Does the story build, or does it drop out of sight? Where is the story placed in the newspaper or televised coverage? Do you think the story reflects good science? Is it fair and balanced? Document your findings.

2. Read the front section of a city newspaper and watch a national news broadcast for the same day. Take notes. What are the lead stories of each? What information do you get from the paper that you do not receive from the television, and vice versa?

3. Choose a different historical time period or country in which the beliefs and perspectives are very different from your own. Research the time or place so that you know specifics about the social or historical context. Pretend you are from that time or place while watching a current TV show or movie. Aside from the obvious confusion (the time or people may not have had TVs or movies!), write about the conventions and beliefs that confuse you as you watch the program.

Spacecraft Exploring Mars

Courtesy: PhotoDisc/PhotoLink

WORKSHEET

Deconstructing the Media

I Have a Dream

File: Dream

Reflect and comment on your reaction to the speech by answering the following questions:

1. Why do you think Dr. King chose to say "five score years ago"? What does this phrase mean? Does it sound familiar to you? Where have you heard something similar?

____

____

____

2. Metaphors are powerful symbols that are used to represent other things. For example, Dr. King uses a financial term, "promissory note," to symbolize the promise of justice. What is a promissory note? What other metaphors does Dr. King use to make his points?

____

____

____

____

3. Repetition is a powerful rhetorical device. It drives home the speaker's points again and again and makes them memorable. List the places where Dr. King uses repetition to his advantage in the speech.

____

____

____

____

4. List and explain examples of language in Dr. King's speech that creates an emotional appeal. What kind of audience do you think would be most affected by an emotional appeal? Who is Dr. King's target audience?

____

____

____

I Have a Dream

1. Five score refers to 100 years. (A score is equal to 20.) A similar phrase is used by Abraham Lincoln in "The Gettysburg Address," causing the audience to reflect back to another powerfully important speech.
2. A promissory note is a written promise to pay someone a specified amount on demand or by a specific time. There are many other metaphors used in the speech. They include: slaves "seared in the flames of withering injustice," a "joyous daybreak to end the long night of captivity," ". . . sadly crippled by the manacles of segregation and the chains of discrimination," living on "a lonely island of poverty," "America has given the Negro people a bad check," and many more.
3. Repeated phrases include "One hundred years later," "Now is the time," "Go back," "I have a dream," and "Let freedom ring."
4. Most of the metaphors conjure emotional pictures of suppressed African Americans. These would appeal the most to African Americans and to those sympathetic with King's call for civil rights. These people are his target audience.

5. Answers will vary.
6. Students may remark that they have more time to think about the images when they are able to read it, but they may be moved more by listening to King's powerful speaking voice.
7. Again, opinions will vary, but many will react emotionally to seeing the powerful images of the crowd at the Lincoln Memorial, King's face, and the scenes of racial violence and "whites only" signs.
8. Students may concentrate on words less, but they may connect more strongly to the emotions conveyed, and they may empathize more with the crowd.
9. This is an interesting question to explore. Certainly students may think of the newer special effects available today and of the inevitable newscaster's commentary accompanying the actual event. This may be the first time your students have seen historical footage of scenes disallowing African Americans' entrance to restaurants, waiting rooms, bathrooms, and drinking fountains. For those who lived in this historical period, the images can be very powerful. It will be interesting to see just how much they move today's young adults.

5. After you have studied the text of *I Have a Dream*, choose a passage that you find particularly moving and talk about why the passage resonates with you.

____
____
____
____

6. Do you understand the speech better when you can read at your own speed as opposed to listening to it? Does your opinion of the speech change?

____
____
____
____

7. How do you feel when you watch the video of Dr. King's *I Have a Dream* speech? In what ways, if any, do you change your feelings or opinion about the speech?

____
____
____

8. Is the addition of the visual element captivating or distracting to you? Do you find that you concentrate on the words more or less?

____
____
____

9. What do you notice about what is actually televised and how it is positioned (close-ups, shots of the crowd, etc.)? Do you think this event would be televised differently if it happened today? In what ways? Would you have filmed this event differently? How?

____
____
____
____

WORKSHEET

Deconstructing the Media

Logical Argumentation

File: Logic

Think of a logical argument you may have studied before. Read or watch it again, looking for the elements of a logical argument: premises (assumptions or grounds for the argument), supporting arguments or axioms (facts, sayings, proverbs, experiences) that back up the points, and conclusions. In the table below, write down the premises, supporting arguments or axioms, and conclusions you find in the argument.

Premises	Supporting Arguments or Axioms	Conclusion(s)

Logical Argumentation

You may need to direct students to arguments that are considered logical. "The Declaration of Independence" is one frequently used, as it has clear arguments, evidence, and conclusions. Scientific evidence generally follows a logical argument of theory, gathering evidence, and arriving at conclusions. Students may want to look at the work of Rachel Carson or respected environmental groups to find examples. Historical texts also use examples to arrive at conclusions about events.

You may want to remind students that logical arguments are not necessarily right. Rather, their method of presentation is different from emotional appeals. See if students can think of arguments that have been presented in a logical format but with which they do not agree. History is a great source. When once all students used to accept that Christopher Columbus should be a national hero, for instance, because he "discovered America," today's students may use new evidence to suggest that he did not discover America or that he does not deserve high praise because of the barbaric tactics he and his crew used against natives.

Lesson 3 Lights, Camera, Action! *The Tools of Audiovisual Media*

What's Ahead?

Goals: This lesson introduces students to some major tools of filmmaking. By taking a closer look at lighting, editing, camera angles, music, and sound effects, students will learn how each of these components plays an integral part in shaping how the audience will respond to a specific scene.

Disciplines: The contents in this lesson pertain to language arts, history, and technology.

Objectives: Upon completing this lesson, students will be able to:

- Define key media terms associated with film production.
- Realize that there is an assortment of filmmaking tools such as lighting, editing, sound, and camera angles that affect how a scene impacts the viewer.
- Deconstruct various film clips to analyze how a few specific filmmaking tools impact a scene.
- Create their own dramatic scene using audiovisual techniques.

LESSON 3

Lights, Camera, Action!

What's Ahead?

While watching a movie, you probably find yourself having different reactions to various scenes. One minute you're wide-eyed with anticipation; the next, you're cringing, afraid of what you might see. What is it that makes us react this way?

While movie plots are written to be romantic, suspenseful, or funny, they are enhanced by numerous techniques that further intensify the genre. In this lesson, you will learn about a few of the many crafts involved in movie making and how they play an integral part in swaying audience responses.

Main Points to Ponder

- Movies can be classified into different genres that set up certain audience expectations. Action/adventure is one genre, and viewers know to expect an hour and a half of nonstop, nail-biting action.
- The director's use of filmmaking tools, such as sound effects and film scores, will heighten the emotional experiences of the viewer.
- Through the use of various camera angles, the director attempts to shape the viewer's responses. Camera angles can let viewers know where the action is taking place or help form opinions about a character's qualities, without a word of dialogue being spoken.

18 MEDIA MATT

Ask students to create a list of their favorite films or films that had the most impact on them. Have the students explain what it was about the films that left such an impact. Try to get the students to be as specific as possible. Note how many refer to the actual devices of creating a film in their comments prior to reading this lesson.

Have the students make a list of the different genres or categories of filmmaking. After making the list, ask the students what they normally think of when they think of each category. Do certain categories of movies have certain reputations with students? Along the same lines, when they think of actors, do they expect a certain type of performance from them?

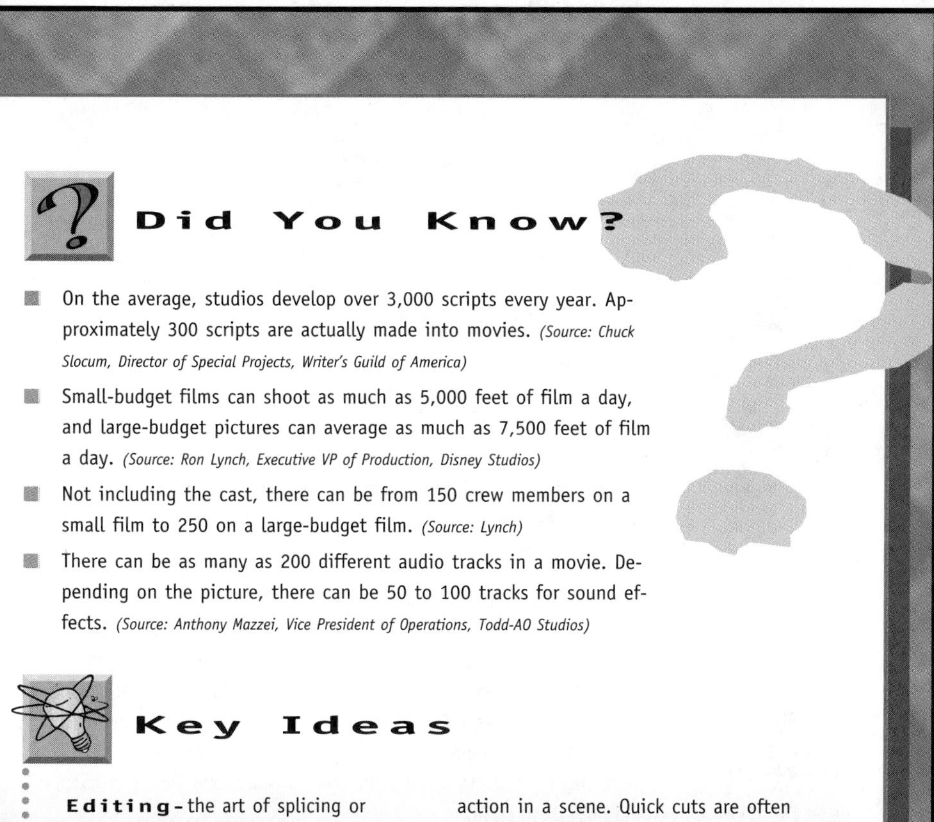

Did You Know?

- On the average, studios develop over 3,000 scripts every year. Approximately 300 scripts are actually made into movies. *(Source: Chuck Slocum, Director of Special Projects, Writer's Guild of America)*
- Small-budget films can shoot as much as 5,000 feet of film a day, and large-budget pictures can average as much as 7,500 feet of film a day. *(Source: Ron Lynch, Executive VP of Production, Disney Studios)*
- Not including the cast, there can be from 150 crew members on a small film to 250 on a large-budget film. *(Source: Lynch)*
- There can be as many as 200 different audio tracks in a movie. Depending on the picture, there can be 50 to 100 tracks for sound effects. *(Source: Anthony Mazzei, Vice President of Operations, Todd-AO Studios)*

Key Ideas

Editing - the art of splicing or putting together film clips in a sequential order to tell a story. Today most films are edited on computer.

Film Score - background music for a movie. Often it includes a theme song.

Foley Artist - technician who creates the sounds that can't be recorded properly during the shoot.

Pan - to rotate a camera from side to side to create the impression of a continuous view, or to follow an object with the camera.

Quick Cuts - a series of very quick shots from many angles that follow the action in a scene. Quick cuts are often used in chase or high-action sequences.

Still - either a photograph blown up from a frame of motion picture film or a photograph taken by a photographer of the production set and used for promotional purposes.

Zoom-in/Zoom-out - zooming refers to changing the framing of a shot. Zooming in moves from a wide-angle shot to a telephoto, or close-up, shot. The effect is to draw attention to the person or object receiving the close-up. Zooming out is the reverse technique, used to place the person or object in a larger context.

LESSON 3: LIGHTS, CAMERA, ACTION! 19

Did You Know?

The information shows students just how much crafting and shaping goes into the final product.

Key Ideas

Discuss the terms and ask students to give examples.

Ask the students to list as many different jobs on the movie set as they can think of. (For fun, you could show the closing credits at the end of a full feature movie and look at some of the more unusual jobs listed.) Then have the students narrow down their lists to the four or five jobs that they think have the most impact on them as the viewer. Ask why they chose their particular list.

Materials

This lesson uses:

- Film clips from TNT's *The Day Lincoln Was Shot* and CNN's *The Making of The Cold War* that illustrate color, lighting, camera angles, edits, sound, and music (Video clips #3-11 - 16:45 total)
- Complete text of interview with Mark Steven Johnson (File name *Johnson* on R&R disk)
- Soundtrack from CNN's *The Cold War* (Audio CD Track #2)
- Film Techniques Worksheet (File name *Filmtech* on R&R disk)

Get Started

Have students recommend a film that they have seen recently and explain to the class what it was about the movie that made it worth suggesting. Ask:

- When you go to the movies do you pay attention to the lighting, camera angles, editing, score, or sound effects?
- Do you think any of those components have an impact on you?
- What are some of the memorable components in suspense or action/adventure films that you have seen?

Break It Down

Use the worksheet **Deconstructing the Media: Film Techniques** section by section as you show and discuss the numerous short clips that illustrate the filmmaker's tools.

Working from the emotion list, show "Color and Lighting" clips and ask the students to associate emotions to the film based solely on the light and color. Chances are that they will arrive at the same conclusions as the filmmakers: bright colors tend to conjure happy thoughts, and dark colors are more reflective and somber, even mysterious.

Have the students refer to the worksheet to further break down and analyze how the different filmmaking tools impact the scenes. Be sure to rerun the clips after students have volunteered their answers, to see which responses were more accurate than others. Have the class continue to refer to their emotions lists to see what techniques correspond to which emotions.

Get Started

How is it that a movie audience can scream in terror at one scene and laugh out loud at another? While an audience may not think about this question, a film's cast and crew may work together for over a year to create a film that will elicit the desired response.

Before a frame of film is ever shot, the director meets with the director of photography, the production designer, and the costume designer to discuss the look and mood of the film. They take into account how the color of the sets and costumes, along with the lighting, will cause the audience to react. Once principal photography has begun, the director and director of photography rehearse scenes and determine what camera angles will be most effective in complementing the actors and their dialogue.

During filming or after principal photography is complete, the director works with the movie's editor. After selecting the best "takes," the director and editor splice together the different angles to establish a rhythm that complements the scenes. For example, an action scene will consist of quick cuts to give the scene a frenetic feeling. In a dramatic sequence, there may be more zoom-ins, stills, and only a few cuts, because the dialogue is most critical to moving the story forward, and excessive cutting would be a distraction.

During or after the process of editing, sound effects and the film score are added. Sound effects, such as rustling leaves or a clock's alarm, are used by the director and editor to accentuate and make real what is taking place on screen. Some people would argue that the score is the single most influential component of the process. Imagine *Jaws* without John Williams' frightening film score or *Titanic* without James Horner's lyrical music.

As you can see, the emotions you feel as you watch a scene unfold aren't just left to chance. A careful, deliberate choice of music, sound, light, color, costume, editing, and camera angles by the director and his or her creative team contributes to your response and ultimately determines the film's success.

"I am a camera with its shutter open, quite passive, recording, not thinking."
Christopher Isherwood, from *A Berlin Diary*

Break It Down

Now that you have a better understanding of how films are put together, analyze some film clips from the TNT Original *The Day Lincoln Was Shot* to discover how the director's tools direct not only the film, but also the emotional responses of the viewer. As you watch, answer the questions on the worksheet **Deconstructing the Media: Film Techniques** (p. 27) for each production element discussed.

Video clips #3–9
TNT Originals
The Day Lincoln Was Shot

Color and Lighting

In preproduction, remember, one of the first things the director does is to collaborate with the director of photography and the production designer to determine color and lighting that will create the desired effects. How do directors know what colors to use?

After answering questions one and two on the worksheet, watch the clips your instructor plays for color, lighting, and corresponding emotions created by the scenes. Compare these observations to your answers to the first two worksheet questions. How do your answers compare with the director's choices?

Lance Henrikson as Abraham Lincoln in the TNT Original *The Day Lincoln Was Shot*

Camera Angles

Where to place the camera and what to show of the scene or actor are conscious decisions intended to evoke specific responses. If the director is successful, you will feel just what he or she has in mind.

High-angle shots—when the camera is placed above the scene and pointed toward the action—can make the subjects look small and powerless. Low-angle shots— pointing the camera up toward the subject—have the opposite effect, allowing the subject to appear strong, large, and superior. Panning allows a camera operator to capture a wide scene. It can also mirror how a character may scan an area, or it can reveal something that was previously hidden or unknown.

Identify emotions you associate with the next film clips based solely on the camera angles.

"The best thing about the future is that it comes only one day at a time."
Abraham Lincoln

Nine separate film clips are provided to demonstrate the numerous techniques described in this lesson. Use various combinations to illustrate the techniques. Most can be used more than once.

Clip #3 - The opening scene of *The Day Lincoln Was Shot* includes good examples of quick cuts, sound effects, close-ups, and use of shadow and light. In it, Booth makes his escape; then the film cuts to his death scene.

Clip #4 - A ballroom scene in which an elated John Wilkes Booth declares his love to Lucy Hale. Techniques demonstrated are use of color, continuous camera, close-ups, and zoom-out.

Clip #5 - As President Lincoln comments on the fall of Richmond, the camera operator uses a low-angle shot to make Lincoln appear larger than life.

Clip #6 - Booth is shown in a rage. This scene is effective in its use of camera angles, quick cuts, and sound effects.

Clip #7 - A dream sequence in which Lincoln foresees his death. Editing uses a jerky, slow motion and black and white film to suggest the dream. Sound effects are also important here.

Clip #8 - After Lincoln is shot, this clip juxtaposes the frenzied crowd against the calm shock in the balcony. As Lincoln is brought through the crowd, cuts go from individuals to the crowd.

Clip #9 - The murder of Booth moves rapidly from a frenzied scene in the burning barn, using unnatural camera angles and effects, to a somber, quiet scene using dark against light and blurred backgrounds against the sharper focus of Booth's hands and his face.

Clip #10 - Michael Narduzzo, dubbing mixer for *The Cold War* series, shows the use of a soundboard.

Clip #11 - Series producer Martin Smith and composer Carl Davis talk about the film score for *The Cold War* series. **Audio CD Track #2** contains musical excerpts from the Soundtrack.

Editing

The way the director and editor piece the different camera angles together creates the pace, energy, and excitement of a scene. Quick cuts and plenty of camera movement are the main ingredients in creating an action sequence that grabs the viewer's attention. Just as powerful, however, are close-ups and few, if any, cuts of an actor watching a loved one say goodbye.

While watching the next film clips, identify your emotional responses and the editing techniques you observe. Are the techniques successful? Would you do the scenes differently? Why and how?

Video clips #10 and 11
CNN's *The Making of History: The Cold War*

Sound Effects

You may often associate certain memories with sounds. When you hear a particular sound, such as breaking glass or a siren, it triggers a specific response. The director and sound editor are well aware of the impact sound has on a viewer, and they work closely to elicit specific emotional responses. Additionally, accurate sound effects add to the realism of a movie.

Watch the clip on *The Cold War* sound technician Michael Narduzzo as he demonstrates a soundboard. Discuss your worksheet answers in class.

Film Scores

Even when films were silent, a lone piano player in the theater would heighten the mood with appropriate pieces of music associated with comedy, danger, love, and suspense. Think about your favorite movies. Can you remember the music played in them? How was music used? How did it evoke emotional responses that corresponded to what was happening in the film?

Listen to the musical score on audio CD that your instructor will play. After answering question 11 on your worksheet, watch the video segment on the musical score from *The Making of History: The Cold War,* and complete the worksheet. In class, discuss the comments of the documentary's composer.

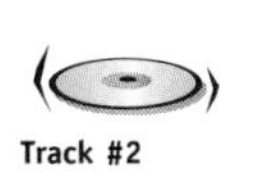

Track #2

CNN's *The Cold War* soundtrack

IN THE SPOTLIGHT

Mark Steven Johnson, Writer/Director

Mark Steven Johnson wrote the screenplays for *Grumpy Old Men* (1993), *Grumpier Old Men* (1995), *Big Bully* (1996), *Jack Frost* (1998), and *Simon Birch* (1998). In his interview he talks about directing *Simon Birch.*

Chuck Slocum, director of special projects with the Writers Guild, states that everything originates from the script. As both a writer and director, do you agree with his statement?

Yes, everything has to come from the page. When I met with the director of photography for *Simon Birch,* all he would do is reference the script and the ideas that he got visually from reading the script.

Can you explain the creative and collaborative process that goes on between the director and the different department heads?

With the director of photography I discuss the kind of look I want for this movie. For instance, with *Simon Birch,* we really wanted to get across that feeling of early sixties Americana.

With the editor, I talk about the style. Clearly, *Simon Birch* is not *Armageddon.* There won't be quick cuts every one to three seconds. This movie takes its time.

The same thing goes with the production designer. *Simon Birch* opens very kind of "once upon a time-ish." The first flashback scenes are very stylized and even. This gives the movie a kind of surreal quality. When we get into the meat of the story, it takes on a realistic look, both in the production design and photography.

***Simon Birch* makes use of low camera angles where the camera's looking up at the adults, the rooflines of houses, the canopy of trees, and the church steeple. Why is that?**

Our story involves two friends. One is described as the smallest person we've ever seen. At times, we want to show what his world is like. That's why I chose those angles.

The complete text of this interview is on the Readings & Resources disk, File: Johnson

© *Hollywood Pictures*

IN THE SPOTLIGHT

The entire interview can be found on the R&R disk (file name *Johnson*) to be photocopied for students. After they have had a chance to read the whole interview, discuss how Johnson emphasizes the importance of the tools they have studied.

Have your students review their list of the different job titles that appear in the closing credits of movies. Have them narrow it down to two or three different job titles that they find appealing and might be interested in pursuing. Once they had the position, what types of movies would they want to make, and what kinds of emotional impact would they like to leave with their viewers?

Sum It Up

Based on their analysis, students should be able to identify the filmmaking tools and how they affect audience reactions. Also have students choose their favorite filmmaking tool and explain why.

Most students will come to realize that they now know a lot more about filmmaking techniques and their impact. Ask students if their broadened perspective will change the way they watch movies in the future.

Put It Together

Divide the students into two or three groups and have each group choose a specific genre/category and set of emotions (for example, the Suspense/Thriller genre and emotions such as nervousness, tenseness, uneasiness). Once the group has reached a consensus on an idea for a story line, have them start writing the scene.

Have each group assign job responsibilities. The responsibilities are as follows: Director (oversees the entire production), Actor(s) (performers in the scene), Director of Photography (sets the lights, determines camera angles), Production Designer (determines the colors for the sets and costumes) Foley artist (determines the sound effects), Film Composer (determines the film score).

Sum It Up

Once you have viewed the different film examples, evaluate the exercis using the following questions:

1. Which filmmaking component had the most impact on you? Why?
2. Which film clip did you find the most convincing? Why?
3. Which element had the least effect on you? Why?

Compare what you know now about filmmaking to what you knew befor this lesson. What have you learned? Will you ever be able to watch mo quite the same way again? Do you think you can still fall under the spe of the film even as you notice and appreciate the techniques that help rect your responses?

PRODUCTION NOTES

From Page to Screen

Many popular books become the seed ideas for successful movies. *Simon Birch* is based on *A Prayer for Owen Meany* by John Irving. Many movie versions of *Frankenstein* have been created, all based more or less on Mary Wollstonecraft Shelley's 1818 novel. What other novels can you think of that have extended their shelf lives to the movie theater?

You are certain to have both read and watched the film adaptations of several novels. Think of the one that is clearest in your memory, or quickly review it by checking the book out of the library and the movie from a video rental store. Review the elements of a novel: plot, characters, setting, conflict, point of view, rising action, climax, and resolution. How are these conveyed in the movie? How does the novelis author the emotions that in the movie are conveyed by the direct tools? How do the events and plc differ from the book to the movie Do you agree with the director's cisions where changes are made t the original text? Which did you more enjoyable: the novel or the movie? Why?

24 MEDIA MATTE

PRODUCTION NOTES

Students have a huge array of both classic and contemporary book/movie combinations from which to choose: *Gone with the Wind, The Client, War and Peace, The Color Purple, Beloved,* and *Frankenstein* are just a few possibilities. Use this feature as a basis for a class discussion, or you can turn it into a larger project by having students watch a movie based on a novel, and then read or carefully review the book. Students should come to see that scriptwriters and directors often take great liberties with the original works, completely dropping scenes or characters and changing details or endings. For example, while there are approximately 60 movies named *Frankenstein,* only the 1994 production by Kenneth Branagh has attempted to be faithful to the novel (according to James Marksbury in his essay "What She Really Meant by *Frankenstein*").

Put It Together

Now that you have a better understanding of how films are put together, you are ready to create a scene on your own. In groups, write and produce a scene (one to five minutes in length) that reflects a specific emotion or emotions, and videotape it to show to the class.

While writing your script, remember that all media have a purpose and are carefully created to convey that purpose. Is your script meant to inform, persuade, or entertain? Who is your target audience? What is your script's primary message? What is the best way to convey that message?

GROUPS

Once your group has decided on an emotion and written a short script, gather the production elements or tools that you will need to reinforce that emotion. Which colors will you select from your color wheel for the sets and costumes? How will you use sound effects to heighten the emotional impact of the scene? What kind of background music will you select to set a mood for your script? How can you alter the classroom lighting? Rehearse your piece before taping it.

Depending on the equipment available to your class, use a camcorder or your school's television production equipment to record the scene. Experiment with the techniques you have learned in class. After showing your video to the class, ask students what kinds of emotions your scene evoked, and why. Then share with the class the emotions and messages your group was trying to convey. Evaluate: Were you successful? Why or why not? What might you have done to improve your work? What tools were not available to you that might have heightened the effects?

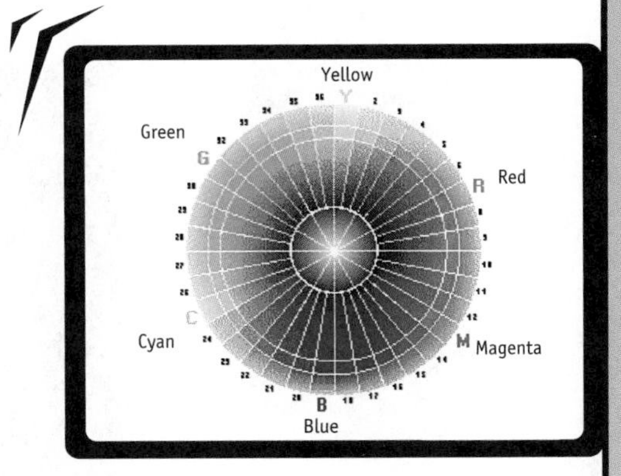

Color Wheel

Remind the students as they start rehearsing their scenes to be conscious of the choices they make in setting up the lighting, costumes, sound effects, and film score to ensure they reflect the emotions and genre/category they have chosen.

For those classes that have access to a single videotape camera, a VCR, and a monitor, have groups choose a camera operator to videotape the performance. For those classes that have access to a full television production studio complete with two cameras, a video switcher, an audio mixer and a VCR, have the students work from their designations to record their performance to videotape. Before the scene is recorded to videotape, be sure to have the students review their cues for where the cameras will be placed, when the sound effects will be heard, when the film score will be played, and what camera will be on what person.

Once the scene is taped, play it back on the monitor and ask the students in the audience to break it down in terms of color, light, sound effects, camera angles, and film score. When reviewing the scenes, keep in mind your students' prior experience with video equipment. Film-making techniques take much time and practice to perfect. Do look for students to at least experiment with the various techniques they have learned to the best of their ability and according to the available equipment.

Take It Further

These extension activities are suggested for classes that have time to study media education in depth, over several days.

1. If your class has access to a production studio, include editing. In the editing studio, students can dub in the music and sound effects using an audio mixer. One suggestion for a simple scene is to have a student walk slowly down a set of stairs. With frightening music and sound effects, this scene could be suspenseful; with carnival music, it could be funny. Changing the lighting from dark to light on this scene would also affect the emotions it evokes.
2. This is a deconstruction exercise that lets students apply what they have learned to their own viewing preferences.
3. The purpose of this writing activity is to have students think critically and analytically in order to recognize just how much their daily lives are impacted by the movie and television business.

Take It Further

GROUPS

1. In groups, create a 30- to 60-second scene that is general enou to be used with different types of sound effects, lighting, and music scores. Select a few sound effects, a piece of music, and lig in the classroom to evoke a suspenseful mood. Now tape the scenes wit a video camera. Play your video for the class, and evaluate its success b discussing the elements you used.

   Now use the same scene and add different sound effects, music, and lighting to create a humorous mood. Again, evaluate the scene and you techniques.

2. Take notes on your favorite TV show as you watch it this week. Jot down which tools are used to create various scenes, and con sider their effectiveness. Do they achieve their purposes? How?

3. Write an essay about how the movies affect you. Have any movi influenced the way you dress, expressions you use, music you lis ten to, opinions you hold, or fads that you enjoy?

From CNN's *The Making of History: The Cold War*

WORKSHEET

Deconstructing the Media

Film Techniques

File: Filmtech

Directors use many specific tools to create the effects they want in a piece of film. Analyze several film clips to discover the techniques behind the film, and evaluate their effects on you, the viewer.

Color and Lighting

1. List as many emotions as you can.

____

____

____

____

2. Using the color wheel as a reference, write down emotion-color pairs.

____

____

____

____

3. After viewing the clips in class, describe what is happening in the scenes. Do the colors and lighting complement the events in the clips? How?

____

____

____

4. What colors are used in the film clips' set designs and costumes, and how do they impact you as the viewer?

____

____

____

Film Techniques

1. The list could include happy, sad, joyful, frightened, romantic, tired, bored, upset, silly, and many more.
2. Some examples might include red—passion, danger, anger; white—innocent or vulnerable; black—mysterious, scary, angry, evil; green—alive, natural, renewed.
3. Students should recognize some correspondence between intended emotions of fear, anger, joy, rage, sadness, etc., and the director's use of color, lighting, and shadows.
4. Booth is surrounded by dark and fiery colors during his flight and his rage, but he is shown amidst the colors of a ball when declaring his love to a young woman. Darkness surrounds Lincoln when he learns of Richmond's fall and when he is shot.

5. Depending on the clip being viewed, camera techniques include close-ups of main characters, pans, slanted angles (during Booth's rage), choppy cuts to allude to a dream sequence, and others.
6. Encourage students to discuss the effects these techniques have on their interpretations of the scenes. Also discuss the first clip that begins with sound only. Ask students whether this causes them to focus more on the words to understand what is happening. At what point do they know which scene they are hearing?
7. Some examples: Booth's rage scene uses quick cuts and the slanted angle to present his unbalanced state of mind. The death scene is slow and quiet to reflect the action, as is the scene of Lincoln hearing the news about Richmond, in which he is both relieved and sad.
8. As well as discussing the intended reactions and how they are evoked by the techniques, have students consider alternative readings. Could they, for example, sympathize with Booth at his death scene? Can they feel for his desperation to get away, as he must know he is destined to be killed for something he believed was the patriotic thing to do? How might a Confederate sympathizer view these scenes?
9. Examples will vary widely. Loud sounds may cause students to become startled; they may associate bells with school; etc.

Camera Angles

5. What angles are used? What is happening in the scenes? Do the tools work? Why?

6. How do you feel when you watch the clips? How do you think the angles contribute to your reactions?

Editing

7. What kind of tempo or rhythm is used in the scenes? Why?

8. What reactions do you have to the scenes? Do they match what the director intends? Why do you think they do—or do not?

Sound Effects

9. Write down any strong associations you have when you hear a particular sound. What is the sound, and what does it make you feel? (For example, the sound of a baby crying may make one person feel protective and another feel annoyed.)

28 MEDIA MATTE

10. What sound effects did you notice in the clip with sound technician Michael Narduzzo? Do you think the sounds he included made a difference to the final production of the film?

Film Scores

11. After listening to the musical score that corresponds to this chapter, write down your response to it. How does it make you feel? What kind of movie do you imagine would go with this music?

12. What do you think of the music composed for *The Cold War*? Do you think it fits its subject? What did you learn from the interview with the composer of the score?

10. Narduzzo adds footsteps, crowd noise, and camera flashes. The additions make the scenes feel more realistic.
11. Play the score before showing the video clips on the Cold War so that students are not influenced by composer Carl Davis's explanation of the theme music.
12. Opinions will vary according to individual taste. It will be interesting to note what students thought of the music and how it might be used, as compared to what Carl Davis says about it.

Lesson 4 The USA, Media Style: *American Society as Portrayed by the Media*

What's Ahead?

Goals: Television, music, movies, video games, advertising, and a wide array of print media are filled with embedded values, stereotypes, and cultural attitudes that convey to the public—and more specifically, children and teenagers—what are the "normal" and "acceptable" beliefs and standards. In this lesson, students will examine messages about their culture as delivered by the mass media, discuss the ramifications of those messages, and then create new and more accurate media messages. The purpose is to motivate students to recognize the impact of the media on their lives and to enable them to think critically about media messages.

Disciplines: The contents of this lesson can be easily integrated into existing curricula such as language arts, American history, economics, and health.

Objectives: Upon completing the lessons in this lesson, students will be able to:

- Define media vocabulary as listed in the **Key Ideas** section.
- Identify current celebrities and the media's role in their fame.
- Analyze values and stereotypes embedded in many media messages.
- Recognize and evaluate materialistic messages in their culture.
- Create a media message that accurately portrays today's teenagers.

Did You Know?

Discuss the statistics and ask students what the implications might be. As they read the figures on just how much television is a part of American life, pose this interesting rhetorical question to your class: do television, movies, and other mass media *reflect* or *create* who we are? Ask students if they can think of examples of both. Some may argue specific series reflect real-life situations that teens and adults face. Popular series such as *Star Trek* may be seen as creating the Trekkie craze and conventions. Some students may

LESSON 4

The USA, Media Style

What's Ahead?

If visitors from another country (or planet) were to search our media messages to learn about the United States, what would they determine to be the characteristics of our culture? Certainly they would notice some prevailing standards, values, and relationships regarding personal appearance, lifestyles, behavior, language, family life, and financial priorities. What would these visitors say were our defining cultural features?

We ourselves might have a hard time answering that question. Just as fish don't notice the water they swim in, most of us have grown up in a society so saturated with messages and images from mass media—movies, ads, newspapers, magazines, posters, billboards, bumper stickers, buttons, comic books, and more—that we rarely notice their impact. In this lesson you will learn to pay attention to the attitudes, standards, and values portrayed in mass media so that you can evaluate them and make choices about their fairness and influence. As you read and complete the exercises, ask yourself the following questions: How much do media *reflect* our culture? How much do they *create* our culture?

30 MEDIA MATTE

Main Points to Ponder

- Celebrities play a significant role in U.S. culture. When we admire them, we often try to imitate their appearance, style, actions, and beliefs.
- Some media messages contribute to unfair stereotypes, biases, and prejudices. These are frequently seen in situation comedies. However, other media messages work to dispel common stereotypes.
- Materialism is prevalent in the attitudes and behaviors of media characters, as well as in the attitudes we adopt from receiving so many advertisement messages.

- Regular television broadcasts began in 1939.

(Source: www.mediahistory.com)

- In 1951, there were 1.1 million TV sets in the U.S., ten times the amount of the previous year.

(Source: www.mediahistory.com)

- Ninety-nine percent of all U.S. households now have at least one television.

(Source: Changing the World through Media Education, *Colorado: Fulcrum Resources, 1998.)*

- "From television ads we know that everyone in America smokes," Georgina Becci, age 13, Buenos Aires, Argentina.

(Source: quoted in Sue Lockwood Summers, Media Alert! *[Castle Rock, Colorado: Hi Willow Research and Publishing, 1997], 40)*

argue that violent series simply reflect real-life situations that teens and adults face. Others may note that the depiction of violence actually glamorizes it.

Materials

This lesson uses:

- A clip of a Miss Teen USA crowning (Video clip #12 - 0:36)
- A CNN feature about Miss Teen USA/Vermont (Video clip #13 - 2:38)
- A CNN feature about Russian fashion (Video clip #14 - 3:48)
- Celebrities Worksheet (File name *Celebs* on R&R disk)
- Stereotypes Worksheet (File name *Stereo* on R&R disk)

Key Ideas

Discuss the **Key Ideas** and ask students for examples of each.

The inundation of daily life by media messages contributes to perceptions about U.S. culture. Explain that you will be examining U.S. culture by analyzing three specific categories predominant in contemporary mass media: celebrities, stereotypes, and materialism.

Ask your students:

- Do you consider yourself a devotee of any particular celebrity? Who, and why?
- Are there any widely held beliefs in the school about particular groups of students or others outside the school? What are they, and why are they prevalent? Do you believe them? Why or why not?
- Are you a materialist? In what senses? What, if anything, are you wearing today that displays a designer label? Are you willing to buy and wear sneakers, jeans, or shirts not produced by a popular designer? If yes, where and when? Why are labels important to students?

Challenge your students to examine their independence in light of mass media appeal. Can they really be independent when the media instill conformity? (Clothes and make-up fads create a kind of "uniform," though most would fight against school uniforms.)

Get Started

This section introduces students to a broader understanding of celebrities, stereotypes, and materialism. Prior to this class, try to find a couple of magazines that contain photos of many popular celebrities that would interest your students. Hold up the photos and ask the class to identify each celebrity. Discuss their appeal and ask students how the media enhances them, making them desirable.

In his book *Visual Messages: Integrating Imagery into Instruction,* media literacy educator David Considine of Appalachian State University discusses the importance of recognizing stereotypes:

"If a culture is stereotyped and misrepresented in a film, it is necessary for teachers to challenge these inaccuracies. Teachers can also look at films from other countries to see how they depict their own culture and the United States. . . . As a dramatic medium with a limited time to develop a story, movies traditionally rely on cliches, conventions and stereotypes. By repeating and reinforcing stereotypes (racial, occupational, religious, national, gender etc.) movies potentially impede the way children see the society they live in and the diverse groups and individuals they must live with. School systems dedicated to promoting cooperation and a multicultural society cannot afford to ignore media representations of those cultures."

Ask the class for media examples of stereotypes, both new and old. Here are some examples to get you started:

- Superman rescuing Lois Lane (women need strong men to protect them)
- Archie Bunker (a character who lives by stereotypes about women, religious groups, nationalities, etc.)
- Music video depictions of love and romance
- Old cowboy and Indian movies

Again using those magazines, hold up examples of products that are likely to be popular in your students' lives. Ask them if they pay attention to ads in magazines and newspapers and if they buy products that they see advertised frequently. Discuss features about the ads that create the appeal for the products. Examples include

Get Started

Movie stars and celebrities have always held our attention. It seems th[at] people just cannot get enough tabloid articles about and photos of pop[u]lar stars such as Brad Pitt or Julia Roberts. People still flock to Gracela[nd,] the estate of the late Elvis Presley, and many participate in Elvis look-alike contests. The Three Stooges remain popular, even though the trio were stars of the 1940s and 1950s.

Some celebrities use their status to draw attention to world problems. Princess Diana used the media to highlight the danger of unexploded la[nd] mines and to promote the needs of the terminally ill and the tragedy o[f] eating disorders. Others gain worldwide notoriety through negative beh[av]ior. Think of Mike Tyson biting off part of Evander Holyfield's ear durin[g a] boxing match.

Key Ideas

Materialism - a philosophy suggesting that matter is the only reality; even thought and feelings are explained in terms of matter. Materialism also refers to the pursuit of material things rather than intellectual or spiritual goals. Comforts, pleasures, and wealth become the highest goals in life.

Product Crossover - when two or more otherwise unrelated companies join together to market items that benefit both businesses (also called "cross-merchandising").

Public Service Announcement (PSA) - a message, similar to an ad but not selling a product, created to inform or alert the public.

Sitcom - a television comedy series.

Stereotype - an idea or belief held about a person, group, or place that allows for no individuality or differentiation.

People learn about the unique traits of the stars—where they live, who they love, what they eat for breakfast. At the other end of the media spectrum are stars who have been categorized or stereotyped as belonging to certain groups. While many groups do share certain characteristics, the stereotype can be harmful because it also attaches value judgments to these groups, often drawing sweeping conclusions such as "Kids with good grades and glasses can't be good athletes," "Beautiful blonde women are unintelligent," and "Men can't cook and take care of a home as well as women." None of these statements is true. But perhaps you know people who still hold such beliefs. Do you think movies have anything to do with the persistence of these ideas? Or do movies help dispel them?

> "A celebrity is a person who works hard all his life to become well known, then wears dark glasses to avoid being recognized."
>
> **Fred Allen**

Both the celebrities and the stereotypes can, by what they wear, say, and enjoy, perpetuate materialism in our culture. Millions are made when media consumers choose to buy stuffed animals that look like beloved cartoon characters or jeans or sunglasses like those a popular actor wore in a movie. Think back to when you were a child. Did you request toys that were based on your favorite stars or movie characters? And now, do you ever want clothes or items that you first saw in a movie or TV show?

THEN AND NOW

The American Family

We can learn a great deal about our culture—how it has changed and how it remains consistent—by comparing the media messages of today with those of the past. One subject worth investigating is the American family. Many of the series from the 1960s and 70s are frequently aired on cable stations. Examples include *Father Knows Best, Leave it to Beaver, The Dick Van Dyke Show,* and *Happy Days.* Try to watch one or more of these shows and learn what you can about the roles of women, men, and children during that time; out-of-school activities; young people's concerns; and fashions. Write about the culture portrayed in the show and ask an adult to tell you how accurate that picture is. Write about the adult's evaluation in your conclusion.

Earlier in this chapter you were asked to consider what an alien might make of U.S. culture based on media messages. Some TV writers have done just that, resulting in shows such as *My Favorite Martian, Mork and Mindy,* and *Third Rock from the Sun.* You can ask older adults about the aliens' observations in the earlier shows if you cannot find them on television. You can probably watch an episode of *Third Rock.* What are some of the alien characters' observations? What makes them so humorous?

LESSON 4: THE USA, MEDIA STYLE

- Connecting beauty with the product (such as beautiful women with shiny hair for a shampoo ad)
- Connecting a higher lifestyle with the product (real estate ads usually show a happy family in front of their newly acquired, large, stately home)
- Connecting success with a product (sports superstars frequently promote brands of shoes and food products)

THEN AND NOW

This feature may provoke a lively class discussion about the portrayal of families by the media, past and present, and about real families. If you own a tape of an older sitcom family show, show it to the class and ask students how these characters differ from today's TV families, and from their own families. They are likely to see that women rarely worked outside the home or dealt with finances or discipline. The father's word was final, and the children obeyed him without much dispute. In today's shows, there are often blended or single-parent families, and women have careers and more say in the household decisions. Kids, especially teens, seem much more mature and are often involved in romantic situations.

Break It Down

Celebrities

You may want to discuss the notion of the hero with students and distinguish it from that of celebrity. In *Media Alert!,* Sue Lockwood Summers defines the celebrity as "[a person] who is widely known or recognized" and who may or may not be a societal leader and good role model. Heroes, she says, "can be real or fictional" and "often feature positive personal traits."

Write students' celebrity choices on the board and note how many times each person mentioned comes up on students' lists. If several have a large number of votes, ask students why these celebrities are so popular with them. You might want to ask:

- Why is the public fascinated with celebrities?
- Are there certain characteristics that all the listed celebrities have in common (good looks, achievement, power)?
- Which celebrities on the list are role models?
- What does this list of celebrities tell us about our society?

Stereotypes

The first clip **(video clip #12)** is likely to reinforce any preconceived notions that students have about pageants. Before showing the feature clip on Charlotte Lopez, Vermont's Miss Teen USA **(video clip #13)**, give students time to voice their feelings about beauty contests. They may express many stereotypes, such as "Pageants are disgusting," "Contestants are stupid women with sexy bodies," etc. The Miss Teen Vermont segment is especially likely to surprise students and provoke discussion. While beauty pageants may downplay women's intellectual abilities, some women use the system of pageants to their own advantage, earning money for college and gaining a powerful platform from which to deliver messages that are important to them.

You may want to ask students to consider media messages that stereotype other groups. For example, programs that feature African Americans often show them one-dimensionally. Bill Cosby has said of them, "Clearly none of these images happen to be the kind of people that you can imagine graduating from college." Additionally, many groups with a significant American population are underrepresented, such as Asian Americans and Hispanics.

Break It Down

Celebrities

Which people come to your mind when you hear the word "celebrity"? Make a list of these people, then discuss your list and the following questions in class. Remember that you can include sports figures, world leaders, and others along with stars of stage and screen.

1. What makes a person a celebrity?
2. Do you have heroes? Are heroes and celebrities the same?
3. Do your heroes or celebrities provide an accurate portrayal of your culture? Do you want them to? Why or why not?

Answer the questions found on the **Deconstructing the Media: Celebrities** worksheet (p. 38), and support your answers with specific examples.

Stereotypes

Video clip #12
Crowning of Miss Teen USA

If you had just beamed down to the United States from another planet and knew nothing about women except what you saw in a beauty pageant, what conclusions would you draw? Watch the clip on the crowning of a Miss Teen USA contestant; then take a few minutes to write down your impressions.

Analyze your own feelings about beauty pageants by writing answers to questions 1 and 2 on the **Deconstructing the Media: Stereotypes** worksheet (p. 40). In class, divide up by common judgments and debate the relative merits and disadvantages of beauty contests.

Video clip #13
CNN Profile: Charlotte Lopez

Now watch the film clip about Miss Teen USA from Vermont. Does this clip do anything to change your first impressions? How does it work to overcome stereotypes? Answer the remaining questions on the worksheet.

Materialism

In a later lesson you will examine more carefully the power and influence of advertising. Here we will look at how ads and other forms of media contribute to the buying craze in our country that has caused one critic to say, "America is moving from a nation of citizens to a nation of consumers."

Think about your favorite television shows, films, and magazines. What fashions and products do they promote? Do you think that the popularity of shows and films contributes to people's desires for the fashions and material things used in them? Why or why not?

Look at the clothing and accessories worn and used by students in your school. Make a list of companies, teams, organizations, or products you see advertised by those students. Don't forget to include hats, shoes, pens, backpacks, key chains, buttons, stickers, and other items. Compare your lists in class. Give reasons why you believe that people intentionally buy and wear clothing that displays advertising messages (such as the name of the designer, a company, a rock band, etc.).

Companies with little in common sometimes combine their efforts at merchandising. For example, fast food restaurants may include toys that are characters from a new movie. In this way, the restaurant increases its sales of children's meals and the movie becomes a part of the children's culture, thus making the movie a "must see." Think of examples of such "product crossovers."

"I was the kind nobody thought could make it. I had a funny Boston accent. I couldn't pronounce my R's. I wasn't a beauty."

Barbara Walters

um It Up

a scale of one to five, evaluate how much you think that

- the media portray an accurate view of U.S. culture.
- celebrities portrayed by the media influence U.S. society.
- stereotypes depicted in the media influence U.S. society.
- Americans buy a product based on its media image.
- celebrities portrayed by the media influence you.
- stereotypes depicted in the media influence you.
- you buy a product based on its media image.

Materialism

Students in the United States have been so bombarded throughout their lives with materialistic messages that it can be difficult for them to separate their personal characters from material considerations; that is, they can fail to distinguish who they are from what they own. The exercises in this section help them become more aware of the influence and role of material things in their lives. As they add up how many popular items they wear or own, ask them to consider those students who do not have these kinds of items. Are such students included among their friends? Are such students judged harshly? This is a great opportunity for young people to see how powerful mass marketing is, even influencing their judgments of others who may not have the money or inclination to buy popular products.

Ask students if they have ever bought one product to get another. Certainly many people flocked to McDonald's when the restaurant offered free Beanie Babies with their kids' meals, and many of those threw the meal away. This is a great example of material waste.

Sum It Up

Here students evaluate how much the mass media influences their society and themselves. Ask them to assess the clips and exercises as well. Which clip did they find the most informative? Which exercises taught them the most about themselves? Did any of the activities cause them to change the way they think about people or products? In what ways?

Put It Together

Have students work in groups consisting of at least one male and one female to create their public service announcement. Before they begin, discuss familiar PSAs so that they have a better idea of the project. Some examples are the PSAs they see in magazines and on television encouraging people not to smoke, take illegal drugs, or drink and drive.

Allow groups some time to rehearse their PSA. Remind them of the importance of presentation. They should be using tools that they discovered in the first three lessons.

If video equipment is available, have groups work during or after class to tape their presentations. If not, allow class time for each group to present its skit. Be sure to allow the class to discuss each presentation in terms of its message and delivery.

Put It Together

Now that you have analyzed and evaluated many American media messages, you should have a better understanding of how our culture woul look to an outsider. You might be surprised at how influential celebriti have become in our society. Perhaps you feel outraged about the inadequate portrayal of certain subsets of our population. You may have noticed an abundance of materialistic messages aimed at youth.

Take action! Create a media message that is realistic and positive. In groups, construct a 30- to 60-second scene for a TV series or a public s vice announcement. You might share something that someone did to h the community. You might invent a celebrity spokesperson who is positive, intelligent, and respectful. You may choose a message that encou ages people to be content with what they have.

Remember to use the tools of good media construction: Decide on a pu pose, a message, a target audience, and the best way to deliver your m sage within the time constraints. Background, props, characters, script, and style are all important. If the message isn't interesting and able to capture the attention of the viewers, it won't be watched. Share your f ished product with your class and evaluate your work.

WORLD VIEW

Designing Russians

While Americans are known for their consumer culture, many other nations are busy imitating U.S. products and ideas or designing their own. Watch the feature video clip on the new world of Russian fashion design. Discuss these questions in class:

1. Do the contents of the feature surprise you? What were your previous ideas about clothes in Russia?
2. Discuss the stereotype presented in the first few seconds of the feature and ways in which it has changed.
3. Do you think the changes in Russian fashion and beauty concepts are a result of Western influence? If yes, do you think this is a good thing?

Video clip #14
CNN clip on Russian Fashion

WORLD VIEW

While the United States is guilty of being the most consumer-oriented country on the globe, other countries also show their own material desires through their ads, styles, and media. The CNN feature clip on Russian fashion **(video clip #14)** is a telling look at how Russians are trying to break from their past Communist restrictions in dress. Adults may enjoy the humor of the first few seconds of the clip the most, but some students will also be familiar with the stereotype of large, black-clad Soviet women. When discussing this clip, help students to notice that many Russians, while they like the new trends, don't have the money to follow them.

Take It Further

1. Watch your favorite television show. Don't leave during the commercials. While watching, take notes on the following questions:

- Who is the target audience for this show? How do you know?
- What are the situations presented on the show? What are the characters' values? Are they similar to or different from your situations and beliefs? In what ways?
- What are the commercials shown during the show? How many ads are shown in the 30- or 60-minute time period? Who is the target audience of each ad? How do you know? What do the advertisers use to capture your attention?
- How many of the items presented in the commercials do you either own or want to own?

2. Interview your parents, grandparents, or other adults to determine who their celebrities were in the past, and why. Also ask them about their teenage heroes and role models. Compare their answers to your own. Evaluate the differences and similarities.

3. Create a new holiday to draw attention to and promote awareness of a specific subset of U.S. culture. Holiday examples include "Family Day," "Disabled Americans Day," or "Vietnamese Awareness Day." Brainstorm ways to celebrate the day and promote it to the school or community. Contact organizations that can provide information or work with you to promote your positive message.

Take It Further

Numbers one and two are deconstruction (or "Break It Down") exercises; number three is a construction ("Put It All Together") activity.

1. Look for students to show an understanding of "target audience" in this exercise. They should also be able to compare and contrast their lives and situations to those on the television show, citing the differences between reality and fantasy. As they deconstruct commercials, they should point to some of the techniques they learned about (such as camera angles, lighting, film edits) to discuss how the ads appeal to their audience.
2. This is another exercise that asks students to compare and contrast as they analyze. If students are unfamiliar with writing essays that compare and contrast, review with them the techniques of writing a parallel-style essay (analyzing first one subject and its parts, then the other subject and its parts in the same order) or a point-by-point essay (alternating between subjects, addressing corresponding parts individually).
3. Help students to brainstorm about groups that are either underrepresented or misrepresented in American media. Remind them where information can be found: the Yellow Pages, public offices, the World Wide Web, newspapers, magazines, etc.

Celebrities

1. Answers may include celebrities' popularity; their contributions to music, sports, TV, or film; and their frequent appearances in the media. People find information on celebrities in the news, in magazines, and on TV, the Internet, radio, and other sources. Responses on influence will vary.
2. What students choose as criteria for making a celebrity will influence their decision on whether or not a student can become a celebrity, but chances are that the criteria will lead to a "yes" answer, as students, as well as adults, can distinguish themselves in sports, acting, writing, art, and influencing civic actions.
3. Students might name well-known cartoon characters, such as Mickey Mouse, or puppets, such as the Muppets. If they answer "no," look for reasonable explanations for their opinion.
4. Consumers often admire and want to be like their favorite celebrities. Buying products that they endorse can be a way for followers to identify with the celebrities.

W O R K S H E E T

Deconstructing the Media

Celebrities

File: Celebs

Celebrities entertain us, provoke us, teach us, and influence us. Think of some people who are celebrities, and answer the following questions about them.

1. Of those that come to mind, what makes them celebrities? What media give you information about them? Have they influenced you in any ways?

____

____

____

____

2. Can a student at your school become a celebrity? How? What are criteria for "making" a celebrity?

____

____

____

3. Can a fictional character be a celebrity or a hero? If you say yes, name at least one. If no, tell why not.

____

____

____

4. Why do you think that advertisers use celebrities' endorsements to sell products?

____

____

____

5. If this were the late 1700s, without any electronic communication systems to reach the public, do you think that one woman, such as Princess Diana, would have had so much influence? What mass media spread the word about celebrities during that period in U.S. history?

6. Is a celebrity always a positive role model? Think of some celebrities who are known by their negative attitudes or behaviors. What impact can such people or fictional characters have on individuals?

7. Make a list of celebrities you've seen endorse products. Next to each name identify the product. Indicate whether you believe the celebrity was a good choice to endorse the product; explain why or why not. Did any of the celebrities influence you to purchase the product?

5. It is highly unlikely that Princess Diana would have had such influence in the 1700s, not only because there was no electronic mass media, but also because she was a woman. Newspapers and magazines were the primary sources of popular culture at that time.
6. Celebrities can certainly be negative role models, as evidenced by Mike Tyson and Dennis Rodman. If kids had admired them previous to the negative publicity, they may tend to excuse the poor behaviors.
7. Some examples include Michael Jordan's endorsement of Gatorade and MCI; Sarah Ferguson's ads for Weight Watchers; and Ron Howard, Whoopi Goldberg, and Backstreet Boys' milk mustache ads.

Stereotypes

1. This is an interesting lesson, because while we try to teach that stereotypes are unfair, the stereotype of the beauty queen being all body and no brains is one we tend to perpetuate. Many look down on families involved in pageants and teach their daughters that beauty pageants are beneath them.
2. Adjectives that some students may suggest include beautiful, attractive, or fake. See if any attribute intelligence or talent to contestants.
3. Students are likely to be surprised at Charlotte's tenacity and ability not only to survive, but also to be successful.

WORKSHEET

Deconstructing the Media

Stereotypes

File: Stereo

Stereotypes can be dangerous, because when a person adheres to them, that person fails to see unique and important traits of individuals. Frequently stereotypes involve hurtful judgments about various groups of people based on race, gender, religion, and culture. Answer the following questions before and after viewing the feature clip on Miss Teen USA.

1. What adjectives and judgments come to mind when you think of beauty pageants and contestants? Do you consider them to be "good" or "bad" events? Explain.

2. Do you think that your feelings are based on stereotypes? Can you think of any adjectives that can be applied fairly to the entire group of contestants?

3. Respond to your evaluation of pageants after learning Charlotte Lopez's story.

4. Can you think of sitcoms or dramatic series that evenly mix characters of various racial groups, such as Asians, Native Americans, African Americans, Hispanics, and whites and that evenly mix personality traits among these groups? If yes, list them; if no, comment on why you think these programs might be difficult to find.

5. Make a list of what people from another country (or planet) might believe about American teenagers based on ads, magazines, music videos, sitcoms, dramas, and movies. How reliable are these stereotypes? What material objects seem important to teens on the shows? Next to each item on your list, state whether this conclusion is accurate and fair. If not, explain what is wrong with the perception.

SSON 4: THE USA, MEDIA STYLE 41

4. Aside from some children's programming that intentionally includes a mix of races and cultures (such as *Sesame Street*), it may be hard, or even impossible, for students to think of such a program. They may consider attitudes of the general public as they explore why such shows are nearly nonexistent, remembering that companies create what people will tune into so that they can make a profit on ads.
5. Responses may include the following: teenagers are all attractive and don't have problems with acne or weight; physical attraction is foremost in teens' minds; teens are frequently involved in violent and brutal situations; teens are more intelligent than adults; etc. Material objects may include clothing, fashions, cars, phones, and technical equipment.

Lesson 5 Power of the Press: *The News Media*

What's Ahead?

Goal: This lesson introduces students to a variety of news media. By examining different representations of the same event, students will analyze and evaluate each medium for point of view, accuracy of information, completion of story, and effect of included/excluded details.

Disciplines: The contents in this lesson pertain to language arts, history, world events, and technology.

Objective: Upon completing this lesson, students will be able to:

- Define key media terms associated with news coverage.
- Realize that there are different types of news coverage—hard news, soft news, balanced coverage, editorials—and that different perspectives on the same story will result in different news constructions. (For instance, Indian and Pakistani reporters were proud of their countries' nuclear tests.)
- Deconstruct various types of news media to analyze the content and its effects.
- Construct their own news presentation of a timely local or state news item.

Did You Know?

Ask students to write a definition for "news." Compare definitions and discuss what they include in and leave out of their definitions.

Have students make lists of all the types of news coverage they can think of. What do they normally think of when they use the phrase "the news" or "the media"? They should come to realize that both terms are more inclusive than they probably think, generally speaking.

LESSON 5

Power of the Press

What's Ahead?

Many people use the phrase "the media" to refer to news coverage. You have already learned that media include much more than news. And news is much more than the daily paper. Just what is included in "news"?

In this lesson, you will learn about the different types and styles of news coverage by examining and analyzing many presentations of one news event: the nuclear bomb testing done by India and Pakistan from May 11 to June 1, 1998. As you see and read the various stories, you will recognize that, while each piece seems intended merely to inform, each one presents a different perspective on the same events.

Main Points to Ponder

- Some news is intended to be objective—factual coverage—and some items included in the news are subjective, or opinionated—for example, editorials, commentaries, and TV news discussions.
- Because different countries have different perspectives on events, their coverage will present differing viewpoints that they consider objective.
- Not only which details are included, but also which ones are excluded, determine the perspective and effect of the news story.

Materials

This lesson uses:

Did You Know?

- There are 1,500 daily newspapers printed in the United States, down from 1,770 in 1970.
- According to 1997 statistics, nearly 59 percent of adults read a daily newspaper. Over 52 percent watch news on television, and 25 percent hear the news on morning radio programs.
- Viewership of TV news is declining, especially among young people and computer users. *(Source: Pew Research Center for the People and the Press, 1996)*

Key Ideas

Balanced Coverage - intended to provide the many perspectives of a given event; presenting more than one side of the story. (For instance, a balanced news story about a murder suspect would include not only the facts of the crime and the suspect's apprehension, but also information about the victim and statements by the suspect's friends or family.)

Hard News - reporting on significant state, national, and world events, such as elections, weather disasters, peace negotiations, and major crime.

News - reports of recent happenings and previously unreported information, locally, nationally, and internationally. Topics range from local charity auctions to a Hollywood actor's recent wedding to the bombing of an embassy.

News Media - all the means of communication that provide the public with news: radio, television, newspapers, magazines, the Internet.

Objective Coverage - intended to be factual, without bias.

Soft News - reporting on human interest stories, such as new information on music groups, beauty pageant queens, and citizens rescuing kittens stuck in trees.

Subjective Coverage - opinionated reporting of an event, with a definite bias. Editorials and commentaries fall into this category.

LESSON 5: POWER OF THE PRESS 43

- 5/29/98 clips from CNN on India/Pakistan nuclear situation (Video clips #15 &16 - 7:42 total)
- National Archive clip of "Duck and Cover" (Video clip #17 - 1:06)
- Two CNN Interactive stories from 5/11/98–5/29/98 (File names *Council* and *Talks* on R&R disk)
- Two *NY Times* editorials on the situation (File names *Threat* and *Hypoc* on R&R disk)
- International article on the situation (*The India Times*) (File name *India* on R&R disk)
- Deconstructing the News Worksheets (File names *News1* and *News2* on R&R disk)

Key Ideas

Discuss the terms in the **Key Ideas** section and ask students to give examples.

Bring in a news clipping that involves a topic students are likely to be aware of and make copies so that each student can read the news story. The news event can be local, national, or international. Have students write down everything they know about this event prior to reading the story. Then hand it out and ask students the following questions after they have had a chance to read.

- How did they originally find out about this event? (Print, TV, radio, Internet?)
- What makes this event "news?"
- Is it "hard" news or "soft" news?
- Was the news coverage they just read objective or subjective?
- Was the material "balanced"? Did it offer multiple perspectives?
- Did their knowledge or perspective change about the event after reading the news clipping?
- What are some of the purposes of news stories? (Informative, persuasive/editorial?) What was the purpose of this news story?
- What are the characteristics of each of the forms of media? (With print you can pace yourself and read things again; with video, the pace is already set—usually fast—but there is a visual advantage over print; Internet usually includes photos and links that provide more information, such as details and backgrounds.)

Get Started

Though we have a free press, citizens must still analyze and evaluate the news we read and see to determine how accurate it is. Some sources are more objective than others. You might bring in a copy of a tabloid news magazine and look at headlines or read an article with the class. Most of their stories are designed for shock value, boasting headlines such as "Big Foot Takes Another Victim." Yet they sell, and some people believe them. Ask students to theorize on the appeal of inaccurate tabloids. Why would people choose to believe the information in them? How do others know that the articles are fabricated?

Bring up the concept of "newsworthiness." News producers, editors, and writers use criteria to determine what to keep and what to delete. These include relevance to the audience, immediacy of the event, interest to the audience (this can include controversy, tragedy, humor, unusualness of the topic, irony), and an entertainment factor (the news still has to sell, so soft news features are considered newsworthy).

Discussion Questions:

- Do students believe, as Barron Lytton suggests, that words can be more powerful than actions? Ask for examples.
- Do they value our free press? In which situations do they think the press should be restrained from coverage? (In matters of national security, for example.)
- Do they pay regular attention to the news? Why or why not? Do they think it is important to be informed about local, national, and world events? (Some may be apathetic about news events, saying either that they don't care or that they feel powerless. You might tell them that students have made a difference by, for example, initiating letter campaigns to corporations that use overseas child labor. Ask if they can think of other examples.)
- Do they make decisions based on what they learn in the news? From which media do they receive most of their news? If they primarily use just one medium, do they think it gives them a complete picture of what is happening in their town, state, country, world? If not, why do they depend on it?
- Are there certain newscasters or correspondents they recognize and trust more than others? If yes, what makes these people seem more reliable to them?

Get Started

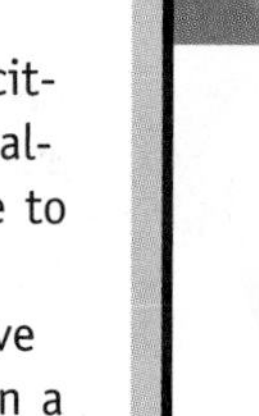

In the nineteenth century, Baron Lytton wrote, "The pen is mightier than the sword." To Lytton's words we might add the saying "A picture is worth a thousand words" to include the photos and video clips that bring us news.

We draw opinions and make decisions based on what we learn from the news media. Without news correspondents and photographers working around the clock and risking their lives to cover wars and crises, we would not know about human rights violations in Bosnia, the Middle East, China, and Northern Ireland; we wouldn't hear about heroism during the forest fires in Florida during the summer of 1998. It would be more difficult to find information on national and local officials. Even news of community happenings would be more difficult to obtain.

In a democratic society, it is essential that citizens be well informed in order to make carefully considered decisions. We ourselves, not a military dictator or an ancestral ruler, determine who will become our politicians and lawmakers. We have a voice in deciding whether or not a new school will be built, whether wetlands will be protected or built up, and whether a Democrat or a Republican will serve as our next president. To make informed decisions, we depend upon a constant and objective flow of information. And to provide that news, the press must be free to cover and deliver information.

"It's amazing that the amount of news that happens in the world every day always just exactly fits the newspaper."
Jerry Seinfeld

What we often forget about, though, is that, like all media, the news is constructed and influenced by many factors. What we learn is dependent upon the expertise of the news correspondent, videographer, and photojournalist. Content is shaped by the amount of time or space allotted for the story and the level of importance producers believe it has. It is affected by the values and beliefs of the media's executive officers, shareholders, and advertisers. In a free society, citizens must think critically about the news they read, hear, and view before they draw conclusions about the events reported.

ꟷreak It Down

/ do you know what you know? That is, how did you arrive at your ıerstanding, beliefs, and opinions about historical and current events?

form an opinion, you have to evaluate the information you receive. must decide whether or not it is reliable, how complete it is, and ıt it means.

show you the need for critical analysis and evaluation, let's look at a ation in India and Pakistan that drew international attention in the ng of 1998. India tested nuclear bombs on May 11th. Pakistan reacted h severe criticism and claimed it would not follow suit. Yet on May h and June 1st, Pakistan also tested nuclear weapons.

ld reaction included both outrage and concern. The superpowers urged countries to sign the Comprehensive Test Ban Treaty.

Video clips #15 and #16

CNN Newsroom:

India and Pakistan

Files: India, Council, Talks, Threat, Hypoc

ysis is needed to evaluate the reliability of

As you view and read several reports on these events, use your **Deconstructing the Media: News** worksheet (p. 51) to analyze and evaluate the news sources. Study the sources carefully—consider the intended audience for the story, advertisers, state/national/international perspective—as you determine the reliability of the information. The following two pages contain excerpts from the articles. The complete articles can be found on your *Media Matters* Readings & Resources disk.

Break It Down

Before using video clips #15 and 16, be sure to view them several times so that you are informed about the historical backgrounds of the India/Pakistan tensions. Like many other current world situations, the present-day problems are a result of decades of mistrust and hostility between the two nations. You might ask students to discuss similar world situations that they know more about, such as the Middle East or Ireland. The first clip concentrates on the May/June 1998 situation in which India and Pakistan tested nuclear devices. The second clip gives historical background information and world views about the current event bomb tests.

Use a world map or globe to be sure students know where the countries are located. Ask what they already know about this area and its people.

Have students read the full versions of the news articles (found on the Readings & Resources disk) so that they can evaluate the complete coverage of each topic. Be sure that they are clear about differences between the hard news and editorials. Also discuss the differences in perspective as they compare the U.S. stories to the one from *The Times of India*. Go over the news components as they are brought up on the worksheets. Refer to **Key Ideas** and ask for examples of the concepts. Give students time to ask questions about the worksheet before they must use it. Students may work individually or in teams.

Be sure to show the video clips to the class at least twice: once in full, and once pausing at each section to discuss the contents and presentation.

Tony Frassrand, Anchor, CNN Newsroom

ARTICLE 1

US stand on N-tests is biased, say scientists

By Srinivas Laxman
The Times of India News Service

File: India

MUMBAI: Many scientists of the Bhabha Atomic Research Centre (BARC) were critical about the discriminatory standards adopted by the Clinton administration with regard to nuclear weapons tests.

These scientists, who requested anonymity, pointed out that the US was adopting a "bullying attitude" towards India by threatening sanctions for conducting three tests at Pokharan in Rajasthan on Monday, whereas "it had displayed utter helplessness when China and France conducted their tests."

. . . According to them, with the five global nuclear powers collectively possessing 36,000 nuclear weapons in their arsenal protests by the Big Powers about the Indian nuclear test had no meaning.

So far, India has refused to give in to global pressure and sign the Nuclear Non-Proliferation Treaty (NPT) and the Comprehensive Test Ban Treaty (CTBT). . .

(The above article has been reproduced by arrangement with The Times of India and is the copyright of the publishers, Bennett, Coleman & Co. Ltd. The Times of India may be viewed at http://www.timesofindia.com.)

46

ARTICLE 2

U.S. calls for Security Council meeting as South Asia nuclear threats heat up

May 29, 1998

File: Council

WASHINGTON (CNN)—Even as the United States worked to convene a high-level meeting to discuss the nuclear arms race in South Asia, intelligence sources said Pakistan may be ready to test nuclear devices again as soon as this weekend. . . They are also expected to be ready to conduct additional tests of their ballistic missiles within the next week, said the officials.

"Pakistan has made no mention of ending our tests," Foreign Minister Gohar Ayub Khan told [CNN's Tom] Mintier, without confirming or denying that future tests were planned. "We have a missile program, and it is in the national interest whatever we want to do."

But the chairman of the Foreign Relations Committee of Pakistan's Senate, Akram Zaki, says Pakistan has written the United Nations to propose a new nonaggression pact between India and Pakistan and new bilateral negotiations. . .

MEDIA MATTERS

ARTICLE 3

ndia proposes bilateral talks with akistan

File: Talks

e 3, 1998

W DELHI, INDIA (CNN)—India offered Wednesday old bilateral talks with Pakistan to reduce tensions in wake of both nations' recent nuclear tests.

The proposal came after a meeting between Indian ne Minister Atal Bihari Vajpayee and Iranian Minis- Kamal Kharrazi, who arrived in New Delhi for talks r a visit to Islamabad.

However, Vajpayee rejected the possibility of let- other parties join mediation efforts between the two nuclear neighbors. Indian Foreign Secretary K. hunath said his country's leaders believe international cerns about the situation in South Asia are exagger- l.

"Life is normal. There is no ground for exaggeration dramatizing the situation," Raghunath said. . .

ARTICLE 4

A Nuclear Threat From India

File: Threat

New York Times Editorial Desk
May 13, 1998, Wednesday

India's explosion of three nuclear devices in the Rajasthan desert makes the world a more dangerous place. By arrogantly challenging international efforts to control the spread of the most lethal weapons, the new Hindu nationalist Government of Prime Minister Atal Bihari Vajpayee may win applause at home from those who confuse military might with self-esteem. But for a paltry and short-lived domestic gain, India now faces a ruinous cutoff in foreign aid, a self-defeating arms race with Pakistan and isolation even from friends. . .

ARTICLE 5

U.S. Nuclear Hypocrisy

The New York Times Editorial Desk
June 10, 1998, Wednesday

File: Hypoc

"Every Nation's Just Another U.S.," your June 7 Week in Review article on the report faulting the Central Intelligence Agency, noted the "everybody thinks like us" mind-set that was said to underlie the agency's failures.

However, if India were "just another U.S.," it would have conducted hundreds of nuclear tests over the last several decades and not just five last month. It would also have wanted to be so globally peremptory as to demand that all other countries behave not as it practices but as it preaches. As ineffectual, tokenist and obsolete as India's decision to test may have been, the one good fallout it has had is to rattle the United States.

The writer is chairman of the English department, University of Delhi. . .

Sum It Up

Based on their analysis, students should come up with a list of criteria for evaluating a "news story."

Chances are that students will rate the video clip the highest, because it includes the story, historical perspectives, and reactions from around the world. Be sure they also see that more details can be put into print news articles because television news must condense all of the day's stories into roughly 22 minutes.

Most students will have surely learned more about the situation than they knew previously. As they voice their opinions, ask them to consider what real information they are basing them on. Chances are that they will have added this new information to ideas they already have about nuclear weapons from past learning. Ask them how accurate and reliable they think their old information is.

Sum It Up

"For most folks, no news is good news; for the press, good news is not news."
Gloria Borger

Once you have deconstructed each example of the news media, evaluat using the following criteria:

- Which one was the most balanced? Why?
- Which one offered the best coverage? Why?
- Which format did you prefer? Why?

Compare what you know now about the situation in India and Pakistan what you knew before this lesson. What have you learned? What difference has it made to you? Has gaining more information altered your o ions, perspectives, or fears about nuclear warfare? Has it made you mo interested or aware of actions you would like to see our country take?

ETHICS IN ACTION

Propaganda

Because we live in a free democracy, we tend to believe we are always told the truth. Propaganda—spreading ideas and information in support of certain causes, institutions, or persons—may indeed be accurate. (Think, for example, of the public service campaigns that promote awareness of the risks of smoking or the dangers of drug use.) But we also know that propaganda can be used to distort or even lie. Think about historical situations you have learned about in which citizens have been told misleading or false information.

Can you think of occasions when the U.S. government used propaganda to mislead citizens? Watch the film clip from *Duck and Cover,* a 1950s U.S. government film used extensively in classrooms to instruct school children about the atomic bomb. As you watch and hear the information presented, what do you think of the content? Interview an adult who was in school during the time this film was used. Did this adult believe the information as a child? Why do you think that the government released this propaganda? Do you think that the government could get away with similar propaganda in this decade? Why why not? Can you think of meth you can use to avoid believing p paganda that you may encounter

Video clip #17
Duck and Cover

ETHICS IN ACTION

Propaganda. While current usage of the term "propaganda" refers to negative or inaccurate information, instruct students that the true definition is neutral and refers simply to widespread dissemination of beliefs or information. You can refer students back to the ethics feature in Lesson 2 entitled "The Power of Language," which discusses misleading uses of language. The *Duck and Cover* footage in **video clip #17** is pulled from CNN's *The Cold War* series, so it includes interviews that may help students better understand the historical context of this propaganda film.

'ut It Together

ık of a newsworthy story that has occurred recently at your school, lo-
y, statewide, nationally, or internationally. In groups, present the
/s item in one of the ways that you have studied. Be sure to consider
of the media techniques and news media key terms you have studied
constructing your own news story.

sent your story to the class, either in print, audio (as a radio piece),
eo (or live, if video is not available), or using a computer. Be prepared
answer questions about your presentation's contents and methods. Use
questions on your **Deconstructing the Media: News** worksheets pp. 51
52 to be sure you have covered all the essential information.

ou are performing a news piece appropriate for video, be sure to re-
rse and consider video elements such as clothes, light, and props when
ating your feature. If you are writing, remember to edit! Think carefully
ut the words you choose, background information that may be neces-
, pictures that could be helpful, and links (for Internet presentations).

PRODUCTION NOTES

arching the Internet

Do you know how to conduct research on the Web? When you go on-line, you will see a rch" icon in the tools on your ser. If you click it, a "search ne"—a program that uses key s to search for matches any-e on the World Wide Web—will ar on your screen. Some well-n engines include *Yahoo, Ex-AltaVista,* and *Lycos.* Type your words into the box provided, click on "Search" or press the "Enter" key on your keyboard. You will then be given a listing of sites that have information about the words that you typed into the box. As you go through them, use the brief summaries provided to decide whether or not this may be a useful site. As you have learned throughout your study of the media, not all sources are equally reliable.

Another way to narrow your search is to go to sites you believe have information about your topic and use their internal search engines. For example, if you are looking for information about a news event, you might choose to find the Internet site of *Time, Newsweek,* the *New York Times,* CNN, *The Wall Street Journal,* the Associated Press, or another reliable news source. When you arrive at the site, use their search engine in the same way that you use a World Wide Web search engine.

Put It Together

Have students brainstorm ideas for a newsworthy story that has occurred at the school, locally, statewide, nationally or internationally. Arrange students into groups, and assign each group to cover the story using a different form of news coverage studied in this lesson: newspapers, TV news, Internet. To give students practice in editing and making choices about what to include, you can request wire service "ticker tape" information from a local paper and raw footage from a TV station to create the broadcast productions.

Students should construct a news story for their assigned medium using the components of a news story already discussed.

Each group should present its project in an appropriate way. (Written pieces should be handed out to each student; Web pieces could be stored on a disc; TV items can be created with a video camera and shown with a VCR; or, if these are not available, they can be presented live to the class.)

Using their list of criteria for evaluating a news story, students should analyze the coverage of each presentation. They should evaluate student news stories for accuracy, construction, contents, completeness, balance, etc.

PRODUCTION NOTES

Searching the Internet. You may find students that are more savvy about search engines than you are! On the other hand, some students will not have much online experience, and they will need this practice. Try pairing students that need to learn about search engines with peer tutors who are knowledgeable about them.

Some of the resources for their analysis of the India/Pakistan talks are found on the World Wide Web (WWW). Be sure that they know how to type in the URL—Universal Resource Locator, or "address" of the Web site—to find the articles. Ask them to check out related sources when they are given within articles by clicking on the underlined hyperlinks to other sites.

Take It Further

These extension activities are suggested for classes that have time to study media education in depth, over several days.

1. Review the concepts of emotional appeal and logical fallacies (found in Lesson Two text and web activities). Editorials can be emotional or they can have a distant, cool tone often found in logical arguments. Ask which the class thinks is the more effective style. How do the editorials compare to the hard news stories? What is similar, and what is different?
2. Ask students why they think soft news is so popular. Why, for instance, do people care about famous actors' lives? Why do they stay tuned for the Paris fashion show of models wearing clothes that they wouldn't dream of wearing?

   Your evaluation of this piece would be very different than for a balanced, objective story. Soft news has a group appeal and frequently even advertises a product (a movie review, for example). Consider how effectively the piece appeals to the emotions and to mass culture. Then question the students: How do they feel about such a creation? Are they comfortable with it? Can they (or have they) done a soft piece with positive social value?
3. Help students brainstorm a list of questions. Try to obtain a bio of your guest speaker ahead of time so the class can be somewhat familiar with his or her work.

Take It Further

1 Find a commentary or editorial about an event that is currently in the news. Read about the event in at least three other different news sources. What are the similarities and differences between the sources? How do they compare to the information you found in the editorial? Check the editorial piece against the more objective pieces you read. Does it seem to be based on facts? Does it leave out important information? Write your own editorial about the news item that either refutes or supports the editorial you chose. Ask yourself: How will I choose my information? Am I intentionally leaving out information? Am I being fair and accurate in my editorial?

Many important current events require critical analysis and evaluation.

2 Form several groups in class and create your own live soft news talk show piece to perform for the class. You might choose to create a scene from a morning talk show or evening variety show. Present your skit, then be prepared to discuss the following questions: How did you choose your topic? What did you think about when deciding on questions (if you create an interview situation)? How much did you need to consider your audience? What was the purpose of your soft news piece?

3 Invite a local news reporter, editor, or news anchor to your class. Ask your guest how he or she selects and constructs news stories using the techniques you have learned.

WORKSHEET

Deconstructing the Media

News, Part 1

File: News1

The basic parts of any news story include answering six key questions about the subject: Who, What, When, Where, Why, and How. Use these questions to find the essential information of the news stories:

1. Who is the story about?

____

____

2. What is the story about?

____

____

3. When did the events take place?

____

____

4. Where did the events occur?

____

____

5. Why did the events take place?

____

____

____

6. How did it happen?

____

____

____

LESSON 5: POWER OF THE PRESS 51

News, Part 1

1. The news feature is about Indians and Pakistanis.
2. The story focuses on the nuclear bomb tests conducted by India and Pakistan.
3. The time frame is May 1998.
4. The tests occurred within the countries' own borders.
5. Both countries feel the need to protect themselves from one another. They also express the need to protect themselves from China and other powerful neighbors.
6. Pakistan conducted its tests secretly after condemning India for conducting nuclear tests. India had been open about their intentions to further their nuclear program, but again, the actual tests were announced after the fact.

News, Part 2

1–6. All answers on this worksheet will vary, depending upon the news article each student chooses to deconstruct.

7. Students may determine credibility based on their respect for the news source. They may also check the information they find against information found in other sources.

8. Photos and newsreels can influence one's emotional reaction to a story. Additionally, the extra information found in a full-length newspaper or magazine story, as opposed to a short radio or television feature, can influence a consumer's reaction.

9. Editorials tend to use persuasive and emotionally charged language, whereas hard news reporters try to use neutral language and situational facts.

W O R K S H E E T

Deconstructing the Media

News, Part 2

File: News2

In addition to answering key questions, there are other elements to analyze for a complete evaluation. Use the following questions as you deconstruct a news story:

1. What is the headline, and what effect does it have?

2. What photos or video clips are used, and how do they make you feel?

3. Is the story presented in a balanced fashion? How do you know?

4. Is it subjective or objective? Why do you think so?

5. How much is covered, and what is left out of the story? Why do you think these choices were made?

6. Is it a hard news or soft news story? Explain your answer.

7. Is the story believable? How do you determine its credibility?

8. How does the medium itself impact the story and your reaction to it?

9. What differences do you notice in language between hard news and editorials?

Lesson 6
Let Us Entertain You: *Entertainment in Television and Film*

What's Ahead?

The expansion of cable television programming, video rentals, and home videocassette recorders have given rise to unprecedented choice and cheaper, convenient access to films once limited to theatergoers. With the push of a remote control button, a master storyteller—television—can transport a viewer into real or imaginary places and times. Ranging from classics such as *The Wizard of Oz, Gone With the Wind,* and *Casablanca* to *Saving Private Ryan, Star Wars,* and *Good Will Hunting,* movies can exercise one's imagination by bringing a story to life, recreating time periods or creating alternative worlds, and producing memorable characters, settings, and fashions.

Goals: This lesson explores the concept of entertainment, enabling students to be more active, thoughtful, and intentional viewers rather than passive consumers of media. By comparing their own lives, dreams, and interests to what they watch on film, students can discover why they make their particular entertainment choices. Additionally, by contrasting their opinions to other students', they can gain more respect for dissenting viewpoints.

Disciplines: This lesson can be used for subject areas in social studies, language and performing arts, business, and video production.

LESSON 6

Let Us Entertain You

What's Ahead?

Take a minute to list your top ten favorite forms of entertainment. No fair reading ahead until you finish your list!

Chances are that your list included going to the movies, watching movie videos at home, and watching television. Full-length feature films and television shows have been entertaining audiences for decades. According to *American Demographics* magazine, "nearly half of teenagers go to the movies at least once a month, compared with just one in four adults." But what you enjoyed ten years ago probably doesn't interest you now, and your current favorites may not interest you when you are older. To be successful, those in the entertainment industry have to understand just what appeals to people at various ages and stages.

In this lesson, you will examine your prior and current recreational viewing experiences with television, film, and video entertainment media. You will explore successful entertainment media and compare them to your own preferences. Why are certain kinds of entertainment so successful? How and why do your choices differ from other people's?

Objectives: At the end of this lesson students will be able to:

- Define words in the **Key Ideas** section.
- Discuss the role of demographics in the construction of media messages.
- Integrate feelings, reflections, and personal judgments about media representation—how media texts relate to or distort reality. They will be able to recognize when they identify with or live vicariously through movies and TV series.
- Recount, examine, and reflect on the entertainment value, meanings, and attitudes associated with their viewing experiences.

Main Points to Ponder

- Certain messages and subjects, such as romance and violence, have high entertainment value that appeals to a variety of viewers.
- Because of our unique backgrounds and experiences, we may interpret a film very differently than the writer and director intended. A film can often support many different interpretations.
- Entertainment media may have a positive or negative impact on individual viewers.

Did You Know?

- The highest-grossing movie of all time is 1997's *Titanic,* at over $600 million as of June 1999.
- In 1936, Selznick International Pictures paid $50,000 for the movie rights to *Gone with the Wind,* the largest price paid for a first novel at that time. Margaret Mitchell won a Pulitzer Prize for the book in 1937; in 1940, the film won ten Academy Awards.
- The longest-running science fiction TV show is *Dr. Who,* at 36 years.
- All of the top 10 home videos for June 1999 in the recreational sports category were *WWF* or *WCW* wrestling videos.

Key Ideas

Codes and Conventions–familiar techniques used by media to convey certain ideas or a particular impression. Symbolic codes include such things as lighting, sound, and dress.

Demographics–the statistical characteristics of human populations, such as classifying by age, gender, race, income, health, or education. These figures are widely used in market research.

Entertainment–something that holds one's attention and gives pleasure, diverts, or amuses.

Escapism–flight from the responsibilities and routines of real life, often through imaginative activities.

LESSON 6: LET US ENTERTAIN YOU 55

Did You Know?

Students might enjoy comparing their favorites to those cited in this section.

Key Ideas

Discuss terms. You might use the following questions:

- Do your students have favorite genres? Ask for examples of films that represent those genres. What conventions are used in creating the different genres? (For example: cowboy and Indian costumes, frightening music in horror shows, dark clothes and makeup for "bad guys." This last example raises another interesting question: Does the use of darkness for the evil characters advance a stereotype that causes people to be more fearful of dark-skinned or dark-featured people?)
- Have you ever used demographics in research papers? How can they be helpful? (Answers: by helping people recognize general trends for research, creating helpful programs for various groups, and for developing marketing). In what ways can they be misused? (Answers: when they are used without consideration for unique traits of individuals; when they are used to create stereotypes)
- Everyone needs a break from time to time. What are your favorite forms of escapism?

Materials

This lesson uses:

- Clip from WCW wrestling (Video clip #18 - 5:17)
- Warner Brothers clip from *Gone With the Wind* (Video clip #19 - 0:25)
- Entertainment Worksheet (File name *Entertain* on R&R disk)
- Wrestling Worksheet (File name *Wrestling* on R&R disk)
- Motion Picture Production Code of 1930 (File name *HaysCode* on R&R disk)

Get Started

Encourage students to define the term "entertainment" for themselves. As they consider programs and films that they once enjoyed as compared to their current favorites, they should recognize that their definition of entertainment has probably not changed; rather, as they have matured, the specifics that fit their definition change. See if students can pinpoint the conventions that entertain young children in their shows, particularly educational programming. Embedded in the antics that preschoolers enjoy is new knowledge—about the alphabet, numbers, language, manners—that can bring them acceptance, empowerment, and self-esteem. What is in the shows your students now watch that compares to that? This is a useful question for students to ponder!

Consider using the following activity, written by Richard Fehman, University of Northern Iowa Instructor, in his article, "Celebrating the Viewer/Learner in Critical Viewing Instruction," *Telemedium, The Journal of Media Literacy,* (Volume 43, Number 1, Spring 1997):

Have students write a media autobiography, dividing it into three parts corresponding to their early years/middle years/late years. This allows them to see how developmental the process of viewing is. After the students have finished their report, break into group discussions to share findings and then gather the whole class to determine what individuals share in common as a community of learners.

Get Started

How do you personally define "entertainment"? Something that makes you laugh? Cry? Something that frightens you? All of the above? How is that possible? While your nephew or niece may find *Barney and Friends* delightful, chances are slim that *you* voluntarily watch it! Programming that entertained you as a child no longer interests you, and what you enjoy now may bore you ten years from now. Does this mean that your definition of entertainment changes?

What is entertaining about the movies and TV series that you enjoy? Is it the characters, the situations in the scenes, the genre, the information you learn, the questions the shows raise, the humor?

Sometimes we watch because we *identify* with a character or situation. You may have a favorite show with characters who are similar to you. Sometimes the scenes may be foreign to your life, but you can still identify with a character's conflicts or feelings. Watching movies with identifying traits can help you to gain a new perspective on your own life.

Sometimes we enjoy *living vicariously* through film. Movies set in faraway lands or different time periods can transport viewers to worlds very different from their own. Sports shows can allow viewers to imagine themselves as professional athletes. Do you find yourself drawn to a doctor, lawyer, or police series? Perhaps it is because the shows let you imagine how it would feel to be one of the characters. Shows with more outlandish characters, such as pro wrestling or sensationalized talk shows, let fans *escape* from their own difficulties and problems for a while.

Viewers anticipate codes and conventions in media, correctly interpreting gestures, music, and situations that are funny, suspenseful, romantic, and so forth. However, viewers may interpret messages differently depending on their experiences, interests, and knowledge. Some people love to watch car chase scenes. Others, perhaps because they have been in a car accident, can't sit through one. Your interpretations may also vary due to family backgrounds and beliefs.

After thinking about these ways of enjoying entertainment media, answer the questions on the worksheet **Deconstructing the Media: Entertainment** (p. 62). Discuss your answers in class.

Break It Down

Let's analyze a very unlikely entertainment video clip, the last thing you might expect to study: professional wrestling. Take a minute to write down what you believe about this kind of programming: the wrestlers themselves, the action, the viewers, the popularity of the shows, the purposes and messages of the programs, the reality or fantasy of the action. Have you ever watched pro wrestling on cable, on videos, or live? Are you a regular viewer? Why or why not?

Why should you analyze and evaluate something as noneducational as professional wrestling? Consider these statistics:

- Pro wrestling is the most highly rated programming on cable television, consistently in the top five regularly scheduled shows.
- Roughly 40 million people watch wrestling programs each week.
- Wrestling programming is available in 85 countries, in over ten languages.
- Over 250 live shows per year tour the United States, performing for full-capacity crowds.
- Consumers spend roughly $1 billion every year in wrestling-related merchandise: action figures, electronic games, videos, clothing, greeting cards, trading cards, magazines, and pay-per-view shows.
- The citizens of Minnesota voted retired wrestler Jesse "The Body" Ventura as their state governor in 1998.
- While the largest demographic watching pro wrestling is males ages 18 and over, 25 percent of the audience are women, ages 18 and over, and 24 percent are children ages 2 to 17.
- Households with an income of $20,000 to $50,000 make up 43 percent of the audience.

(Sources: "Lords of the Ring," Time, *June 29, 1998;* USA Today, *August 6, 1998; World Championship Wrestling promotional material)*

"I am simply the most majestic, the most popular and the most distinguished performer that this game [pro wrestling] has ever seen."

Lionheart Chris Jericho

Love it or hate it, professional wrestling has a significant presence in mainstream U.S. society. The wrestlers have developed characters and story lines. World Wrestling Federation owner Vince McMahon says that

Break It Down

Show **video clip #18** on World Championship Wrestling. While students may be surprised and amused at the choice of video, there are specific reasons for the pro wrestling selection. Many students will dismiss pro wrestling as "stupid," and some may admit to enjoying it, but none will be able to deny the impact of this programming once they read the statistics. The purpose of pro wrestling is clearly entertainment, and it should be interesting for students to discuss just why such a spectacle appeals to so many people of differing demographics. Historically, violent forms of entertainment are nothing new. You might remind students about the gladiators that entertained Roman citizens in ancient times. In the case of television and movie violence, however, the action is simulated, not real. A & E has aired a documentary on pro wrestlers in which the wrestlers discuss their roles as actors. Terry "Hulk Hogan" Bollea says, "If somebody gets hurt these days, it's an accident" (*The Wall Street Journal*, 6/5/98).

What are the specific elements of this entertainment? Certainly the physiques and costumes draw attention, both those of the wrestlers and of their female cheering counterparts. (WCW has the sexy "Nitro Girls.") Perhaps more importantly, wrestling presents a simplified moral universe, in which men are either good or bad, brave or cowardly. The story lines trace the rise and fall of heroes and villains who, through an ongoing soap opera of shifting loyalties and betrayals, arouse the full range of the audience's emotions: anger, fear, hope, and joy. After Hogan's years as a "good guy," he changed characters and became a "bad guy" dressed in black whose character attempted to take over the WCW. Pro wrestling is certainly a form of escapism, just as serialized romance novels or afternoon soap operas are.

What of the violence of the wrestlers' moves and the violent threats and challenges they hurl at each other? Though most admit the action is staged, WCW's Eric Bischoff says, "People like to forget it's pretend" (*USA Today*, 8/98). Discussion may help students to understand their own feelings about the seemingly contradictory coupling of violence and enjoyment. Few could deny the pleasure they feel as they watch Zorro's extravagant swashbuckling or Wyatt Earp and his followers' shoot-outs with the bad guys in *Tombstone*. Where one "draws the line" is largely a matter of personal opinion, and it will vary depending on individuals' upbringing, beliefs, and values. Remind students to be respectful of others' opinions as they discuss this controversial topic.

Discuss the worksheet questions and student answers. What else influences their attitudes and how they think? What percentage would they assign mass media for creating their values, beliefs, and preferences?

Hulk Hogan
Courtesy: World Championship Wrestling

the shows "should be looked upon as live-action adventure soap opera." Writ-ing about the fans, TV writer Lyle Harr observed, "There are cute little kids standing on chairs, white-haired grand-mas wearing WCW T-shirts, families out for a night on the town, clean-cut college boys on summer break, and a few good old boys who seem to be on a pe manent break from reality." Harris inte viewed fan Taylor Harris of Birmingham who said, "Americans need something t believe in; we all do. It makes you feel good. We need to believe in something even if it's fake. It brings everybody to gether."

Video clip #18
World Championship Wrestling

Watch the clip of pro wrestling, and answer the questions on your work sheet **Deconstructing the Media: Professional Wrestling** (p. 64). Discu your answers in class.

- In a 1998 CNN/USA Today Poll, 75 percent of Americans believed there is a relationship between the national crime rate and violent programs on TV.
- According to the Center for Media and Public Affairs, a child will witness 8,000 murders on television by age 12.
- In a 1998 health survey conducted by the Kaiser Family Foundation and ABC Television, 74 percent of Americans said they believe that TV programs encourage irresponsible behavior.

Sum It Up

1. Explain how pro wrestling is "carefully manufactured and packaged".
2. What is the point of view of pro wrestling? Of the characters in the segment you viewed?
3. Do you think the moves in pro wrestling are real or fictitious? Why?
4. On a scale of one to five (low to high amount), how do you rate (1) pro wrestling, and (2) your favorite movie or TV series for:

- entertainment value?
- technical achievement?
- violent content?
- romantic or suggestive content?
- realism?
- similarity to your own life?
- positive messages?

Before studying this lesson, had you thought about your viewing preferences in these ways? What have you learned about the movies and programs you enjoy? Do you think they influence you or others? In what ways? Has this lesson changed the way you think about entertainment media? How?

Courtesy: WCW

"I have come up with a sure-fire concept for a hit television show, which would be called 'A Live Celebrity Gets Eaten by a Shark.'"

Dave Barry

Sum It Up

Students' evaluations will vary. Be sure they show an understanding of this exercise by asking them to explain their evaluations using media vocabulary and deconstruction techniques.

Put It Together

Encourage students to choose any medium they find entertaining, rather than feeling limited to television and movies. Though they have not explored all forms of media, they have thought about what entertainment is, and they can apply those ideas to any format.

If this activity is too time-consuming for your schedule, you can shorten it by, for example, having students only write the letter to the agent or outline their idea without writing a more complete chapter, episode, directions, etc.

Put It Together

What kind of media message would you like to see become an entertainment hit? Develop an idea for a screenplay, TV series, game, or novel. Using what you have learned and your own definition of entertainment, create a proposal and sample for your idea. (Work alone or in a group.)

For a novel, include a plot outline, character descriptions, and one written chapter. A screenplay sample should be formatted like a script and should also include directions for the setting, cameras, and lighting. Games would require sketches, the object of the game, and directions for play.

In an introductory letter to an entertainment agency or publisher, convince the agent that your work should be produced. Include your beliefs about entertainment, but highlight features that would appeal to a large audience.

THEN AND NOW

Video clip #19

Turner Entertainment
Gone With The Wind

Hollywood Romance

One of the greatest films of all time is *Gone With The Wind,* based on the best-selling novel by Margaret Mitchell. The movie, which premiered in 1940, was recently re-released in 1998 due to its great appeal and ability to transcend time periods.

Set in the South before, during, and after the Civil War, *Gone With The Wind* depicts the conflicts of southern Americans as they confront slavery, the golden age of the plantation, bitter civil war, and northern carpetbaggers during Reconstruction. In the forefront is the magical romantic triangle formed by strong-willed Scarlett O'Hara, philosophical Ashley Wilkes, and the controversial Rhett Butler.

Vivian Leigh and Clark Gable *Gone With The Wind* © 1939 Turner Entertainment Co. All Rights Reserved

Many scenes from the movie are unforgettable. One of the best is when Rhett requests a kiss from the unwilling Scarlett amidst the famous backdrop of Atlanta burning from General Sherman's march to the sea. In its time, this was considered to be a highly provocative and controversial scene. Watch the clip twice in class: once to be involved in the content, and a second time to consider the technical tools used—lighting, music, dialogue, and camera angles. How do you rate the effectiveness of this clip in terms of content and production? Do camera techniques and lighting contribute to viewers' perceptions of gender roles in the movie? How does it compare to today's scenes depicting romantic attraction? Which do you like better, and why?

MEDIA MATTERS

File: HaysCode

THEN AND NOW

Hollywood Romance. Students are probably familiar with *Gone with the Wind* (see **video clip #19**). If you have time, this is one movie worth showing in its entirety, deconstructing scenes for lighting, camera angles, costumes, etc. If not, recommend that students watch it and write a critique for extra credit.

Depictions of love, romance, and attraction were so different during the heyday of *Gone with the Wind* and many movie classics, which were produced under the strict guidelines of the Hays Code of 1930. It will be interesting to see how students react to the kissing scene on the movie clip. Ask what they find more romantic and emotional: a clip such as the one from *Gone with the Wind,* or a modern one that leaves little to the imagination? Have students read the Hays Code general principles (found on the R&R disk). Would any movies in theaters today meet these requirements? Why do students think the code was repealed?

Take It Further

1. Watch an hour's worth of children's cartoons, noting how many times characters are killed, come back to life, experience real pain, and are punished for violent behavior. Using your statistics, write an essay in which you defend or oppose violence in children's cartoons.

2. Watch a movie classic. You may use *100 Greatest Films* found on the Web at www.filmsite.org/, as a reference. Critique the film for content (plot, characterization, setting, conflict, themes) and technical merit (camera angles, lighting, color, costume, music, etc.). Explain why the film has transcended time.

3. Imagine that you own a new cable channel. Identify a target demographic and write summaries of your lineup of five new shows. Explain how they will appeal to the chosen demographic.

ETHICS IN ACTION

Truth, Fantasy, and Consequences

Market researchers in the entertainment industry study what entertains people in various demographics. They must ask, "What do young women want to see? How does that differ from what young men will watch? How can I combine these elements to create a larger viewing audience?" Because producers must sell their concepts to advertisers and sponsors, they may be more concerned with what sells—what the largest number of people will pay to see—than with the social value of the content. While there are numerous viewing experiences that can both entertain and teach us something about ourselves, many blockbuster films and top-rated televisions series contain violent or graphic images that may negatively impact certain individuals.

In early stages of child development, youngsters do not have enough experience to discriminate clearly between fantasy and reality. They really do believe in Santa Claus. Even older viewers may not have sufficient experiences to recognize the difference between fiction and reality. When character Jennifer Lindley on *Dawson's Creek* is crushed by her loss of boyfriend Dawson Leery to Joey Potter, some adolescent viewers might feel her pain. A 40-year-old viewer is more likely to view the scene as a minor incident that will soon fade away. Viewers who watch violent or dangerous scenes could try to duplicate the action with tragic, even deadly, consequences. Research has also drawn connections between teenage girls' eating disorders and the movie and magazine images constantly put before them of extremely thin, successful, beautiful females.

Imagination is essential to people, allowing them to consider various points of view and to increase their own creativity. When people cannot separate imagination and fiction from reality, however, it can create dissatisfaction or, at its worst, tragedy. In class, discuss stories you have heard that connect mass media images with real-life tragedies.

LESSON 6: LET US ENTERTAIN YOU 61

Take It Further

Numbers 1 and 2 are deconstruction exercises; number 3 is a construction activity. In the first exercise, students will need to tabulate their own set of statistics and use them in their evaluation of violence in children's programming. In the second choice, they will need to refer back to techniques learned in Lesson 2, "Lights! Camera! Action!" Activity 3 will allow them to use the newly learned concept of demographics in creating their cable channel. Look for them to explain the association between the demographic chosen and the rationale for the programming.

ETHICS IN ACTION

Child development professionals teach that young children cannot distinguish between fantasy and reality. But, young children are not the only ones who cannot always separate fiction from reality. In "Gone Too Soon," an article about teen suicide, the *Atlanta Journal Constitution* states:

> Given the way young people can feel invulnerable, and the way violence is portrayed so casually in today's media, some teenagers don't fully appreciate the permanence of suicide. "They don't realize that dead is dead," says Iris Bolton, . . . director of the Link Counseling Center in Sandy Springs. "We had a case where a 13-year-old girl committed suicide. She said people were being mean to her, so she'd just kill herself, and when she came back in three weeks, they'd all be nice to her." (10/12/98, p. C1)

Entertainment

1. Students may or may not identify with specific character traits, the region, urban or rural setting, or events in the movie they choose. They may note that the stars in the movie are more glamorous than they or are involved in more sensational situations.
2. Because students can choose their own media sample, answers will vary widely. Look for them to use specifics from their sample to discuss its implications in their lives.
3. Characters chosen will vary according to what is currently airing on television. Certainly students will find stereotypes in which the successful characters are thin and beautiful. See if they can think of any programs in which the glamorous actors do not necessarily win in the end.

WORKSHEET

Deconstructing the Media

Entertainment

File: Entertain

What is it in entertainment media that makes us laugh, cry, fear, and come back for more? As you examine your own preferences, this worksheet will give you the opportunity to think about just what you enjoy, and why. Since some of your answers may be lengthy, feel free to use a blank sheet of paper to complete your answers.

1. Think of a movie or television show with which you identify. What parts are similar to your own life: characters, setting, situations, and so forth? What is different?

____

____

____

____

2. Which movies or shows (or books or plays) have allowed you to live vicariously in their worlds? Which have been most enjoyable to you, and why? Does this tell you anything about yourself? What?

____

____

____

____

3. Make a list of television characters played by teenage and young adult actors. Think about how these different characters are treated similarly and differently. Do you find trends in which the female stars are more attractive and slimmer than costars? Who "gets the guy"? What are the traits of the successful male stars?

____

____

____

____

4. How do the situations in the shows compare to your life? Do you believe that watching so many beautiful, successful characters can make viewers dissatisfied with their own lives? Why or why not?

5. Do you regularly watch any shows that have violent content? What are they? Why do you watch them? Think of a show you have watched that contained violent content. Would you voluntarily watch another program in the same series? Why or why not?

6. List some dramatic series and/or sitcoms that are popular on television and do not have violence or romance as their main features. How do they attract their audiences?

7. Make a list of your top three favorite full-length feature movies. What characteristics do they share? Do they include a glamour/romance/violence formula within their plots? What makes these movies your favorites? Try to determine the demographics for each movie, and explain your choices.

4. Answers will vary, but look for students to justify what they say with details.
5. Answers should reflect individual students' views on the role of violence in the media and their own values.
6. *Wonder Years* is one candidate. Students may find they need to refer to some popular older shows, such as *The Andy Griffith Show, The Brady Bunch, etc.,* that attract audiences through comedy. Other current sitcoms may also apply, but they tend to use sexuality for comic effect more than their predecessors did.
7. Expect many different answers for this question. See if students can find a pattern among the movies they pick for favorites. They should be able to explain why the movies chosen are their favorites.

Professional Wrestling

1. While the purpose of pro wrestling is primarily entertainment, those opposing the shows may have a hard time agreeing. See if they can separate personal taste from an objective answer.
2. While the target audience is young males, pro wrestling's audience demographics encompass many groups.
3. The character of Hulk Hogan is an egotistical man who bullies and insults his opponents. Interviews with the real man indicate that he is a much quieter, less arrogant person.

WORKSHEET

Deconstructing the Media

Professional Wrestling

File: Wrestling

After viewing the World Championship Wrestling clip, answer the following questions:

1. What is the purpose of professional wrestling? Do you think it achieves its purpose? Why or why not?

____

____

____

____

____

____

2. Who do you think is the target audience for the programming? What material is included to appeal to a broader audience?

____

____

____

____

____

____

3. Describe Hulk Hogan, the character. Would you guess that Hulk Hogan, the man, is similar to his character? Why or why not?

____

____

____

____

____

____

4. Describe some of the best creative scenes or techniques used in the clip.

5. Why do you think that professional wrestling is so popular?

6. Should the public be concerned that professional wrestling is so popular among children? Why or why not?

4. The pyrotechnics that introduce the show are certainly entertaining and creative. Students' answers will vary.
5. Pro wrestling creates a simplistic universe in which there are all good and all bad players. Real people live complicated lives and may wish for this easier-to-understand fictional world.
6. Answers will vary. Look for students to justify their answers, whether they say "yes" or "no."

Lesson 7
Come and Get It! *Print Advertising and Broadcast Commercials*

What's Ahead?

Goals: In this lesson, students will analyze both print ads and television commercials to gain a brief historical perspective of advertising and to understand the motives behind ads, the manipulative devices used, and the visual techniques that create the impact of advertisements. The intention is not to teach that ads are bad, but to underscore the need to realize their influence on our beliefs, desires, and purchases. Students can appreciate the humor or creativity of an ad while recognizing that the purchase of the product will not, in fact, make them more beautiful, happy, or successful.

Disciplines: The contents of this lesson pertain to language arts, history and social studies, visual arts, business and economics, health, biology, psychology.

LESSON 7

Come and Get It!

What's Ahead?

Can you sing your favorite commercial jingle? Do you have a favorite ad slogan? You may be surprised to learn that producing a 30-second ad can take as much time as and more money than a 30-minute sitcom. No wonder they can be so catchy and entertaining! Of course, advertisers have a lot at stake. They pay a great deal of money—and the more popular the program, the more expensive the 30- to 60-second time slot—to convince you that you need their product or service, whether you really need it or not.

In this lesson you will learn about the unique world of advertising—its history, reason for existence, and methods of appealing to its audience. With this type of medium, it is especially important to be able to distance yourself from its entertaining aspects to ask yourself these questions: What am I being told about this product or service? Am I receiving information about the product's real qualities, or am I being enticed by implications of success or beauty? Why do I want this item? Do I need it?

Main Points to Ponder

- Media depend upon sponsorship to exist. Because media productions must make money, they are dependent on "selling" their products to the advertisers who will, in turn, try to sell their own products to each medium's audience.
- While advertisements can inform consumers about products, helping them to decide whether or not they should purchase the specified product or service, they can also entice with manipulative persuasion, suggesting that consumers who buy the products will become more successful, beautiful, or happy.
- Advertising is found almost everywhere: clothes labels, billboards, school vending machines, bumper stickers, buttons, book covers, lettering on cars, sports stadiums, public buildings, political campaigns, and elsewhere. Many people feel there should be commercial-free zones, such as schools.

- The average American sees about 32,000 commercials every year.
- The average North American citizen (U.S. and Canada) consumes:
  - five times as much as one from Mexico.
  - ten times as much as one from China.
  - thirty times as much as one from India.
- Five percent of the world's population consumes one-third of the planet's natural resources.
- In 1998, a 60-second ad aired during the Super Bowl cost $2,600,000.

Objectives: Upon completing this lesson, students will be able to:

- Define key terms associated with advertising.
- Identify the persuasive techniques used in advertisements.
- Deconstruct advertisements.
- Understand how advertisements affect our personal choices and our culture.
- Create advertisements to show their understanding of key concepts in the unit.

Did You Know?

The materials in this section are designed to show students the pervasiveness of advertising and the excessive consumption of North Americans, as compared to heavily populated countries around the world. You might ask the students if they believe there is a correlation between the amount and expense of ads (see the statistic about Super Bowl ads) and the high rate of consumption by Americans.

Get Started

To generate discussion about the pervasiveness of advertising in our culture and to define just what an ad is, ask students to brainstorm in small groups a list of places where they find advertisements in their everyday life. Then have the class share their thoughts while you compile a list of their responses on the board. This should be a lengthy list—don't forget to point out to students what they may overlook, such as t-shirts, baseball caps, shopping bags, catalogs.

If students are not familiar with the term "logo," define it and ask students to identify all the logos in the room. Discuss whether they think logos are ads. Finally, ask each student to write a definition for "advertisement." Volunteers may record their definitions on the board for the class to discuss.

After this discussion, provide students with this definition from the American Market Association for the term "advertisement": "Any paid form of nonpersonal presentation and promotion of ideas, goods, or services by an identified sponsor." Analyze this definition in light of the previous class discussion.

Show the CNN clip on the youth market (**video clip #20**). Ask students if they were aware that teens and young adults are so targeted by advertising. How does it make them feel? By recognizing that ads are intentionally created to get them to buy, do they think they will be more critical of products and their promises?

A readily available source of vintage ads is at www.mediahistory.com/advert.html on the Internet. One 1933 Hires Root Beer ad states that the root beer is "healthful"; you may want to point out that there were not then the same restrictions on accuracy that we have today. There are also movie poster ads on this site. Students can look for details that they think would entice consumers. This is also a good way to show commercials unfamiliar to students so that they can begin to see more clearly how they work.

Key Ideas

Be sure students understand the terms by asking them to give examples where possible. Help students become engaged in this chapter by asking questions such as the following:

Get Started

Why does advertising exist? In a society where goods are unavailable or scarce, ads are not needed. But when goods are mass produced, advertising provides buyers for those goods. Prior to the mass production of goods, a shoemaker, for instance, would construct a single pair of shoes for each customer who entered his shop. If he advertised at all, he would advertise his service rather than his product in a printed announcement or a small, simple ad posted on a wall. Goods were not associated with a brand name; people bought shoes, or shirts, or flour, not a specific brand.

Today, we find out about mass-produced goods through advertisements. To keep our attention, advertisers make ads creative and entertaining. To convince us to buy, they often use techniques that are less product related than consumer driven. Many ads appeal to certain needs and desires

Key Ideas

Cropping - the technique used to cut away the surroundings of photos in order to give greater prominence to a specific person, idea, or object.

Focus groups - a small number of people, usually 10 to 20, gathered together by a company to express their opinions and make suggestions about a specified topic or product.

Framing - using borders to limit the background of a photograph.

Jingle - a simple, catchy arrangement of words or light verse, usually put to music, used in advertising to help consumers remember the product.

Psychographics - the study of a target audience's emotional make-up, insecurities, desires, and wants.

Public Service Announcements (PSAs) - a subcategory of ads that promote positive actions and behaviors rather than products.

Unique Selling Proposition - the special benefit a product has that no other product can offer.

Voice-over - a voice that comments or narrates off-camera. For instance, when you don't see the person who is saying the words of a commercial, you are hearing a voice-over.

that have been carefully studied by psychologists, marketers, and experts in the fields of demographics and psychographics. Focus groups test the effectiveness of their ads.

Modern advertisers emphasize the life-style benefits products can offer by appealing to the consumer's dreams and desires. Instead of selling cosmetics, advertisers sell beauty, confidence, and hope. In a car ad, the engine is not described; the message is that if you possess the car, your insecurities about love, appearance, or power will evaporate.

Here are a few of the most frequently used techniques of persuasion that you will find in advertisements. Many will be familiar to you.

- **Bandwagon:** "Everybody has it and if you don't, you will be a social misfit and outcast."
- **Attraction:** "If you buy this car, wear this cologne, drink that soft drink, you will be able to attract that gorgeous woman/man in the background of the ad." This may be the most widely used device in advertising.
- **Happy families:** "Use our product and you will have the love of a perfect family. Everyone will be happy."
- **Something for nothing:** "Act now and you will also receive this free gift."
- **Testimonials:** Celebrities are seen endorsing a product. If the celebrity uses it, you will be like him/her if you use it too.
- **All natural:** These ads respond to the population's growing concern with health. "Buy our product, and be the picture of health and/or stamina."
- **Nostalgia:** "Our product takes you back to a simpler, gentle time when people were truly happy."
- **Patriotism:** These ads contain emotional appeals using the American flag or other national symbols, images, or songs.

Watch the CNN "Youth and Advertising" video clip and discuss your reactions to the information presented. Think of some advertisements you have seen that seem to target young people. What persuasion techniques are used in these ads?

"Good advertising does not just circulate information. It penetrates the public mind with desires and belief."

Leo Burnett

Video clip #20

CNN "Youth and Advertising"

- What is your favorite ad? Why?
- Are there ads you dislike so much that you would not buy the products they advertise? Explain.
- Do you leave the room when commercials come on the TV, or do you stay to watch them?
- Do you think you are influenced at all by ads? In what ways?

Materials

This lesson uses:

- CNN clip on Youth and Advertising (Video clip #20 - 1:08)
- Radio clips from The Ad Council's drunk driving prevention campaign (Audio CD Track #3)
- Ad Council PSA on junk food (Video clip #21 - 0:20)
- Advertising Appeals and Techniques (File name *AdAppeal* on R&R disk)
- Print Advertisements Worksheet (File name *Printads* on R&R disk)
- Television Commercials Worksheet (File name *Tvcomm* on R&R disk)

The File: AdAppeal on the Readings & Resources disk contains a more complete list of ad devices.

Break It Down

Larry Adelman, co-director of a 1998 California Newsreel entitled "Our Ad Ad Ad World," says it is "time for a public debate on the role of advertising and consumption in our society." How would your students line themselves up in such a debate?

Print Ads

Create a "gallery walk" by posting the ads around the room. Have students walk around the room with their notebooks, view the ads, and try to identify the techniques used to persuade the consumer that he/she needs the product. When the gallery walk is complete, return each ad to its original owner. Discuss the students' observations and their experiences with framing and cropping. They may notice that a product receives more attention through these techniques, or that undesirable elements in a photo can be taken out. You can also tell them that much photo manipulation goes into creating the "perfect" product. Fast-food restaurants' burgers, for example, frequently have the seeds glued on individually. Grease is completely blotted off and light oil is sprayed in its place. Many hamburgers are thrown away during the production of a single print ad or TV commercial.

Break It Down

"I do not read advertisements. I would spend all of my time wanting things."
Archbishop of Canterbury

In *The Image Makers: Power and Persuasion on Madison Avenue* (New York: Time Books, 1984), author William Meyers said, "Ad Alley's wizards have firmly established themselves as both the creators and controllers of our consumer culture . . . they are now virtually able to dictate the food we eat, . . . the cars we drive, even the presidents we elect." Just what effect has advertising had on our culture, on what we expect from life, on our values and beliefs?

Print Ads

1. What persuasive techniques can you identify in ads? To find out, bring in an advertisement that appeals to you or that you find interesting. You will have the chance to examine the ads brought to class by other students as well. Note the techniques used to create a successful ad. Use the Worksheet **Deconstructing the Media: Print Advertisements** (p. 75) to further analyze your ad for emotional appeals and techniques.
2. Framing and cropping are two techniques used to further emphasize products and messages about them. Cut a 2½-inch wide by 2-inch high rectangle in a white piece of paper. Walk around the room and use the "frame" to view objects, people, and scenes. Try different angles, close-ups, and long shots. Jot down notes about your experience framing the world. What did you focus on in your frame? What did you leave out? What was it like to see the world in this way?
3. Look at the ad you brought in. How is it framed? Does your ad seem to be cropped?
4. Look at the ads posted around the room, and pay attention to cropping. What might have been left out? Can you guess why? What was included? Why?

Courtesy: the Ad Council

Radio Ads

Voices can convey emotions to correspond to the content. Listen to the drunk driving prevention PSAs produced by the Ad Council. What techniques do they use to get their message across? Compare these ads to radio ads you hear for different beverages. What techniques and messages do they deliver?

Audio Track #3
The Ad Council:
Friends Don't Let Friends Drive Drunk

Television Commercials

Television commercials use the same devices as print ads, but with two powerful components added—movement and sound. Moving images engage a more primitive, less logical part of the human brain than words do, and they therefore have the capacity to arouse the strongest emotions and be more persuasive. Images and sound together are much more powerful than text.

So many ads appear on television (a half-hour sitcom has approximately eight minutes of commercials, each about 15 seconds long) that the first step is to grab the viewer's attention and keep his or her finger off the mute button on the remote. Commercials draw us in with quick camera cuts, special effects, music, mystery, and voice-overs. The commercial then creates a need or desire and "positions" the product as the only thing that can fulfill that need or desire.

1. Watch the television PSA ad about junk food, produced by the Ad Council. Who is the target audience? What techniques are used to get the message across? Compare this campaign to ads for nonnutritional foods you see on television. Who is their target audience, and how do you know? What techniques are used to make those products appealing?
2. Use the worksheet **Deconstructing the Media: Television Commercials** (p. 77) to analyze ads that you find on television.

Video clip #21
The Ad Council:
"Gofer Cakes"

Radio Ads

The ads provided by the Ad Council (**audio CD Track #3**) begin with sound from home videos of happy preschoolers. Next, an announcer tells the audience that a drunk driver killed the child shortly after the film was taped, and follows with the slogan, "Get the keys. Friends don't let friends drive drunk." Students should note the differences between these quiet, tragic real-life ads and the ones they will hear for alcohol that emphasize fun, youth, and success.

Television Commercials

Students should get a laugh from watching the junk food PSA (**video clip #21**). The clip uses parodies of actual ads for junk food that inundate television. When they compare the PSA to real commercials for non-nutritional foods, students should be able to compare and contrast the elements of each: bright, colorful depictions of the foods, happy eaters, "couch potatoes." A major difference is that the product commercials will not depict overweight youth overeating, while the PSA follows the problem of overeating junk foods to its logical conclusion.

You can model the worksheet activity before asking students to do it. Tape a commercial and bring it to show in class. Have students watch it two or three times, and discuss the camera angles, lighting, colors, jingles, voice-over, quality and tone of voice, etc. Have the class discuss how effective the commercial is.

Sum It Up

On a scale of one to five (from little to great extent), evaluate how much you think that advertisements

- affect your purchasing decisions.
- affect your peers' purchasing decisions.
- accurately represent products you buy.
- contribute to consumers' buying things they don't really need or even want.

THEN AND NOW

Mass Production and the Rise of Advertising

The combination of the Industrial Revolution, the rise of a literate population, and the widespread use of the printing press made advertisements necessary, available, and more elaborate. Advertising became necessary because now there were more goods than were needed. Advertisers had to create the need or the desire for this surplus of material objects.

Printers discovered that they could make money both by selling papers and by charging merchants to print ads. They hired agents to sell ad space and paid the established 15 percent commission. Thus was born the ad agency.

When the technology of glass jars and tin cans was developed in the 1880s, brand names arose. Previously, people bought items such as sugar, soap, flour, and candy from large, unmarked barrels in neighborhood general stores. Now, companies manufactured Ivory Soap or Baker's Chocolate and created colorful packaging and images they wanted buyers to associate with their products. Agencies used the work of early psychologists such as Ivan Pavlov and John Watson to refine ads with repetition, jingles, and graphics to entice customers. In fact, Watson was the first person to apply the concepts of psychology to the advertising industry, and in 1924 he became the vice president of J. Walter Thompson, one of the largest ad agencies in the United States at that time.

In the 1950s, ad executive Rosser Reeves developed the concept of the "Unique Selling Proposition" (USP), which was the special benefit the product had that no other product could offer. The Reeves agency coined the word "Gardol," the ingredient in Colgate toothpaste that would fight cavities and that no other toothpaste had. The Doyle Dane Bernbach agency began creating ads with entertainment value. The industry developed rapidly with the proliferation of television. Agencies used marketers to study consumers' demographics so they could design compelling images that would create a consumer "need" for the product (William Jawitz, *Understanding Mass Media,* [Lincolnwood, Ill.: National Textbook Company, 1996], 460–467).

THEN AND NOW

Students may not be able to conceive of a time when ads were not as pervasive as they are today. Suggest that students interview a grandparent or adult over the age of 60 about major products of their youth. Ask them to remember ads and what they promised about the products. Additionally, have students ask them if they recall buying items that were not brand name items. Older adults will recall stores with penny candy, and elderly adults can tell about going to a store and asking for "bread, milk, butter, etc." Ask if students can think of an equivalent to those products from past decades, such as "generic" foods and drugs.

Put It Together

In a small group, create your own ad campaign, using the persuasive techniques and visual elements we have discussed.

Part One

Choose a generic product you will sell (such as hairspray, toothpaste, an automobile, dog food). Then create a Unique Selling Proposition (USP) for the product (see "Then and Now" feature for more information on USPs).

1. What is the market you will be targeting as potential customers?
2. What devices will you use to appeal to this market?

Design the product's packaging. Create a print ad that includes a slogan for the product, and write a storyboard for a 15-second commercial. Try to write a jingle for the product. (Classes with video equipment and sufficient time can actually produce the commercial.)

Present your product and ad campaign to the class, explaining the marketing strategy and persuasive techniques you used.

Part Two

Using the same product, packaging, and potential customers, create another print ad stating only facts about the product. Discuss in your group which you think will sell more of your product and why.

Take It Further

1. Study junk mail and catalogs as a form of advertising. How are they similar to the more traditional forms of advertising you have studied (print ads and commercials)? In what ways are they different?

2. Research the link between advertising and consumerism from an environmental standpoint. For articles on the subject, do a key word search on the Internet or in your library files for advertising,

Put It Together

This construction activity again allows teachers to make good use of multiple intelligences and heterogeneous grouping practices while students learn more about ad creation. Students will need to make use of concepts they learned in this chapter, such as jingles, slogans, and framing and cropping techniques. Additionally, they need to draw on previously learned concepts, such as purpose, point of view, and production techniques (lighting, angles, etc.). Two main concepts to look for in students' work with this activity are as follows:

1. Conscious use of manipulative strategies, demonstrating that they are aware of these persuasive elements and can recognize them in ads they view.
2. Creation of two very different ad campaigns, demonstrating that they can differentiate between emotional persuasion/manipulation and logical information.

Take It Further

1. This deconstruction activity allows students to look at another subdivision of advertising: "junk mail." Some of this mail is highly persuasive (for example, "YOU HAVE JUST WON ONE MILLION DOLLARS! If you have one of the lucky numbers...") See if students ever order from mail advertising and whether or not they are satisfied with their orders. Because of camera techniques, mail order products often look much better on paper than in reality.
2. This construction activity gives students a chance to evaluate consumerism in America and think in depth about its impacts.

3. We all have commercials we enjoy, and this exercise gives students the opportunity to examine just what it is about their favorite ads that they like. Interestingly, more and more commercials seem to be highly creative, but barely concerned with the products themselves (for example, some car commercials and, in magazines, some designer clothes ads). You may want to discuss this trend in class to see if students do or do not notice what the products are.

consumerism, and environment. What are the ecological and global implications of the fact that the richest one-fifth of the world's population accounts for 86 percent of private consumption? Prepare a video that communicates your findings in a PSA.

3 To help people remember products, advertisers try to make the ads creative, catchy, and entertaining. Think of some memorable ads. What do you enjoy about them? Do you remember the product? Can you think of ads that you enjoy, yet you don't associate the product with the ad?

ETHICS IN ACTION

People as Objects

ETHICS Jean Kilbourne, media critic and writer, has lectured frequently on the ways women are depicted in advertisements. She contends that advertisers depict women in these ways:

1. **Canting**—the woman's body is positioned in a way that makes the model look weak, submissive, or insecure, rather than strong and ready to face the world.
2. **Clowning**—the model is positioned to look silly or childish, suggesting that women cannot be taken seriously.
3. **Superiority**—the size, position, and placement of men and women in ads suggests the subordination of women. Women are frequently seen behind or below men.
4. **Dominance/violence**—the implication and threat of violence are used to get the attention of the viewer.

Look through a fashion magazine and cut out at least five ads. Deconstruct the ads using Kilbourne's points. Tell which of the ways the woman is depicted and then tell what values and attitudes about women are conveyed through the ads.

Select one of the ads you deconstructed. Brainstorm some of the ways you can remake the ad to effectively promote the product without demeaning women. Draw your new ad, or reconstruct it using cutouts from magazines or newspapers.

Men are also depicted in ways that promote stereotypes. Look through magazines and study the ads that feature men. Name ways that advertisers use to depict men and boys similar to the ways Jean Kilbourne listed for women. Select one ad that provides examples for each of the ways you list.

Contrast the two lists you have for the depiction of men and women in advertising. Write your responses to the following questions, and follow that with a class discussion.

1. Do you agree with Kilbourne's ideas on the depiction of women in advertising? How difficult was it to find examples?
2. How might the gender roles perpetuated in advertising affect the ways men and women see themselves and the possibilities for their lives?
3. Do you think, as many critics contend, that the depiction of women in advertising contributes to women's dissatisfaction with their bodies?
4. Do you think ads contribute to the prevalence of eating disorders among women?
5. Do you think the depiction of men in advertising contributes to men's dissatisfaction with their bodies? Why or why not?
6. How might the depiction of the sexes affect male-female relationships?

ETHICS IN ACTION

People as Objects. A visit to the Web site www.about-face.org/ can provide many samples of ads in which women are portrayed in the ways mentioned above. There is also commentary on the messages that the ads convey. This may help students understand the obvious stereotypes before they have to search for them. However, depending on the ages of your students and your school policies, you may want to look at the site and just download examples you want to use, without giving out the Web address. Some links can lead to sites where students would find materials that may not be appropriate for them.

WORKSHEET

Deconstructing the Media

Print Advertisements

File: PrintAds

Using the sample ad you brought in for class, analyze what your ad says and how it says it in order to understand how ads work to entice you to buy products. List what you see without making judgments. After you note all the techniques the ad uses, you can evaluate the impact of the techniques and draw conclusions.

1. What emotional appeals does your ad use?

____

____

____

2. How does the ad convey these emotions?

____

____

____

3. Is there any product information given in the ad? If yes, what is it?

____

____

____

4. What product information is *not* given? Why do you think it has been left out?

____

____

____

____

____

____

____

____

____

____

Print Advertisements

1. Look for students to use the list of emotional appeals found in the book and on the computer disk.
2. Answers may include use of color, positioning of images, what is in a position of prominence, what is cut out of the image.
3. Answers will vary. Often there is some objective information about the product, but even this is frequently made fuzzy or irrelevant by weasel words. NOTE: Weasel words and many other ad devices are defined in file name AdAppeal on the R&R disk.
4. Chances are that direct product information is diminished or not present.

5. Answers will vary, depending upon the ad being deconstructed.
6. Generally, images of most prominence will be more lighted and brightly colored than other images.
7. If models are used in the ad, they often have expressions depicting great satisfaction with the product or with their lifestyle as a result of buying the product.
8. Ads tend to use very little copy, and the copy is usually concise and catchy. Many students will find weasel words in their ad's copy.

5. Study the images in the ad. How do they contribute to the ad's message?

6. How is light used in the image? Is high contrast used, or is the image shadowy and dark? Are some parts of the image more lighted than others? Why?

7. Consider the use of close-ups and composition. What expressions are on the models' faces? What does their body language show? Are these postures in any way related to the product?

8. Study and comment on the placement of the words in the ad, the "copy." How does this help convey the ad's message? What manipulative words can you find ("free," "improved," "only," "pure," "virtually," "better," "more," "special")? What do these words mean? Why do you think they are used?

WORKSHEET

Deconstructing the Media

Television Commercials

File: TVComm

Watch a favorite television commercial. Answer the following questions:

1. What devices does the ad use to grab your attention in the first few seconds?

2. What visual images and techniques of persuasion does the ad use?

3. What message is the ad trying to get you to believe?

4. What is the marketing strategy of the ad? Who is it intended for, and how do you know?

5. What information is left out of the ad? Why?

Television Commercials

1. Answers will depend on the commercial chosen and product advertised, but many use quick cuts that give a feeling of energy and entertainment.
2. Techniques may include a story line, quick cuts depicting success and satisfaction, attractive lighting, perfect product examples, and handsome men and beautiful women.
3. Ultimately, the ad wants you to believe that you need the product.
4. Look for the kinds, colors, and ages of models used, the situations depicted, and the pace of the ad to indicate the demographics.
5. An ad is not going to tell its audience that kids will tire of the toy being sold or that a detergent won't really remove every stain, for example.

Lesson 8
Is That So?
TV Talk Shows

What's Ahead?

Goal: Television talk shows have become the "talk" of the television industry. They've grown in popularity, proliferated in number, and caused some heated discussions because of the frequently outrageous content. The talk show phenomenon provides an opportunity for discussing how popularity is measured, how the ratings system works, and what attributes make the shows popular. This last question leads to an exploration of uses and gratifications research—why people watch what they watch.

Disciplines: This lesson relates to knowledge and skills covered in language arts, social studies (economics), and psychology courses.

Objectives: Upon completing this lesson students will be able to:

- Identify the three types of talk shows—celebrity interview, issue oriented, and "ordinary people."
- Define the **Key Ideas** related to the lesson.
- Explain how the Nielsen ratings system works.
- Deconstruct a talk show.
- Identify the various components of a talk show.
- Produce an amateur-level talk show.
- Express their opinion regarding social responsibility and talk show production.

LESSON 8

Is That So?

What's Ahead?

Talk shows have become the fastest-growing genre in television entertainment. As the field becomes more competitive, some producers try to improve their ratings by airing shows that discuss highly controversial topics in an increasingly confrontational way.

There is much debate about the content of these programs and whether or not the more outrageous shows should be prohibited. Their enormous popularity indicates, however, that they will not disappear soon. Thus, it is up to the viewers to decide if they will watch controversial shows and, if so, how they will respond to them.

To understand the phenomenon of talk shows, one must be aware of the types of talk shows, the economics of television, the rating system employed, and the needs of the typical talk show audience.

Main Points to Ponder

- Television can shape our understanding of the world. Frequent viewers of talk shows, especially, could mistake the distorted view of reality and bizarre behavior for the real world.
- The three basic types of talk shows are celebrity interview shows such as *Larry King Live* and *The Rosie O'Donnell Show;* issue-oriented programs such as *Nightline* and *Talk Back Live;* and exposé shows whose guests discuss their personal problems and interpersonal conflicts such as *Oprah* and *Jerry Springer.*
- The economics of television demands that talk shows attract a large audience in order to survive in a highly competitive, ratings driven industry. Media-savvy viewers understand how ratings are obtained and how they influence program content.

78 MEDIA MATTE

Materials

This lesson uses:

- *Talk Back Live* footage with John Glenn (Video clip #22 - 7:11).
- Sally Jessy Raphael magazine feature, excerpts from articles on Roseanne Barr and Jerry Springer

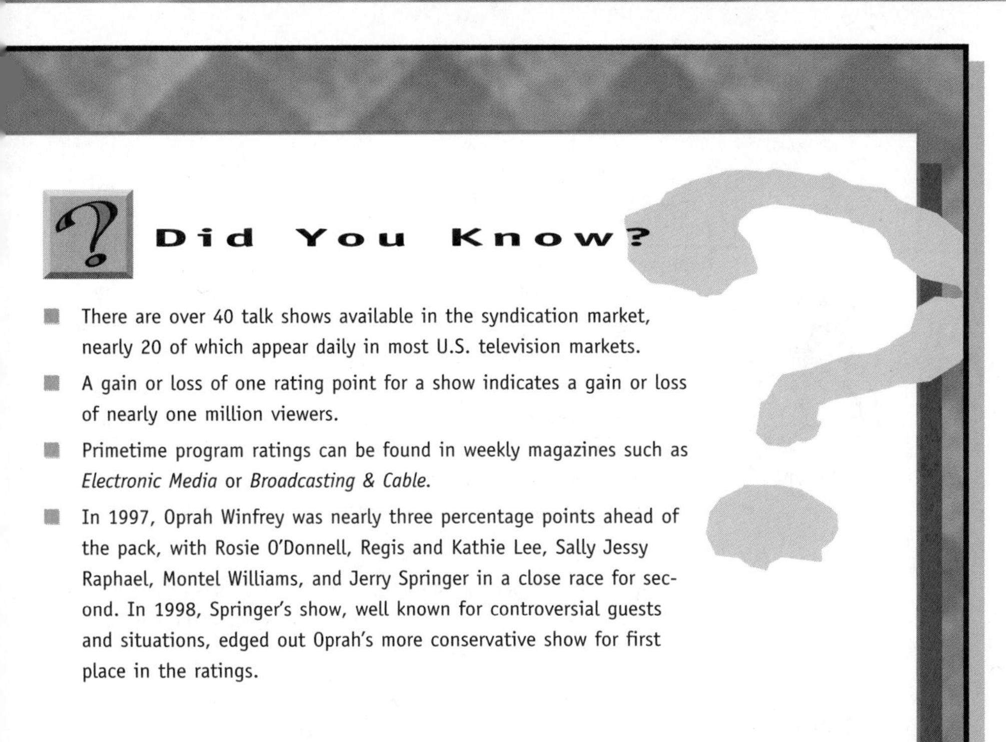

Did You Know?

- There are over 40 talk shows available in the syndication market, nearly 20 of which appear daily in most U.S. television markets.
- A gain or loss of one rating point for a show indicates a gain or loss of nearly one million viewers.
- Primetime program ratings can be found in weekly magazines such as *Electronic Media* or *Broadcasting & Cable.*
- In 1997, Oprah Winfrey was nearly three percentage points ahead of the pack, with Rosie O'Donnell, Regis and Kathie Lee, Sally Jessy Raphael, Montel Williams, and Jerry Springer in a close race for second. In 1998, Springer's show, well known for controversial guests and situations, edged out Oprah's more conservative show for first place in the ratings.

Key Ideas

Nielsen Ratings - The largest and best-known company providing television ratings is the Nielsen Media Research Company. The process it uses to determine a program's ratings is explained in the **Production Notes** feature in this chapter (p. 82).

Share - the percentage of television sets in use that are tuned to a network during a specific time period.

Syndicates - Organizations that supply television stations around the country with programming—some of it first-run, some of it rerun.

Television market - Any geographic area receiving programming from a television program provider.

Uses and Gratifications Research - Research conducted by communication scholars that attempts to answer these questions: Why do people select particular media and programming options? What needs are being satisfied through their use of these media and programs?

LESSON 8: IS THAT SO? 79

(File name *ShowHost* on R&R disk).

- A Close-Up Look Worksheet (File name *CloseUp* on R&R disk)
- Talk Shows Worksheet (File name *Talkshow* on R&R disk)

Did You Know?

Statistics here deal mostly with Nielsen ratings, which are explained in the lesson's **Production Notes** feature.

Key Ideas

Syndicators produce most television talk shows. Tape the closing credits of several talk shows so students can identify the syndicate. Ads for these shows, which appear in *Electronic Media* magazine, often advertise the percentage of certain large U.S. markets that air their programs. If possible, bring in one or two of these ads and discuss the significance of syndicators and television markets.

Distribute copies of the Nielsen ratings for a recent week. You can find these in *Electronic Media* or *Broadcasting and Cable* magazines, or on the web at http://ytv.yhoo.com/nielsen/. Discuss the feature box in the lesson on the ratings. Have students list their three favorite primetime programs and try to find their ratings. How many of the top ten shows for that week are among the students' favorites?

Discuss the importance of Uses and Gratifications Research to television producers and their advertisers (see worksheet question #4 to see a list of reasons given for people's viewing choices). By understanding why people like certain kinds of programming, producers can design programs that satisfy people's preferences and "meet their needs."

Get Started

Ask students how talk shows differ and lead them to see that there are actually three main categories. Ask which variety/celebrity interview and issue-oriented talk shows they've seen. How are the target audiences different?

Ask students if the talk shows they've watched ever dealt with topics that they thought were inappropriate. Were there any topics that they think wouldn't be good viewing for small children? Why are the air times of concern?

Have students note the three positions described in the first paragraph of this section and explain which of the positions they agree with. Discuss the concept of "social boundaries." Are some matters private—and best kept that way? Do the producers of talk shows have any degree of social responsibility in these matters? Have students explain and support their opinions. Remind students to think about personal responsibility and choice: they ultimately determine whether or not they will watch shows that they deem to be inappropriate. Discuss the talk show research that emerged from the study conducted by Michigan State University researchers.

Get Started

The rapid growth of the talk show format and the resulting high level of competition for audience share have led to the airing of increasingly controversial topics, especially on daytime television. A growing proportion of the shows focus on highly personal aspects of people's lives. Some say talk shows are just entertainment, so whatever captivates an audience is fair game. Others maintain that discussion of inappropriate private matters is unhealthy. These critics argue that talk shows are becoming public therapy sessions, which represent, at best, a misuse of therapy for commercial reasons, and constitute, at worst, a danger to both participants and viewers.

A study of 110 daytime talk shows conducted by five researchers from Michigan State University reveals interesting facts about the typical talk show's content, audience, and guests:

- Many talk show guests engage in highly personal self-disclosure. As a result, content is often a discussion of personal problems, interpersonal conflicts, and unusual behavior.
- Some psychologists and sociologists express concern that frequent viewers may conclude that this behavior is normal and lose sight of our society's commonly accepted social boundaries.
- Audience analysis studies show that many regular viewers like talk shows because they view them as "participatory." The viewers appreciate that they are able to make evaluations along with the experts who appear on the shows.
- Talk show guests are often aware that they may face ridicule on the program, but nonetheless seek the sense of power or exhilaration that comes from being on national television.

(Source: Journal of Broadcasting & Electronic Media, *Summer 1997, p. 419.)*

"If there's anything unsettling to the stomach, it's watching actors on television talk about their personal lives."
Marlon Brando

80 MEDIA MATTERS

1. Discuss the growing amount of self-disclosure on talk shows. Ask whether it is possible that the self-disclosure provides "drama" that attracts audience interest. Is it possible that this format is now being used as a cost-saving device? For example, in 1998 a typical episode of ***ER*** cost around 13 million dollars to produce. On a talk show, the guests supply the dramatic story. The producer doesn't incur the expense of a large cast, multiple sets, and several scriptwriters.
2. Do students agree with psychologists and sociologists who fear that frequent viewers may conclude that the aberrant behavior discussed on talk shows is normal and acceptable?
3. Do students agree that talk shows are more "participatory" than most television shows? If so, might this explain some of their popularity?
4. Have students read the article by Sally Jessy Raphael and excerpts about Roseanne Barr's and Jerry Springer's shows. Do they believe that talk shows can accomplish what Raphael and Barr hope to achieve? The attraction of Springer's show is quite different. Have students consider the viewer needs his show meets. (Direct students to question four of **Deconstructing the Media: Talk Shows** p. 87.)

Break It Down

Review the recommended clips and shows to complete these exercises:

Video clip #22
Talk Back Live:
John Glenn

1. Watch the clip of *Talk Back Live* that features astronaut John Glenn, known as both the first U.S. astronaut in space and, after his 1998 shuttle flight, the oldest man to go into space. Who do you think this show would appeal to? Why? The show is aired in the late afternoon. Is most of its target audience available to watch it at this time? How do you judge the quality of the segment? What do you notice about the audience? Defend your rating.
2. Watch one of each of the other two types of talk shows. An issue-oriented show could be *Meet the Press, Nightline,* or *Larry King Live.* For a show that interviews ordinary people, you might watch *Oprah Winfrey, Montel Williams,* or *Ricki Lake.*

Look over and discuss the seven elements of a talk show on the worksheet **Deconstructing the Media: A Close-up Look at a Talk Show** (p. 85). As a class, determine the criteria for quality in talk shows. For example, what criteria would a show emphasizing entertainment include? What about a show emphasizing informational value? Fill out your worksheet to give your analysis and evaluation of one of the talk shows you viewed. For your rating score in each category, use a scale of 1 to 5 (one being the lowest score, five being the highest).

CNN's *Talk Back Live*

Discover your thoughts about talk shows—reasons for watching or not watching, feelings about their content, and so forth—by filling out the more general worksheet, **Deconstructing the Media: Talk Shows** (p. 87). Discuss your differences of opinion in class.

Break It Down

1. Show **video clip #22.** After John Glenn's 1998 space shuttle flight, he was hailed as an American hero. Certainly, the words, the facial expressions on the audience members, and the quotes put onto the screen exemplify this almost reverent feeling. The clip is one of a celebrity-type talk show, but it is unusual in that Glenn is not actually present on the set.
2. Have students watch at least one talk show during the coming week and do the exercise in their workbook. Ask students to decide in advance which shows they will watch so you can be sure each category of talk show is represented. If time is limited, have students do this in class, working in groups of three or four and analyzing a show everyone in the group has seen. Ask each group to appoint a team recorder who will write down their ratings and summarize them.

Review with your students each of the seven components of television talk shows listed in their worksheet. Review the concept of deconstruction, if necessary.

After class discussion of their analyses and evaluations, have each team recorder add the ratings to get a total rating for the show. Note which programs have the highest overall ratings. Discuss these findings. If students did the exercise at home, have each student identify his or her total rating for the show and compare ratings. One of the key concepts of media literacy is that "audiences negotiate meaning" (see Lesson 1). How is that evident in comparing individuals' ratings? Discuss possible reasons for differences in ratings.

Sum It Up

1. After looking at the Nielsen Ratings and determining the most widely viewed talk show for the previous week, ask students which they think are the most "talked about" talk shows. Are the comments made about the show generally positive or negative?

Very often it's the sensational shows that get noticed—and talked about. This increases people's awareness of the show, which can lead to higher ratings as curious new viewers tune in.

2. Sally Jessy Raphael is host of the longest running daytime talk show. Her commentary (on the R&R disk, file name *ShowHost*) defends daytime talk shows. Discuss the trends she mentions. Ask students, "Where will talk shows go from here to attract audiences?"

Ask students to identify the specific criticisms leveled against talk shows that are cited by Raphael. Have them reflect on and discuss the following statements:

a. "...most of us have done countless shows dedicated to saving lives or, at the very least, turning troubled lives around."
b. "With television (being) the leading provider of information in this country, I know more people get vital knowledge about psychology and health from daytime talk shows than they do from reading newspapers or textbooks."
c. "The audience applauds the good people and boos the bad people. The lesson is always that the good guys are right and the bad guys get hurt."

Sum It Up

1. Tabulate your ratings and results from the **Break It Down** exercise. Are there any patterns in the class's ratings of shows? Do any shows receive more positive or negative ratings than others? Discuss the reasons. Overall, how do you judge the main purposes of media (to inform, entertain, or persuade) with respect to each type of talk show?

File: ShowHost

2. Read the feature article by talk show host Sally Jesse Raphael, as well as the excerpts about Roseanne and Jerry Springer that your instructor will provide. After careful consideration of these articles, and in light of your own experience with the talk shows you recently watched, write your own guest commentary in response to Raphael's ideas.

PRODUCTION NOTES

Television Ratings

The Nielsen Media Research Company is the largest and most widely used of the available ratings services. Nielsen Media Research determines the ratings for television programming by installing devices called "people meters" in approximately 4,000 selected households. Nielsen claims that this randomly selected group of households mirrors the interests and viewing patterns of the entire population. While this is debatable, broadcasters consider it the most effective rating system currently available.

The people meter is a small device containing a sophisticated microprocessor that sits atop the television set. Demographic information about each household member is entered into the computer. The information includes age, gender, and other data that marketers find useful. Each household member pus[hes] an assigned button as he or she watches television. Advertisers c[an] thus determine the members of [a] specific target audience watchin[g] any given program. Each day the [in]formation is fed into Nielsen's c[om]puters at 3:00 a.m. By 3:15 p.m Nielsen produces the daily rating report, which becomes available [to] its clients electronically.

PRODUCTION NOTES

Distribute copies of a recent Nielsen rating for primetime television. Explain that each rating point represents 980,000 households, or one percent of the nation's estimated 98 million homes with a TV. The rating number serves as the basis for the cost of a 30-second commercial during a specific program. Nielsen Media Research also publishes Cable Nielsen Ratings and Top Ranked Programs in Syndication. Have students check the latter on the Internet at http://www.UltimateTV.com/news/nielsen/syndication/ to see which talk shows were on the top 20 that week.

Put It Together

Divide into three talk show production teams. Each team will produce a segment from one of the three types of talk shows. Use the items in the **A Close-Up Look at a Talk Show** worksheet (p. 85) to consider important elements. Which of the elements are most important to your show?

GROUPS

Produce your program with the intention of having one additional audience view it after the class has seen it. You might show it to another class in the school, the PTA, the school board, or an elementary school class. Make a plan for that additional presentation (location, equipment needed, how to advertise and promote the program, etc.).

After each presentation, discuss the exercise. What questions and comments do students have about your show? How do they rate it, using the questions from **A Close-up Look at a Talk Show?** What did you learn from this exercise? What might you do differently the next time around?

CAREER PROFILE

The "Queen of Talk": Oprah Winfrey

Oprah Winfrey is regarded as the founder of the confessional variety of talk shows. She began her career in 1984 as the host of Chicago's *A.M.* show. In 1986, the series became *The Oprah Winfrey Show* and entered syndication. Today, Winfrey's show remains extremely popular, and her success has allowed her to enter and influence other forms of media, including books, television specials, and movies.

On the road to success, Winfrey confronted the barriers of gender, race, and appearance. When she began, she was an overweight woman who openly joked about and struggled with this problem. Many women relate to her struggle and admire her candidness on the subject.

More admirable has been her adherence to propriety in a talk show race that seems to become more outrageous by the week. Unlike Jerry Springer, who remains a mystery to his audience, Oprah is as confessional as her guests are. This has created a following that is more sympathetic and caring than many talk show audiences. Arguably, Winfrey has made the talk show format more sophisticated. Her book club, launched in 1996, has propelled 24 books onto the best-seller list in just two years, an indication of her far-reaching influence. She has also successfully motivated viewers to do good deeds with her "Angel Network" and now incorporates a "Remembering Your Spirit" segment in her shows.

In addition to her talk show, Winfrey is producing television movies based on books whose characters act consciously to better their lives. In 1998, she starred in and produced the feature movie *Beloved,* based on Toni Morrison's novel that addresses the terrible effects of slavery.

Courtesy: CORBIS/Mitchell Gerber

Put It Together

Divide the class into three groups: one group to plan and videotape an issue-oriented talk show, one a celebrity-interview show, and the third an "ordinary people" daytime talk show. Make arrangements to have camcorders available for each team. Shows should be 5–10 minutes in length.

Have students divide up pre-production, production, and distribution responsibilities. At specified intervals, each team should submit a progress report so you can see if they are on the right track and will be able to meet their deadline. These reports should use the framework provided in the deconstruction exercise in their **Break It Down** workbook section.

Take It Further

1. After using the seven components listed in **Break It Down** for this exercise, have students identify other important components of talk shows. They might mention pace of the show, music, age of the guests, etc. Have them also apply these in analyzing and evaluating *The Oprah Winfrey Show*.
2. Have students do this exercise in teams of four to six.
3. If students have any difficulty locating the Nielsen Ratings for the past week, have them use the Alta Vista search engine. Again, students can also compare the relative ease and helpfulness of search engines.

Take It Further

1. The two top talk shows, according to the Nielsen Ratings, are *Jerry Springer* and *The Oprah Winfrey Show*. Watch one of these shows and explain its popularity. Refer to each of the seven elements of a talk show that you used in **A Close-up Look at a Talk Sho** or watch an episode from each of the talk shows and compare and con trast the elements of the shows. Why do you think that such different shows are vying for the highest ratings in this category?

2. If you were invited to produce a new talk show that targets yc peers, whom would you get to be the host? Write about the to you would select for your first three shows, and the guests you would have for each show. Give reasons for the topics and guests you'v chosen.

3. Look up Nielsen ratings on the Web and see if you can locate ratings for prime-time programs of the past week. What ratings any, do you find for talk shows?

"Think like a queen. A queen is not afraid to fall. Failure is another steppingstone to greatness."
Oprah Winfrey

Bobbie Battista, Host CNN's *Talk Back Live*

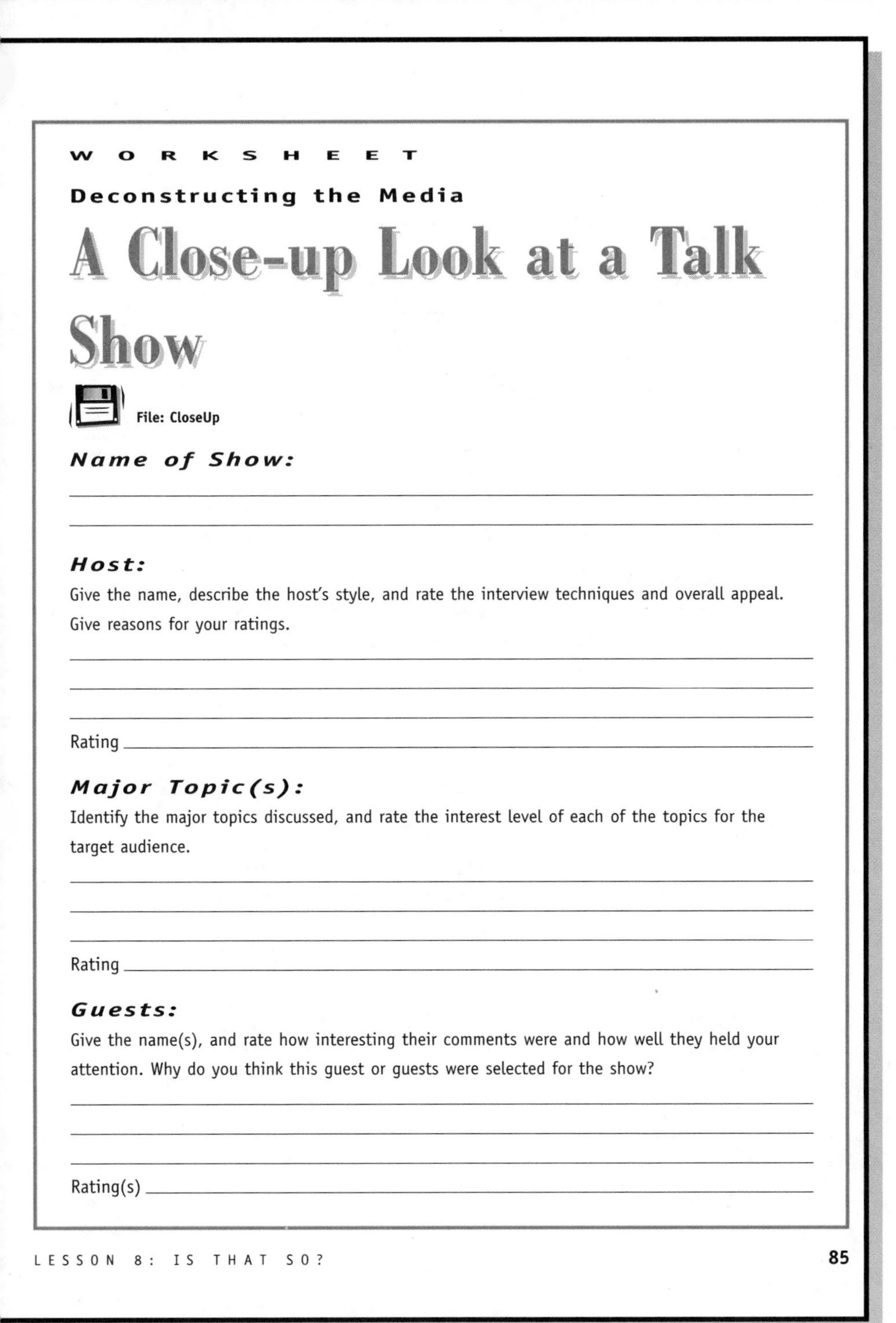

WORKSHEET

Deconstructing the Media

A Close-up Look at a Talk Show

File: CloseUp

Name of Show:

____

____

Host:

Give the name, describe the host's style, and rate the interview techniques and overall appeal. Give reasons for your ratings.

____

____

____

Rating ______________________________

Major Topic(s):

Identify the major topics discussed, and rate the interest level of each of the topics for the target audience.

____

____

____

Rating ______________________________

Guests:

Give the name(s), and rate how interesting their comments were and how well they held your attention. Why do you think this guest or guests were selected for the show?

____

____

____

Rating(s) ______________________________

LESSON 8: IS THAT SO? 85

A Close-Up Look at a Talk Show

1. **Host** Names, styles, and techniques will depend on the particular show that the student views.
2. **Major Topics** Topics will vary according to the type of talk show viewed.
3. **Guests** Guests may be celebrities or not, depending on whether the show watched is an issue-oriented, exposé, or variety program.

4. **Studio Setting** Usually sets for celebrity shows are somewhat more elaborate or elegant than those used for exposé talk shows.
5. **Studio Audience** Generally, audiences are more vocal at exposé talk shows than the other types.
6. **Target Audience** Demographics vary widely according to the type of talk show viewed. Political interview shows appeal to an older, more educated audience than exposés. Look for students to mention language, topics, live audience interaction, and other specifics in determining demographics and appeal.
7. **In General** Again, devices will vary greatly according to the type of show and the target audience. Political talk shows tend to have low-key openings, as compared to the hype and audience noise that opens exposé shows.

Studio Setting:

Describe the set used for the show, and rate its appropriateness for the target audience.

Rating

Studio Audience:

Describe the characteristics of the audience. Why do you think the show has a live audience? To what extent do you think the audience adds to the energy and vitality of the show?

Rating

Target Audience:

Describe the demographics of the audience for whom this show is intended. How could you tell? How does this show appeal to its audience? Give some suggestions for making it even more appealing to that target audience.

Rating

In General:

What devices were used at the opening of the show to attract the audience's attention? What devices did you notice throughout to maintain interest and attention?

Rating

WORKSHEET

Deconstructing the Media

Talk Shows

File: TalkShow

1. Do you watch any talk show(s)? If so, which one(s)? Why do you watch?

2. What attention-getting techniques does your favorite talk show use? (If you don't have a favorite, choose one to analyze.) Do you think these techniques give the show a competitive edge over similar shows? How?

3. Does the show have a Web site? What kind of information does it have on its Web page?

4. "Uses and gratifications research" is the name given to studies that analyze why people use certain types of media and what needs are being met through the use of those media. Here's a partial listing of reasons why people watch television:

- To be amused.
- To see authority figures.
- To have shared experiences with others.
- To satisfy curiosity.
- To find distraction and diversion.
- To find models to imitate.
- To gain information about the world.
- To see others make mistakes.
- To affirm spiritual and cultural values.

(Source: William Fore, Mythmakers. *[New York: Friendship Press, 1990])*

Which of the reasons listed above might help to explain the popularity of television talk shows?

Talk Shows

1. Some students watch the afternoon talk shows because of their outlandish topics. Others will not be talk show viewers.
2. Some use strange stunts, sexual situations, and potential for conflict to interest their audiences.
3. Most talk shows do have Web sites that give summaries of shows and allow people to voice their opinions about topics and shows.
4. Answers will vary. Look for students to explain their answers.

Lesson 9 The World Around Us: *Docudramas and Documentaries*

What's Ahead?

Goals: This lesson introduces students to documentaries and docudramas and to the distinctions between the two genres. By examining clips from both types of film, students will be able to analyze and evaluate each medium for point of view, accuracy of information, and dramatic license.

Disciplines: The contents of this lesson pertain to language arts, social studies, science, and video production.

Objectives: Upon completion of this lesson, students will be able to:

- Recognize different types of documentaries and docudramas.
- Deconstruct documentaries and docudramas and analyze the elements of both.
- Define key terms associated with documentary and docudrama production.
- Construct a documentary or docudrama about a school or local issue.

Have students write definitions of "documentary" and "docudrama." Compare these definitions with those in dictionaries or media textbooks, if available. (The definitions given here have been adapted from the *American Heritage Dictionary*.)

Docudrama: A television or motion picture of events based on fact.

LESSON 9

The World Around Us

What's Ahead?

What do you think of when you hear the word "documentary"? Do you watch these shows on your own at home, or do you only watch them when a science or history instructor shows one in class? Do you know what a "docudrama" is? What are the differences between the two?

Lesson 5 makes a distinction between hard and soft news. The difference is not unlike the distinction between documentaries and docudramas. While both genres are intended to inform, the docudrama allows for far more artistic license, with the principal goal to entertain. Each genre has its own codes and conventions.

Main Points to Ponder

- Documentaries usually look objective, but they still have a point of view. The writer has a specific purpose that is communicated by both what is included and what is excluded. The viewer must determine whether the message is fair and balanced or slanted to promote a particular viewpoint.
- Docudrama screenwriters create dialogue between historical characters to preserve the dramatic structure of the film. They may alter the known physical characteristics of main characters or even change the actual events. This is called *artistic* or *dramatic license.*
- *Historical fiction* is related to the docudrama. A key difference is that the plot and characters are fictional, although they are set in a real time period. An example is *Gone with the Wind.*

88 MEDIA MATTE

Documentary: 1. Consisting of, or based upon documents. 2. Presenting facts objectively without editorializing or inserting fictional material, as in a book or film. A television or motion picture presentation of factual, political, social, or historical events or circumstance. Often consisting of actual news films accompanied by [voiceover] narration.

Ask students for their preconceptions about documentaries. Some may think that they are boring, while others may enjoy documentaries on certain subjects. Ask for suggestions, and make a list on the board of topics and events that interest your students. Ask if they have seen documentaries or docudramas on these subjects, or if they would like to see some.

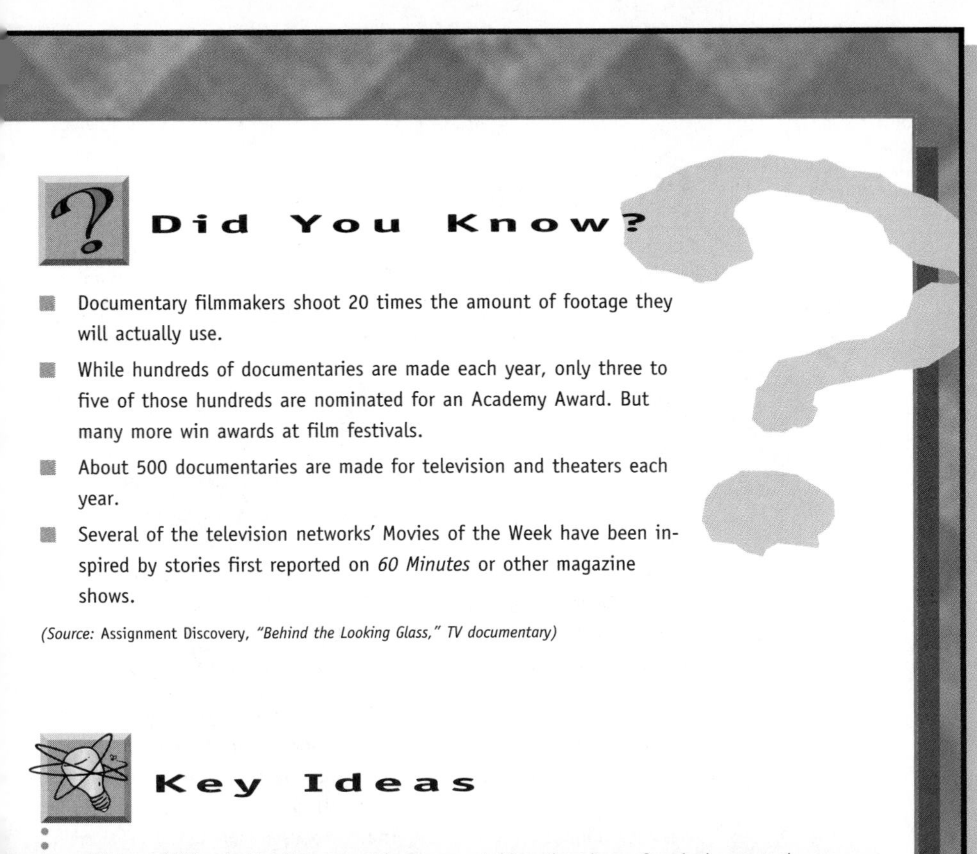

Did You Know?

- Documentary filmmakers shoot 20 times the amount of footage they will actually use.
- While hundreds of documentaries are made each year, only three to five of those hundreds are nominated for an Academy Award. But many more win awards at film festivals.
- About 500 documentaries are made for television and theaters each year.
- Several of the television networks' Movies of the Week have been inspired by stories first reported on *60 Minutes* or other magazine shows.

(Source: Assignment Discovery, *"Behind the Looking Glass," TV documentary)*

Key Ideas

Classified Information- a label used to restrict access to controversial information that might be detrimental to the provider, creator, consumer, or collector of the information.

Drama- a story presented through action and dialogue that deals with complex human emotions and life situations.

Dramatic Conventions- techniques that are used as substitutions for reality. An audience accepts them as real, even though they know them to be fictional. Examples include actors impersonating characters, scenes and props taking the place of real places, and dream sequences or foreshadowing that the audience accepts as real within the fictional context.

Foreshadowing- something that indicates an event that will occur in the future; looking back on the scene, you would view it as a hint.

Voice-over/Cutaway- during the editing phase, one can add narration over existing visuals on film (the voice-over) or add more visuals to go along with existing sound (a cutaway). This usually is done when editing film shot from more than one camera.

LESSON 9: THE WORLD AROUND US! 89

Materials

This lesson uses:

- Clip from Fine Line Films' *Hoop Dreams* (Video clip #23 – 2:06)
- Clips from *The Day Lincoln was Shot* (Video clips #5 – 9-9:24 total)
- Documentaries Worksheet (File name *Document* on R&R disk)
- Docudramas Worksheet (File name *Docudrama* on R&R disk)

Discuss docudramas separately. Many students may not realize they have watched and enjoyed these. Well known ones include *JFK, Nixon, Woodstock, Gandhi,* dramas about Diana Spencer's life, *Gettysburg,* and *Apollo 13*. Docudramas can move an audience to sadness, anger, and joy by developing the characters' human side and by using devices such as foreshadowing and dramatic irony. The use of these devices, however, frequently requires creating fictional dialogues and incidents that diminish historical accuracy.

Students should also be aware that there is a distinction between historical fiction and docudrama. Historical fiction does not attempt to recreate important incidents in the life of a real historical person, but they use real historical backdrops. Such films include *Gone with the Wind* and *Saving Private Ryan*.

Did You Know?

This section will inform students about the size of the documentary/docudrama industry. They may not realize just how large the business is.

Key Ideas

Discuss the terms in the **Key Ideas** box and ask students to give examples. Previously classified materials are frequently sources and starting points for new documentaries. For example, central to the CNN documentary series *The Cold War* are the vast records, documents, and films that were previously unavailable to the public, as well as new interviews from citizens and officials from the Soviet Union and former Eastern Bloc countries. New information can be used to corroborate old sources or to refute them.

Get Started

Have students make lists of all the types of documentaries and docudramas they have seen. (If they are unsure whether certain movies were docudramas or historical fiction, tell them to write them down anyway, and see if anyone in the class knows for sure.) Ask for titles and see how they fit into the categories explained in the students' workbook.

Some examples:

Process documentary: Students may know of programs that illustrate how a scientific theory is proven, how animals survive, how meat is packed, how cars are assembled, or how a sport is played. Perhaps students can think of a process in their community that they could document (a new bridge, a product, coaching techniques, forensic or business education events, etc.)

Biography docudramas can depict inspirational people (*Gandhi*), scientists (*Curie*), political leaders (*JFK, Wallace, Nixon*), film stars, artists, musicians, etc.

Historical documentary examines a historical event, decision, or movement. These can provide excellent introductions for further research. They can involve reenactments as well as historical footage or findings. Examine how many Titanic documentaries are currently available.

Historical docudramas (such as *Gettysburg* or *Schindler's List*) help us see events as if we were there. Most contain elements of biography as well as process.

Event documentary lets the viewer "be" at a specific event or historical moment. (*Woodstock* is a good example.) Special news presentations often run unedited live historical events, such as an inauguration. Event documentaries are created from that footage as commemoratives of special events, with additional analysis or interpretation included. The extensive live coverage of Princess Diana's death found its way into many ensuing event and biographical documentaries. Event docudramas abound as well.

Photographic or travelogue documentaries let us see places for ourselves. If done well, they may make us feel that we have been there; if done poorly, they can misrepresent places we know very well. Ultimately, they let us decide whether we would like to visit for ourselves or do further research.

Get Started

The verb "to document" means to supply factual or textual evidence that proves the truth of something. A documentary is the filmed equivalent. Some of the better known ones include National Geographic's wildlife and regional documentaries and Nova's scientific documentaries. Documentary conventions include interviews with experts and voice-overs during scenes depicting the topic. Historical reenactment is another technique, but the audience is generally told that the clip is not an actual newsreel.

The purpose of a documentary is to create a true picture of a person, process, or event. However, some are criticized for slanting the facts. For instance, some documentaries have portrayed John F. Kennedy as a motivational, inspiring president. Others have relied more heavily on facts uncovered about Kennedy's controversial relationships and connections. Depending on the sources chosen and the balance created, a documentary producer could create very different biographies of Kennedy.

If you pull apart the word "docudrama," you can see that docudramas are meant to be both "true" and "dramatic," portraying real events and people in a fictionalized way. Instead of presenting a series of interviews with experts and reliable sources, historical film footage, and formerly classified information, the docudrama is produced more as a feature movie using actors, recreated settings and costumes, and creative film techniques you learned about in Lesson 3 that increase the emotional impact. To interpret these presentations correctly, you must always be aware that much of what you see is fictional, included to enhance the main idea or to make the story more interesting.

There are several subcategories of docudramas and documentaries. ***Process*** programs document how things are done or made—for example, how cars are assembled, salt is taken from the ocean, or fetuses develop into babies. A second category is ***biography.*** There are several documentaries on the life of Mohandas Gandhi, and his life was popularized in the award-winning docudrama movie *Gandhi,* starring Ben Kingsley.

History is an important subdivision in documentary and docudrama. One example is the CNN 24-part series *Cold War,* which documents nearly 50 years of political tensions and social unrest as the United States and the Soviet Union built their nuclear arsenals. *Cold War* uses interviews of offi-

ts and ordinary citizens on both sides of the issue, as well as previ-
sly classified information and newsreels. Akin to the history category is
t of ***event,*** which focuses on a specific event, such as the wedding of
na Spencer to Prince Charles or the death of Mother Teresa. These are
onicled live by news crews, then are cut and repackaged into documen-
ies that may also include aspects of biography. From that point, many
developed into docudramas, usually released last, because they take
re time and money to cast, set, film, and edit.

Break It Down

ny children and young adults dream of greatness. Perhaps as a child
 dreamed of becoming an Olympic athlete or a world-renowned entre-
neur. The documentary *Hoop Dreams* follows two young African Ameri-
ns through their high school years as they pursue their dreams to become NBA players.

tage and Poster from "Hoop Dreams" courtesy
Fine Line Features

Watch the clip taken from the beginning of the documentary. How is the style different from a feature entertainment movie? What about the film techniques and quality? Do you think the primary purpose of the film will be to entertain, to inform, or to persuade? On what do you base your answer?

Video clip #23

New Line Cinema *Hoop Dreams*

The next clips are taken from the Turner Original Movie *The Day Lincoln Was Shot.* You may have already studied these clips in Lesson 3, but this time you will critique them in terms of docudrama conventions

Video clips #3–9

TNT Original

The Day Lincoln Was Shot

Break It Down

It would be valuable to rent the home video movie *Hoosiers* or *Passing Glory,* which are basketball docudramas. Screen one to find a clip or two that students could compare to the documentary elements they see in the *Hoop Dreams* clip (**video clip #23**) (interviews, real settings and people). Use the worksheet **Deconstructing the Media: Documentaries** with this section.

The segment from *Hoop Dreams* can also provide a valuable digression into an area that students have not studied in the workbook: sports figures as heroes and entertainers, and their role in creating big money for advertisers and media corporations. Talent scouts, high schools, and colleges may make large investments in young athletes in hopes that they will make it to the top, earn huge salaries, and reinvest some of it in the institutions that helped them to get to the big time.

The clips from *The Day Lincoln was Shot* (**video clips #5-9**) present combinations of facts mingled with dramatic conventions, such as period costumes, engaging actors, and foreshadowing. Review the Instructor's Guide section for Lesson Three that summarizes the film clips to choose which ones you want to use in your class. For instance, clip #7 depicts a dream sequence in which Lincoln foresees his own death. This is a great foreshadowing technique to add dramatic tension, but it not something based on factual evidence.

Foreshadow is also used in other scenes you can mention to your class. For example, as Mr. and Mrs. Lincoln depart for the Ford Theatre, Lincoln says "Goodbye" to a security guard.

The man replies, questioning, "You mean good night, sir." Ask students whether these scenes could possibly be based on facts. The answer is that they can, and such incidents are often found in personal journals of people involved in the historic events. Docudrama productions do employ researchers whose job it is to find details that bring the figures to life. However, many scenes are also fictionalized to produce the effects of foreshadow and irony.

rather than for specific film techniques. Before viewing them, take a class inventory to see what you know and feel about the assassination of Abraham Lincoln and about his assassin, John Wilkes Booth. Make use of any class encyclopedias or history textbooks to uncover more information. A brief history of the events can be found on the Internet at http://www.insiders.com/civil/t13person1.htm or through a key-word search for Lincoln and Booth. Have you ever watched any documentaries on this event and these people? What were your impressions based on these?

Watch the clips and take notes on the technical tools used and the dramatic license that fills out the characterizations. Answer the questions on the worksheet **Deconstructing the Media: Docudramas** (p. 97), and discuss your answers in class.

PRODUCTION NOTES

Words from the Masters

When shooting documentaries, the camera operator is generally limited in exercising stylistic control. Vienna-born documentary cameraman and photographer Wolfgang Shuschitzky explains:

With a documentary, you haven't got plasterers and carpenters and wardrobe and make up and that sort of thing. So you must make the best of what you have, which I prefer. I mainly am an improviser, and I decide things when I see them. I don't plan ahead.

W. B. Pollard, a specialist in documentaries, discusses lighting:

There's never enough money for documentaries, and the first economy they always think of is the cameraman's lighting. To be honest, it isn't a bad thing. An overlit documentary looks terribly artificial, like a feature, and loses atmosphere and authenticity. When you haven't much light, you have to use a bit more ingenuity. I quite like working with a director who knows nothing about photography and asks for the most ridiculous things, which are quite unphotographable. Well, that's a challenge, and you have to find some way of doing it.

Documentary filmmaking can be both enlightening and threatening to the powers that be, whether in government or big business. Bill Nichols, in his *Movies and Methods*, (University of California Press, 1976) claims:

The cinema known as documentary, with all the vastness that the concept has today, from educational films to the reconstruction of a fact or an historical event, is perhaps the main basis for revolutionary filmmaking.

(Source: Kenneth MacGowan: *Behind the Screen: The History and Techniques of the Motion Picture.* [New York, Delacorte Press, 1965] 176, 55)

PRODUCTION NOTES

Words from the Masters. This feature offers thoughts on docudrama/documentary production from people involved in the field. Have students think about the technical challenges of the documentary, as discussed in terms of lighting, financing, settings, and language. They need to compete for audiences against lush productions with eloquent actors and expensive Hollywood settings and special effects. Bill Nichols sees the ideal cumulative effect as revolutionary. Ask students how documentaries can be seen as "revolutionary." Can they think of any that significantly changed the way they think about things? The other feature box in this lesson mentions one that truly was groundbreaking: Murrow's *Harvest of Shame*. Can they think of others that have had this kind of effect?

Sum It Up

In your evaluation of the clips you have deconstructed, answer the following questions:

1. Can documentaries move viewers emotionally? Give an example of your answer.
2. Can docudramas clarify facts? Give an example.
3. Could docudramas stick to just the facts and remain as entertaining and thought-provoking as they are? Explain your answer.
4. Should docudramas be used as supplements to teaching history or science? Defend your answer.
5. What makes each type (docudrama and documentary) appealing?
6. Who would be the audience for each?

THEN AND NOW

Docudrama Style and History

Docudrama flourished in the days of the early Hollywood studios, especially the 1930s. Since they needed inexpensive or B films to supply double features for the many theater bills in the United States, Warner Brothers and others turned to retelling historical biographical stories.

World War I was the first war to be filmed. Newsreels were shown at theatres prior to the featured movie. A new genre was born: the war movie. Many found these to be little more than a revamping of the western, often-repeated morality tales that did not tell the true story but only served to create support for the war.

As film developed as a medium for education as well as entertainment, pioneers could see its usefulness in dramatizing social issues. Documentaries and docudramas also gained importance with the emergence of television. Edward R. Murrow's legendary 1960 documentary *Harvest of Shame* embarrassed Americans on Thanksgiving Day by showing poverty in the land of plenty, much as John Steinbeck's novel *The Grapes of Wrath* revealed the plight of Dust Bowl victims in American farm history.

The miniseries was born out of a need to portray historical novels more thoroughly. David Wolper emerged as an American docudrama producer. His *Roots* docudrama of Alex Haley's family history was the most-watched television show in history.

The latest rage in documentary is the developing subgenre called "shockumentary," which airs local newsreels, police reports, and videos shot by private citizens of violent and shocking events such as rampaging circus elephants, deadly storms, and people being attacked by pit bull dogs. The programs are relatively cheap to produce (at $500,000, approximately one-third the cost of a dramatic show) and draw the male audience that advertisers want to reach. *(Time, "When Good Networks Go Bad," February 1, 1999, pp.60–61)*

Sum It Up

Possible answers:

1. Yes, documentaries can move viewers emotionally. One example is that they can get emotionally involved with the boys in *Hoop Dreams*.
2. Docudramas can clarify and bring to light little-known facts or personal stories of the historical figures or events involved. However, they can also add fictional content that people may believe to be true.
3. Answers will vary.
4. Answers will vary.
5. Information and drama are two possible answers.
6. Answers will vary. The audiences for a docudrama and a documentary about the same topic could, in fact, be the same. For instance, someone who enjoyed *Hoop Dreams* is likely to enjoy *Passing Glory*.

Look for these elements in a documentary and docudrama:

Documentary	Similarities	Docudrama
Informative	Opening credits	Entertainment
Facts arranged to present the topic accurately, usually chronologically	Locations	Dramatic license
Experts, reliable sources	Dialogue	Actors
Interviews	Sets	Special Effects
	Scenery	
	Reenactments	
	Narrator	
	Voice-over	
	Simulations	
	Reporting	
	Credits	

Put It Together

This construction exercise will allow students to construct either a short documentary or docudrama, both on the same subject, to learn more about their composition and to compare and contrast their elements.

Ask students to brainstorm topics that involve their school or community, such as

1. A local issue (cutting arts funding, an election);
2. A crisis (suicide, gangs, school violence, etc.);
3. An event (a party, getting a drivers license, interviewing for a job); or
4. A production (a parade, an art project, fund raising, building a garage).

From the list, choose one or two items that will lend themselves to both documentary and docudrama presentations. Divide the class into groups so that there is a documentary and a docudrama created for each topic.

Discuss what features the two presentations may have in common and what differences the audience might expect. Even the common elements may be presented very differently.

Arrange for students to take camcorders into necessary places for filming (for instance, if their program is about cheerleaders, they may want to film parts of a practice or sports event). Help them to realize they are limited by time and are not expected to present a fully polished production.

Ask the groups to discuss how they made their decisions of what to include, what to leave out, and how to best present their material. Have the class determine which genre they think is more effective with the given topics.

Put It Together

As a class, brainstorm some of the topics and events that are important in your school or community. Choose one or two of the topics (depending on your class size). Have one team create a short documentary and another team create a docudrama on the same subject. Narrow down your topic so that you can create a complete feature in about five minutes.

For the documentary, the team should try to create a fair, balanced presentation of the facts. Decide what must be included; choose reliable sources to present evidence and to corroborate facts. Also determine what you do not want to include, and be prepared to defend your decision.

Those creating the docudrama on the same topic will create a fictionalized presentation, casting students as actors to dramatize the story line. What scenes should you create to best get across your message?

You will need to designate scriptwriters, editors, actors or interviewers, researchers, and camera technicians. You may also want a sound person to be responsible for background sound effects and music. Ideally, you will use video recorders to film your documentary. Remember to include appropriate camera techniques. If cameras are not available, write a script that includes descriptions of scenes, techniques, and sounds, as well as dialogue.

Present the projects in class. Discuss the similarities and differences in the productions. Determine the effectiveness of each production and decide which genre you prefer for presenting the particular topic, and why.

THEN AND NOW

Docudrama Style and History. This feature gives some insight into the history of this lesson's genres, as well as some reasons they came into existence. Use the ideas to discuss other documentaries and docudramas.

The topic of "shockumentaries" is well worth a class discussion. In many ways, they are related to the sensationalized talk shows discussed in Lesson Eight: low budget, shocking programs that increase ratings and ad dollars for networks and cable stations. This topic provides another avenue to discussing an essential question, "Why do people choose to watch sensational programming?

Take It Further

1. Find a subject for which you can watch both a docudrama and a documentary. (You may need to get one or both from a video rental store.) After watching both, write an analysis that discusses the differences and similarities, strengths and weaknesses of each production. Determine your preference in this case, and explain your choice. What would you do differently to strengthen either presentation?

2. Choose a topic that is important or interesting to you. Research it and create either a documentary or a docudrama proposal for it. Discuss and defend your choice of genre and techniques.

3. Change your TV viewing habits for a week, and substitute documentaries and docudramas for the other genres of shows you typically watch. You can find them on stations such as History, A&E, Discovery, PBS, CNN, and TNT. Sometimes networks also carry these types of shows. Write about your experience. Did you find any documentaries entertaining? Which ones, and why? Did you question any of the facts presented? Which ones, and why? Are you likely to change your viewing habits to include more of these productions? Why or why not?

When shooting documentaries, camera operators are limited in the stylistic control they can exercise.

Take It Further

1. The first activity is a deconstruction that allows the student to watch productions in their entirety, a good way to analyze and evaluate docudramas and documentaries. They may want to use a Venn Diagram to illustrate some of their findings.
2. This construction activity is another group activity. Have students reflect on the types of documentaries and docudramas discussed in **Get Started** as they choose their subject. In their presentation make sure they explain and defend the decisions they had to make to produce their film.
3. This exercise challenges students to broaden their viewing habits by paying significant attention to a category of media that most may not normally choose. By restricting their viewing to documentaries for an extended period, they are compelled to give genuine consideration to a genre that can potentially broaden their critical understanding of both the media and the world.

Documentaries

1. Depending on students' preferences, answers may include personal profiles, nature shows, history, or science documentaries.
2. Chances are that students will at least think the subject is appropriate for a docudrama, but answers will vary.
3. Answers will depend upon individual reactions to the boys. Many will find them likeable because of their goals and desires both for themselves and for their families.
4. Neighborhood scenes are included to give the viewer a sense of the boys' backgrounds. Slow motion is used to show one of the boy's ability. Interview is also important to this documentary.
5. It would be easy (and probably successful) to dramatize the events surrounding one or both of the boys' attempts to reach fame.

W O R K S H E E T

Deconstructing the Media

Documentaries

File: Document

Documentaries employ techniques that are very different from those used in dramatic movies. Answer the questions on this worksheet to discover what is unique about this medium.

1. Think about the documentaries you have viewed. Which stand out as your favorites? Why?

____

____

____

2. Write down your impressions about the theme of young, disadvantaged children dreaming of making it to the top. Is it a useful theme for a docudrama? A documentary? Explain.

____

____

____

3. Do you have an emotional response to the boys in *Hoop Dreams?* What details move you or keep you from getting involved with them?

____

____

____

4. What techniques are used in the film clip? Are they effective? Why or why not?

____

____

____

5. How might one create a docudrama about the same topic?

____

____

____

____

____

WORKSHEET

Deconstructing the Media

Docudramas

File: Docudrama

Docudramas make use of fictional techniques, such as dramatic dialogues, foreshadowing, and dramatic irony. They may also change the physical characteristics of historic personalities or the outcomes of events to create a particular response in the audience.

1. Write down your knowledge and feelings about Abraham Lincoln, John Wilkes Booth, and the assassination of Lincoln before doing any research.

____

____

____

2. Write down additional facts you learn after checking a couple of readily available sources about Lincoln and Booth.

____

____

____

3. What dramatic and cinematic devices are used in the clips? How do they enhance or discourage historical accuracy?

____

____

____

4. What responsibility do you think a docudrama producer has in telling an audience that the story is not completely true?

____

____

____

____

____

Docudramas

1. Students should know that Abraham Lincoln was president during the Civil War and that Booth assassinated him in Ford's Theatre.
2. Many more facts about both men are readily available in encyclopedias, history books, and online.
3. Camera angles, lighting, costumes, and dialogue are among the devices used to bring the events to life. They can enhance historical accuracy when they are true to actual words spoken (such as having a character recite a speech that historians agree was spoken by that person in history). They can discourage historical accuracy when the audience believes in the historically inaccurate material as they are drawn into the cinematic effects.
4. Answers will vary. Most are likely to agree that at least some notice of historical inaccuracy should be noted at the beginning and/or conclusion of the film.

Lesson 10
Radio Revisited: *The Medium of Radio Broadcasting*

What's Ahead?

Goals: This lesson will introduce students to the medium of radio—its history, its uniqueness, and the impact it has on its listeners. Most of your students probably have a favorite station they listen to almost every day. This lesson helps them to distinguish the differences in effect and influence between radio and other media.

Disciplines: Language arts, social studies, psychology, and technology are related to this lesson.

Objectives: After studying this lesson, students will be able to:

- Define **Key Ideas** associated with radio.
- Explain the impact of radio personalities with respect to a show's overall voice, content, and audience.
- Deconstruct various types of radio messages.
- Create an audio media message.

LESSON 10

Radio Revisited

What's Ahead?

Almost 100 years old, radio is one of our most common media formats. Ninety-nine percent of all homes in the United States have at least one radio. Listeners rely on radios for information, entertainment, and companionship. Since it has no visual element, radio's early efforts relied only on sound and the imagination of its listeners as it popularized the art of storytelling for all ages, and in all genres: comedy, drama, mystery, and science fiction. Soap operas and drama have migrated to television, but talk show hosts and disc jockeys continue to expand the radio medium.

Today, radio targets specific audiences based on various demographics, including age, gender, ethnic background, listening habits, and personal interests. In this lesson, you will learn about the power and effects of audio. Words and sound can produce long-lasting images and feelings.

Main Points to Ponder

- The average home has 5.6 radios, making radio one of today's most pervasive media formats.
- People gathering information from radio may draw different conclusions than those receiving their information from TV. We may interpret visual cues in different ways than we analyze audio ones.
- Radio is almost entirely live—straight from the sound studio to the listener without the advantages of edits and retakes.

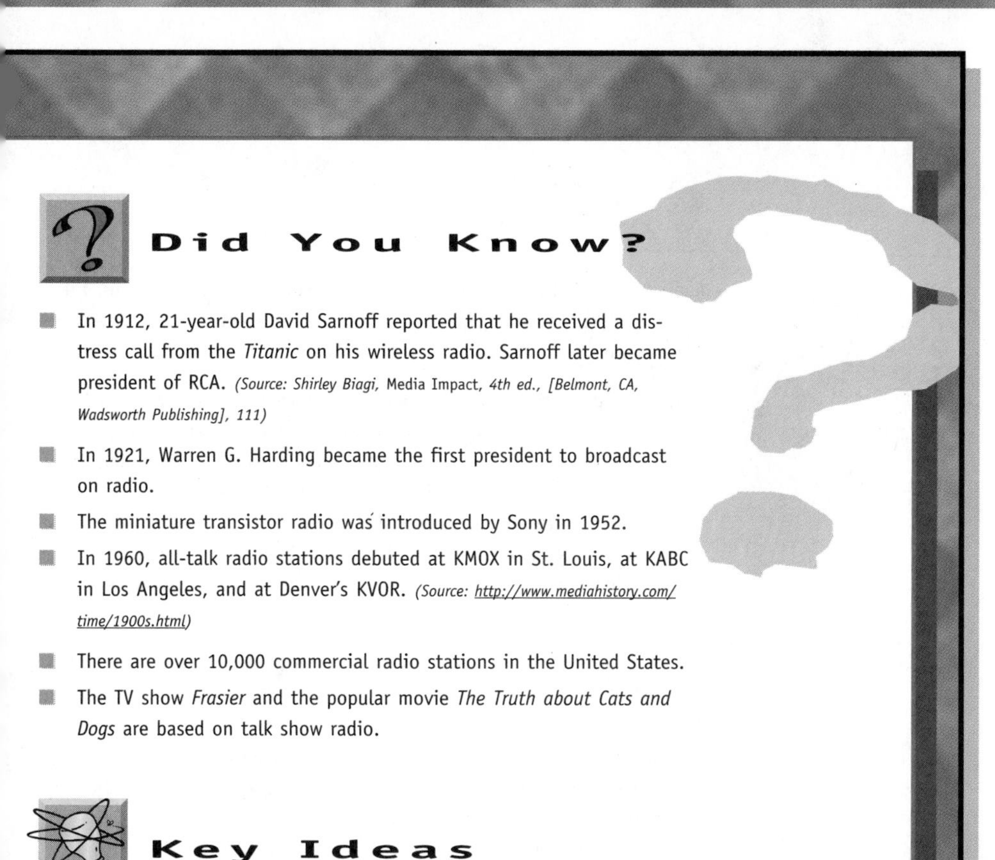

Did You Know?

- In 1912, 21-year-old David Sarnoff reported that he received a distress call from the *Titanic* on his wireless radio. Sarnoff later became president of RCA. *(Source: Shirley Biagi,* Media Impact, *4th ed., [Belmont, CA, Wadsworth Publishing], 111)*
- In 1921, Warren G. Harding became the first president to broadcast on radio.
- The miniature transistor radio was introduced by Sony in 1952.
- In 1960, all-talk radio stations debuted at KMOX in St. Louis, at KABC in Los Angeles, and at Denver's KVOR. *(Source: http://www.mediahistory.com/time/1900s.html)*
- There are over 10,000 commercial radio stations in the United States.
- The TV show *Frasier* and the popular movie *The Truth about Cats and Dogs* are based on talk show radio.

Key Ideas

Format - the overall focus of a station. Radio stations today air programming that targets specific markets based on various demographics, including music preferences and other interests such as sports, news, and talk shows.

Narrowcasting - segmenting the audience based on their radio interests.

National Public Radio (NPR) - the only major noncommercial radio network in the United States.

RealAudio - software that allows Internet users to listen to and/or record over 100 radio stations from several countries.

Sound Bite - a short audio message that encapsulates a key point or main idea.

Theater of the Mind - visual images people create in their minds "to fill in the blanks" between the words and sounds they hear on radio. The effect is similar to the one that occurs when people attend live theater.

LESSON 10: RADIO REVISITED 99

Did You Know?

Facts illustrate the importance and prevalence of radio. Harding was the first president to broadcast on radio, but this tradition continues today. The Emergency Broadcast System also continues to maintain a network to help and inform citizens in the event of an emergency.

Key Ideas

Ask students for examples of the **Key Ideas** section. Even though the days of dramatic radio are passed, students can still discuss "Theater of the Mind" in terms of how they envision disc jockeys, talk show hosts, and their guests.

Materials

This lesson uses:

- CBS footage of the Nixon/Kennedy debates (Video clip #25 - 2:17)
- CBS audio recording of the Nixon/Kennedy debates (Audio CD Track #4)
- CNN radio news clip on Kosovo (Audio CD Track #5)
- CNN feature "Media Circus: Talk Back Radio" (Video clip #24 - 5:09).
- News article on Kosovo (File name *Kosovo* on R&R disk)
- Excerpts from "Stealing Calm: An Ode to Radio" and "Why Radio Thrives" (File name *Whyradio* on R&R disk)
- Radio Worksheet (File name *Radio* on R&R disk)

Get Started

This section discusses the relevance of radio and its ability to survive despite waves of newer, more sophisticated technologies. Ask students:

- How many listen to radio daily? How often? Why?
- If they listen to music, why don't they listen to their favorite CDs instead? (One answer: they are likely not to own all of their favorite music, and radio stations are constantly introducing new music.)
- Have they ever needed to listen to radio in an emergency situation; for instance, when power went off and they had to depend on battery-operated radios? How do they think they would have felt without the radio?

Copy and have students read the article excerpts on radio (on the R&R disk). "Why Radio Thrives" gives many examples of how radio has adapted to maintain an audience in spite of new media. "An Ode to Radio" is more philosophical, suggesting that radio is a more demanding medium than television. Ask students to consider and respond to Shenk's suggestion that "video trumps thought" and radio listeners "must become truly engaged... [Radio] requires more of a commitment."

Get Started

Radio is one of the oldest of the electronic media, and it is, perhaps, the one most taken for granted. This old-fashioned medium is thriving despite the arrival of home computers and cable TV. Why?

First, radio provides information and entertainment in a transportable format. While commuters cannot watch television, they can and usually do listen to their car radios for news, traffic reports, weather, and entertainment. Radio has consistently adapted quickly to changes in popular tastes, adjusting to the way people live and work. Families no longer gather before the radio at night to hear their favorite mystery or comedy program, but they tune in regularly for their favorite call-in show or "top 40 countdown."

Early on, radio's ability to report information instantaneously established the medium as a popular news source. From the 1920s through the 1950s, Americans learned about local events, the nation's economy, and international affairs primarily from radio. It is still an important resource during crises, natural or man-made, since most homes have at least one radio that runs on batteries. A disaster in Syracuse, New York, on Labor Day 1998 is one of countless examples that demonstrate this fact. At 1:15 a.m. a major storm blasted the city with winds of 70 to 90 mph, gusting up to 115 mph. An estimated 140,000 homes and businesses were without electrical power for days. Local radio stations, powered by generators, were able to stay on the air and provide critical information and comfort.

In place of the big band sounds that dominated the airwaves 50 years ago, today's listeners have a multitude of music choices such as country, southern gospel, jazz, hip hop, rock, easy listening, and oldies. Most stations now use narrowcasting to cater to various target audiences.

Finally, radio thrives because it fills the mind with images that allow listeners to personalize whatever they hear, be it announcer, commercial, call-in listener, or song. That fact has not changed since the first radio program was broadcast on Christmas Eve 1906. Let's examine how that happens.

Break It Down

The Kennedy-Nixon debates of 1960 illustrate the critical difference between seeing and hearing. Aired on both television and radio, the four debates were available to almost everyone in the United States. In the days that followed the debates, diametrically opposite conclusions emerged. Those who watched television said John F. Kennedy won the debates. Radio listeners, on the other hand, concluded that Richard F. Nixon was the winner.

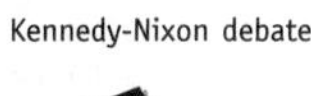

Audio Track #4

Kennedy-Nixon debate

What caused the discrepancy, given that both radio listeners and TV viewers heard the same words? Try an experiment to discover the differences between the broadcasts. Half the class will listen to the debates, and the other half will watch the television clip. Afterwards, come together to discuss who you felt won, and why.

Video clip #25

Kennedy-Nixon debate

Now trade sources. Pay attention to your own behavior with each medium.

1. Did you listen as attentively to TV as you did to radio?
2. How did you visualize the candidates on radio?
3. How did that make you feel about the two men?
4. Summarize what you heard on radio. Do the same for TV, and compare the two. How much do visuals alter your interpretation of what is said?

Kennedy-Nixon Debate, CBS News Archives

"If we cannot end our differences, at least we can make the world safe for diversity."

John F. Kennedy

Break It Down

Kennedy/Nixon debates (Audio CD Track #4, Video Clip #25): For sighted persons, vision is the dominant sense. As a result, what they see can have more weight than what they hear. To some extent, this explains why those who saw the Kennedy/Nixon debates concluded that Kennedy was the winner. Kennedy's youthful appearance, when compared to Nixon's rougher features, was a powerful, perhaps misleading visual cue that Kennedy was the more positive candidate. See if your students can analyze the effectiveness of Nixon's speech in the radio format. This may be difficult, as the clip is very short, but they are still likely to have some comments about the differences. Certainly they will be amazed at the change in television quality from 1960 to the present. Also ask them to analyze the content of the debate. Who wins based on what is really said?

Radio News (Audio CD Track #5): Both television and radio are criticized for the short bites of information they give about the news of the day. Additionally, they are criticized for including too much "soft news," and not enough "hard news" (see lesson five). If possible, take today's main story from both the radio and the newspaper. Compare them for depth of coverage. Is either insufficient in any way? How and why? For a more complete study, have students listen to today's news on the radio, watch it on television, and read it in today's paper. Ask: Which is more complete? What are the advantages of each?

Students will have to cut a significant portion of the copy on Kosovo (on R&R disk) to create a radio news item. Most news bites are only two to three sentences long. Ask them if they think they are able to convey all the important information about the news by cutting as much as they must.

Talk show hosts: Most of the call-in radio talk shows are on AM radio. Similar to television talk show shows, they maintain their popularity by remaining controversial. Ask students to discuss the nature of outrageous hosts and topics after watching the CNN clip on talk show hosts (**video clip #24**). Do they think that the topics and their treatment are important for us to ponder as citizens? Are they necessary? Do they deserve on-air time? Why or why not?

Radio News

For many busy people, radio is the number one source of news. Do you ever listen to radio news? What are the similarities and differences between radio news, TV news, and newspapers?

Audio Track #5
CNN Radio

Listen to the audio clip from CNN News. What do you think of the information you hear? Is it newsworthy? Why or why not? What are the advantages and disadvantages of radio news?

File: Kosovo

Now read the news article on Kosovo (on the Readings and Resources disk). What information is in both sources? What is left out on the radio? What is the impact of the cuts on a listener's knowledge about the events? How do you think the story would be covered on TV?

Talk Show Hosts

Video clip #24
CNN: Media Circus, Talk Back Radio

Talk shows, both on radio and on television, are one of the most popular genres of entertainment today. One reason is that they allow the audience to become involved. Audience members can voice their opinions, tell their personal stories, and actively approve or disapprove of the content. Talk show personalities appeal to particular audiences by carefully selecting topics for their shows. This appeal to the known values and beliefs of a specific group is called creating a "niche market." Talk show radio has been criticized for providing a forum for controversial hosts. Some hosts have been accused of provoking the public to acts of violence. Others have been censored by the FCC and eliminated by many radio networks due to obscene program content.

Tom Leykis: Talk Radio Host

1. Watch the CNN clip on radio talk show hosts. Did you think that these hosts were intentionally trying to stir up controversy? How do you feel about it?
2. Do you listen to any talk show programs on the radio? If not, do you know anyone who does? Whose show(s) do you listen to? What is the slant of the show? Why do you listen? Discuss the possible consequences of controversial and inflammatory content on talk radio.

3. Another kind of talk show features interviews with notable personalities. These talk shows do not necessarily allow the audience to call in. Examples include National Public Radio's "Fresh Air" and "All Things Considered." Listen to a radio interview and compare it to TV celebrity interviews.

Disc Jockeys

Do you have a favorite DJ? What traits do your favorite DJs have? Given three radio stations with similar content, many listeners choose their favorite based on the personality "spinning the hits."

Who do you like to listen to on the radio? Why? What makes you tune your radio to another station?

Radio as Theater

The "Theater of the Mind," as radio was often dubbed, used to bring memorable stories such as serialized mystery and science fiction tales, dramas, and comedy to listeners prior to the advent of television. Listeners had to be able to "see" the action via sound. Voices were critical. The pace, pitch, and inflection of speech combined to create the visual image of a character in listeners' minds.

Experiment in class. Try smiling. Have one team turn their backs to the class and individually recite several lines from a textbook. Predetermine who will smile throughout the reading, and ask the rest of the class to pick out the one smiling.

Sound effects and music completed the package. Music established romantic, scary, or mysterious moods, while sound effects filled in the gaps. An episode of *Suspense* dealt with creatures that could turn people inside out whenever eye contact was made. To create this gruesome and gory effect, the sound engineer used a surgical glove, peeling it off his hand into a bucket of water. Total cost: 14 cents. Today's sound effects—everything from airplane takeoffs to waterfalls—are available prerecorded.

Create your own sound effects by using a cassette recorder at home. You can use the actual item to represent a sound (for example, record a blender for the sound of a blender) or be more creative (use items to represent sounds, such as the surgical glove example). Bring your tape in, and have the class guess what the sounds represent.

Disk jockeys: Radio shows need someone to fill the gaps between each entertainment or information segment. That is the role of disk jockeys, or radio personalities. Ask students what it is about them that is likable and unlikable. Who do they like, and why?

Radio as Theater: It would be hard to find a radio station today that broadcasts drama and fiction, though there are readings produced on NPR. However, sound effects are certainly part of radio broadcasts, especially among DJs who include funny monologues and dialogues. Ask students if they can think of any sound effects they have heard recently on their favorite radio stations. Also ask them to be on the alert for sound effects over the week, and report them back to the class. How effective are they? Do they add to the enjoyment of the listener?

Sum It Up

Answers will vary. Students may feel that visual images influence them over content; therefore, radio gives more accurate information. On the other hand, television can display images that help people to clarify situations in their own minds. Any students who listen to radio on a regular basis are bound to be influenced by the content from announcers, participatory audience members, commercials, and music.

Sum It Up

Evaluate the impact of radio using the following questions:

- Which do you think gives you the "truer" picture: radio or TV? Why
- How important do you think radio is in society?
- How important is radio in your own life?
- In what ways do you think radio influences people?

Now that you have studied the medium of radio, have you changed you opinions about it? Has this chapter influenced how, why, or how much you listen to radio or what programs you listen to? If yes, in what way

THEN AND NOW

A Brief History of Radio

The technological foundations for radio were established before World War I by inventors such as Guglielmo Marconi, Lee DeForest, Reginald Aubrey Fessenden, and Edwin Armstrong. During the war, the use of radio among the various armed forces transformed the medium from a novelty into a necessity. By 1922 the government had licensed more than five hundred stations. Live music was the staple of early programming, but soon vaudeville-trained comedians were attracting larger audiences and serving as effective on-air spokespersons for products. George and Gracie Allen and Jack Benny and Fred Allen were some of the first radio comedy teams to become successful. Advertising time was sold on the basis of the estimated popularity of programs, and networks and sponsors used ratings to determine a performer's success.

Ken Hamblin: Talk Radio H

Network news departments emerged as World War II approached. Edward R. Murrow, a 27-year-old CBS correspondent, introduced a new sophistication and sense of immediacy to radio news with his coverage of Hitler's march to Vienna in 1938. Murrow's live reports from the Battle of Britain in 1940 brought the war directly into American homes.

As the war ended, another powerful information medium—television—loomed on the horizon. By 1950, radio's profit and popularity were declining. The introduction of inexpensive AM-FM radios in the 1960s, however, favorably impacted radio sales and rescued the medium from obscurity. Today, radio stations are readily distinguished by format as well as call letters. Among the 10,000-plus commercial radio stations, some 30 distinct formats have been identified. New ones emerge as frequently as listeners develop new tastes. In 1997, radio revenue peaked at $13.6 billion, more than doubling 1985 revenues. Radio currently reaches 75 percent of consumers daily and 96 percent every week.

THEN AND NOW

A History of Radio. This section gives students some background on how radio became a major media force, as well as how it manages to survive in today's high-tech world. Joggers and bikers can take their news and music with them via a headset and tiny radio, but there is no way for them to safely and inexpensively carry their television or computer while they exercise or drive their cars. Radio continues to be the best choice for information and entertainment in situations such as these.

Put It Together

Now that you know what radio can do and a little about the elements that make it work, it's time to create something for air. Fortunately, radio requires relatively little equipment. If you do not have access to a recording studio, here are the basics:

- Audio cassette recorder (records, plays, erases)
- Blank audio cassettes
- Hand-held microphone to plug into the tape player (optional)
- Stopwatch or clock with a second hand

Recording Tips

- **Microphones:** If you're using an external mike, make sure it's not too close to the speaker's mouth. Don't shout, because that distorts the sound. Be sure to speak clearly. Remember, an external microphone is plugged into the "mic" input or "line in" on your recorder.
- **Levels:** If the tape recorder has a VU meter, test the recording level. Every VU meter has a red zone. If the needle stays too long in this zone while you're recording, the sound could be distorted, or as the pros say, "too hot." If the needle is barely moving, the level is too low. Sound will be distant and weak. Try to keep the needle just right of center. If you don't have a VU meter, make a sample recording.
- **Microphone stand:** If two people are using a single script, use a microphone stand. If you don't have a stand, one person can hold the mike. Keep it an equal distance from both people, and don't lean into the microphone when you speak. *Hint:* Take a drink of water before starting to record.
- **Silence:** When you're ready to record, put the tape recorder into Record mode and let the tape roll for a few seconds. You'll get a more professional sound with a second or two of silence at the beginning and end of the tape.
- **Music:** You can add music and/or sound effects by playing cassettes on another tape recorder as you record the script. Keep the music loud enough to be heard, but low enough so that it does not compete with the voices.
- **Location:** A closet or a room without windows works best.

Put It Together

Students will need to think about the elements that make radio influential: content, radio voices and personalities, and background music and sounds. They should also consider the limitations of radio, particularly its lack of editing and visual content. Radio messages need to be thought out carefully, as they are not usually pre-recorded. Students should have a clear purpose in mind—information, entertainment, persuasion—when they begin to compose their radio piece.

In radio, sound and credibility are all-important. Listeners become loyal fans of DJs and talk show hosts because they believe in them. And they believe in them either because they "sound" believable or likable, or because the listeners know something about the hosts that appeal to them. Emphasize to your students that a radio voice is important; it carries the same weight that physical attractiveness carries in film. This is an advantage to many radio personalities who are not physically attractive, but possess a great radio voice.

Job Responsibilities

- **Producer—**in charge of the overall development of the broadcast.
- **Sound engineer—**in charge of the technical aspects of recording the broadcast. Also responsible for sound effects, overall sound quality, and contributing to the program content.

GROUPS

Divide into four groups. Create a short radio piece that reflects one of the radio spots discussed earlier—news, interview, disk jockey piece, or talk show. Each group should determine the various job responsibilities, in addition to writing the spot. Include music and/or sound effects where appropriate.

After you decide on the content, fill in the details. Where, when, and how often will the completed spot air? Who is the target audience? What do you want them to do or to remember, and how do you want to deliver the message—funny, dramatic, or straightforward? What is the purpose of your media message? Remember to create a complete piece, with a beginning, middle, and end. Keep the final time under five minutes.

IN THE SPOTLIGHT

Richard Benson, Operations Manager

"I love my job!"

After ten years in the industry, that's how Richard Benson still feels about his work in radio. "It's fast-paced and there's always something going on," says the Operations Manager for CNN Radio in Atlanta, Georgia. "It's a thrill to know that people all over the country are hearing late-breaking news that you just got."

Radio isn't all tinsel and glamour, however. "In school you don't have a sense of how hard people work," says Benson. "We're on the air 24 hours a day, but we're not a big staff. So everybody does it all—sports, business, weather, features."

Now responsible for day-to-day operations at the radio network, Benson started as a college intern in 1989. "I liked the 'now' effect of radio," he says, "but I also felt that I would have a chance to do more and to learn more than I would in television."

Benson recalls that his intern experience was very rewarding. Radio veterans showed him the ropes, taught him how to conduct telephone interviews, and helped him to write better. Within a year Benson was hired as a part-timer. An eager and earnest worker, he soon became an editor, responsible for telephone interviews, news conferences, and press statements, among other duties.

When a producer slot was created, Benson stepped in. He was promoted to Operations Manager two years ago. Benson's advice to students seeking a career in radio is simple: "Go to your local or school station and introduce yourself. Tell them you're willing to do anything," he says. "And if they should turn you down, just keep going back."

IN THE SPOTLIGHT

Richard Benson Interview. Benson's words demonstrate his delight with the medium, though he also addresses the challenges. Ask if any of your students are interested in going into radio as a career. They might be able to interview a local DJ or radio technician to find out more about the job requirements.

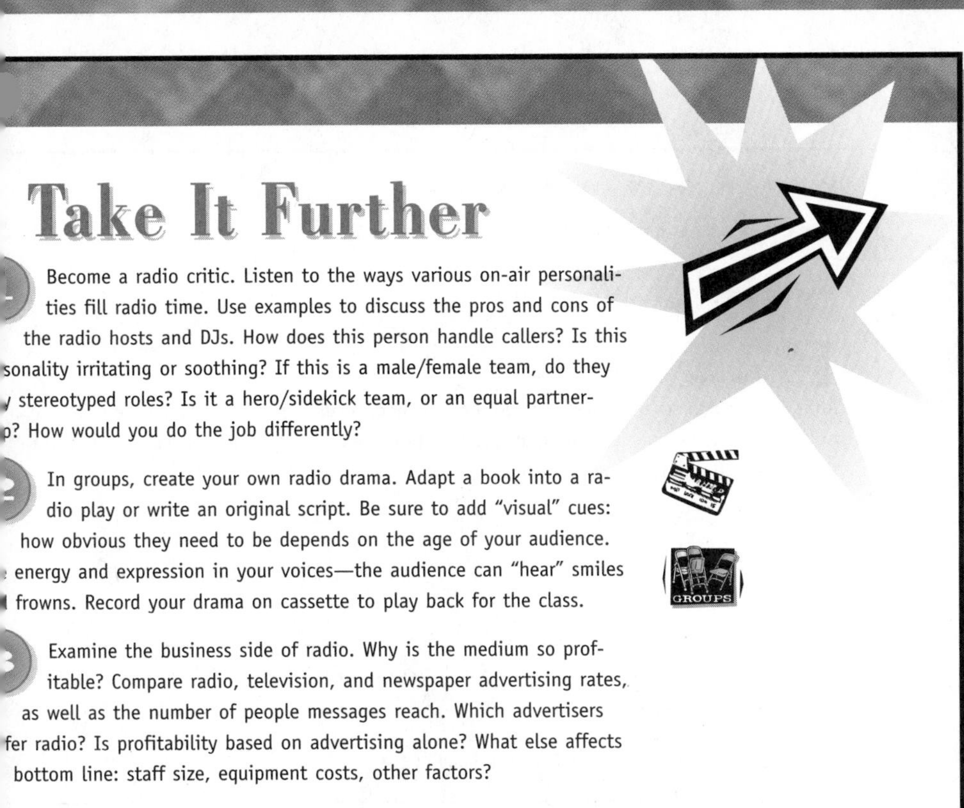

Take It Further

Become a radio critic. Listen to the ways various on-air personalities fill radio time. Use examples to discuss the pros and cons of the radio hosts and DJs. How does this person handle callers? Is this sonality irritating or soothing? If this is a male/female team, do they y stereotyped roles? Is it a hero/sidekick team, or an equal partnerp? How would you do the job differently?

In groups, create your own radio drama. Adapt a book into a radio play or write an original script. Be sure to add "visual" cues: how obvious they need to be depends on the age of your audience. energy and expression in your voices—the audience can "hear" smiles frowns. Record your drama on cassette to play back for the class.

Examine the business side of radio. Why is the medium so profitable? Compare radio, television, and newspaper advertising rates, as well as the number of people messages reach. Which advertisers fer radio? Is profitability based on advertising alone? What else affects bottom line: staff size, equipment costs, other factors?

Controls in a recording studio

SSON 10: RADIO REVISITED 107

Take It Further

1. This exercise asks students to deconstruct the job of a radio host. They are then encouraged to invent their own radio personality in the "What would you do differently?" question. Look for them to consider key elements of radio—voice, contents, credibility—as they create a better radio host.
2. This construction exercise can be a fun one for students. Though the era of dramatic radio shows is gone, they can imagine what it would take to create a successful audio program. Voices, characterization, exaggeration, music, and sound effects are all key elements in creating the mood that best matches the theme of the drama.
3. This third exercise is research based. Encourage students to call the business offices of local radio stations to discuss the questions they need to answer. They also need to listen to a fair amount of radio and take notes on advertisements to determine who advertises the most on radio stations. Certainly, radio ads are cheaper then television ads, because they require considerably less in production costs, having no video components. An interesting question to ask students is this: which commercials do they tend to remember more: radio or TV ads? Many may remember TV ones, because of the visual component. But radio advertisers probably give a bit more thought to the verbal content of their ads, and auditory learners may recall the details of radio ads better.

Radio

News

1. Most news stories are told in the third person, though they may include first-person quotes or interviews.
2. Answers may include the tone of the announcer, the language, and extra sound effects or interviews.

On-Air Personalities

1. Announcers may talk about recording artists, concerts, local or national news, sports, and international events.
2. Often morning shows include two DJs who create a kind of variety show using banter, celebrity interviews, practical jokes, and a recap of the previous evening's news. Afternoon music radio stations tend to play more music with less talk.

W O R K S H E E T

Deconstructing the Media

Radio

File: Radio

After listening to several types of radio programming, including story clips, commercials, public service announcements, and on-air personalities, identify the various elements that make them work, and evaluate their effect on you.

News

1. As you listen to a news story, what voice do you hear? Is this a first-person narrative or a moment-in-time story?

____

____

____

2. Besides music, what other cues set the mood of the story?

____

____

____

On-Air Personalities

1. Pick out several stations and compare on-air personalities. What kinds of topics do the announcers and DJs talk about?

____

____

____

2. How do announcers and topics differ among the various air times? Compare a morning drive with afternoon drive time or the mid-day periods.

____

____

____

3. How can you tell which market—age, gender, or ethnic—is being targeted?

Commercials and PSAs

1. What types of products and services are particularly well suited for radio advertising? Why?

2. How do radio commercials grab your attention?

Narrowcasting

1. In your listening area, how many different kinds of stations are available, to your knowledge? To what kinds of demographics do you believe the particular stations cater?

2. Do you listen to more than one type of radio station? For what reasons?

3. Ads provide clues to the target audience. So does the type of music or talk and the DJ's point of view.

Commercials and PSAs

1. Car services, grocery stores, and restaurants are among the best-suited ads for radio because many people listen to radio while in their cars and may be tempted to go directly to these types of businesses.
2. Radio ads often use humor to get the listener's attention.

Narrowcasting

1. Chances are that most students can think of at least five types of stations in their area, including rock, jazz, country, talk, news, and oldies. Demographics may vary according to the region in which students live.
2. Many students will listen to several stations because they have several types of music or information in which they are interested.

Lesson 11 From Rap to Rachmaninoff: *The World of Music Media*

What's Ahead?

Goal: This lesson is intended to help students recognize the influences, both positive and negative, that music and the music industry have on their lives. Students will become more aware of lyrics in songs and of disturbing conventions used in music videos to sell the musicians' CDs. They will also have the opportunity to construct their own positive music messages.

Disciplines: This lesson pertains to the study of language arts, music, video production, psychology, science, and social studies.

Objectives: After studying this lesson, students will be able to:

- Define key terms in the lesson.
- Deconstruct music in terms of mood and meaning conveyed through the genre and lyrics.
- Determine the effects of various types of music on their lives.
- Construct a music message.

LESSON 11

From Rap to Rachmaninoff

What's Ahead?

Are you a blues fan? A Top 40 follower? Or do you dismiss the middle road, preferring alternative, rap, or classical music?

Chances are that you spend time listening to music every day. Humans' attraction to rhythm and music is as old as humanity itself, though we will probably never know just what music sounded like in the ancient world. We have art and literature that show us music did exist, but, of course, no recordings. Even from the more recent era of classical masters such as Beethoven, we have only written musical compositions, and we can only guess at how the music sounded and affected its listeners. Music is a powerful medium that affects not only our feelings, but also our attitudes and actions.

Main Points to Ponder

- Lyrics have been used not only to articulate romantic joys and sorrows, but also to deliver social and political commentary, promote religious beliefs, and consider harmful behaviors such as drug use, heavy drinking, hate crimes, and violence.
- Music videos' primary purpose is to sell the music cassettes and CDs of the artists. Videos employ many of the devices of advertising.
- Because music has such a powerful grip on its listeners, throughout the ages people have feared possible negative behaviors resulting from listening to music and lyrics.

110 MEDIA MATTE

Materials

This lesson uses:

- excerpt from "This Kiss" music video (Video clip #26 - 0:45)
- "This Kiss" music (Audio CD Track #6)
- "This Kiss" lyrics (File name *Thiskiss* on R&R disk)
- Analyzing Music, Lyrics, and Music Videos Worksheet (File name *Music* on R&R disk)
- Music Survey Worksheet (File name *Survey* on R&R disk)

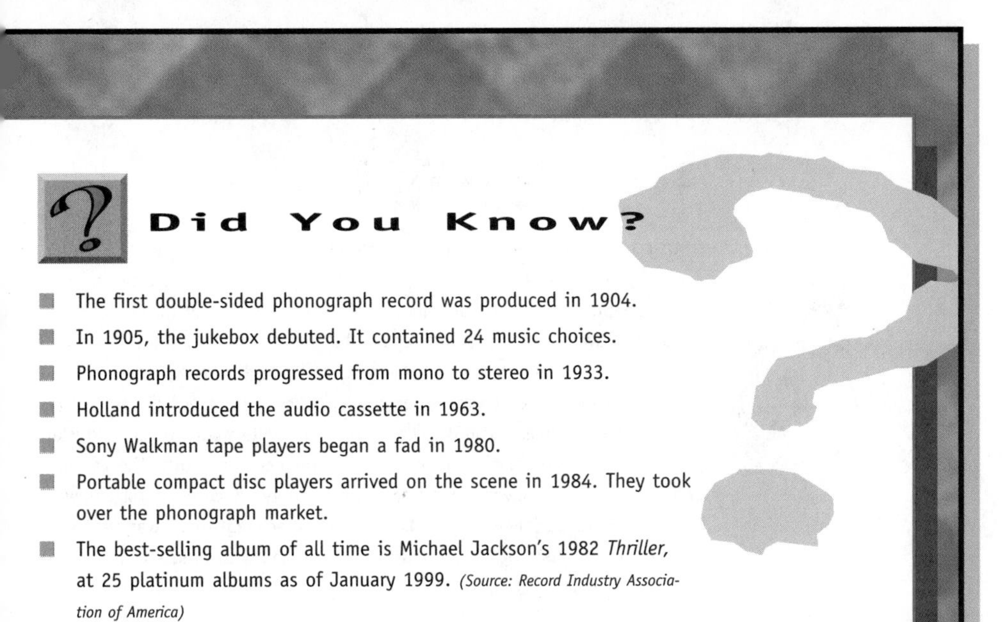

Did You Know?

- The first double-sided phonograph record was produced in 1904.
- In 1905, the jukebox debuted. It contained 24 music choices.
- Phonograph records progressed from mono to stereo in 1933.
- Holland introduced the audio cassette in 1963.
- Sony Walkman tape players began a fad in 1980.
- Portable compact disc players arrived on the scene in 1984. They took over the phonograph market.
- The best-selling album of all time is Michael Jackson's 1982 *Thriller,* at 25 platinum albums as of January 1999. *(Source: Record Industry Association of America)*

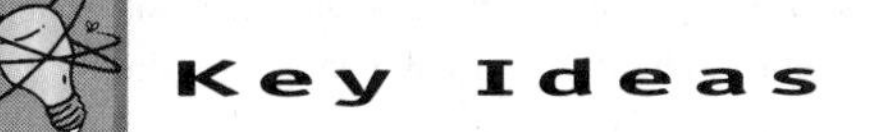

Key Ideas

Agent-a person who has been authorized to act for another person or group of people. In the music industry, an agent is one who books appearances and negotiates contracts for musicians.

Choreography-the carefully arranged, detailed movements of a dance.

Crossover-a music product that is a blend of two music genres; for example, a song that combines country/western with pop.

Hip Hop-(1) the music that accompanies rap; (2) the culture of rap, including clothing and art.

Lyrics-words put to music.

Music Video-a multimedia genre that combines songs with videos. Sometimes the video tries to depict the words of the song or show an artistic or symbolic representation of it. Sometimes the video has little to do with the lyrics, but joins together a song with something desirable to the viewer, such as fantasies of popularity, success, or love. Most videos also include clips of the artists singing and playing the song.

LESSON 11: FROM RAP TO RACHMANINOFF 111

Did You Know?

The historical facts presented allow students to put the development of music as an industry into context.

Key Ideas

Students are likely to be very familiar with these terms, but ask them to provide examples of the different kinds of genres, lyrics, and videos. Also ask them what terms they think are important to music literacy. In the world of popular and contemporary music, they may well know more than you do! If you have favorites of your own that they are unlikely to know much about (opera, for example), you can tell them about your favorite genre's characteristics and key terms.

Get Started

This section begins by demonstrating that music has always been both loved and criticized. Students may feel that parental disdain for their music is something new, but even Plato scorned any music that was not created for contemplating the sacred. Along with concerns about immorality in music, musicians have been censured for creating compositions with critical political content, such as various Russian composers during the Soviet period and 60s rocksters criticizing the Vietnam War.

Students interested in learning more about scientific studies of music may want to look at the University of California, Irvine's Web site devoted to this subject at http://musica.uci.edu/. There is an article indexed about the effect of doing homework with music playing in the background. The conclusions are that it is not distracting and can even be helpful to extroverts, but that introverts should tend to work in a quiet space. Additionally, students can find research about how listening to classical music (especially Mozart) may improve memory.

Ask students what they think about a rating system on CDs. They are likely to disapprove of it. Then ask, "Do you think there should be a rating system on movies?" While they may not want to admit it, most probably think the movie ratings are necessary, though they might want to make some changes in them. Challenge them: If it is okay to X-rate sexually explicit movies, why shouldn't music containing strong violence and sexual content also be rated?

Get Started

Music has been loved and criticized throughout history. Ancient Greeks were convinced that music had the power to heal, stir the emotions, and sway people to both positive and negative actions. The medieval Christian church allowed and encouraged chant, but banned instrumental accompaniment from religious services. The nineteenth century composer Johann Strauss was criticized by many for popularizing that "immoral" dance, the waltz. In the 1950s and 60s, pioneer rock and rollers such as Elvis Presley and the Beatles were condemned as bad influences on youth. The popular *Ed Sullivan Show* showed Elvis from waist up only, since his gyrations were considered to be indecent. The Beatles' shoulder-length hair was seen as disrespectful. Much other pop music is connected with drug abuse and violence.

Perhaps music receives so much attention because it truly is a powerful medium. Research done at the University of California, Irvine, has indicated that children who take music lessons are better able to understand concepts that are also necessary to understanding math and science principles. Scientists have also found correlations between music and epileptic seizures, psychological therapy, memory, and risk-taking behaviors.

"There are more love songs than anything else. If songs could make you do something we'd all love one another."
Frank Zappa

Many adults are concerned that listening to rap, heavy metal, and offensive lyrics can lead to antisocial and violent behavior. This concern led to the 1985 formation of the Parents Music Resource Group, which lobbied for a labeling system similar to movie ratings. Parents have tried to sue music stars Ozzie Osbourne and members of the group Judas Priest for marketing songs that they believe led their children to commit suicide or act violently.

Contemporary music gained a new dimension with the advent of music videos and MTV. Just as television added an extra factor to an audience's judgment of political figures, televised music videos prompt listeners to consider the quality of music groups' appearance, their performance, and their interpretations of their music. The videos are also powerful devices for selling music CDs, and as such, many use the ad technique of linking success, power, and romance with the music.

112 MEDIA MATTERS

You may not be allowed to show music videos that students need to be aware of the most. While many videos are truly creative (such as Madonna's song *Frozen*, in which she morphs into different animals), far too many depict women as things that can be used and tormented, and who live only to sexually tease and please men. These videos create fantasy worlds, and they work much as advertisements do, causing less media-aware viewers to expect the same in their own lives as they buy and listen to the music. Ask students to carefully consider the values created in music videos and to deconstruct them in the same way that they would analyze stereotypes, violence, and sexual content found in movies and ads.

Break It Down

Music Videos

Listen to the song "This Kiss" by Faith Hill. Discuss your impressions of the song. Think about how you might create a music video for this piece. Then watch the excerpt from Hill's music video. Does the video enhance or detract from the music, in your opinion? Deconstruct the video in terms of acting, camera techniques, and special effects. Answer the questions on the worksheet **Deconstructing the Media: Analyzing Music, Lyrics, and Music Videos** (p. 118), and discuss your answers in class.

Audio Track # 6
Faith Hill, "This Kiss"

Video clip #26
Faith Hill, "This Kiss"
(Warner Brothers Nashville)

File: ThisKiss

Big Business of Bubble Gum

Adults in their thirties and forties may smile or groan when reminded of the "bubble gum" musicians of their time: the Monkees, the Partridge Family, the Jackson Five. Their counterparts in the 1980s and 1990s are teen idols 'N Sync, New Kids on the Block, and Backstreet Boys. Many music fans and producers may sneer at such groups, preferring "serious" music, but these young bands have staked their ground with light pop sounds, playing to sell-out crowds and making millions on CDs, videos, and lunch boxes covered with their images.

The bands have similar images. There's usually a cute guy with dimples, a good dancer, and a member with a tough-guy edge to him. Coincidence? Not usually. Music producer Louis Pearlman, known as "Big Poppa" to his protégées, carefully constructs his groups, choosing members by such details as height, weight, hair color, and personality. They are trained by "teams of choreographers, vocal coaches, personal trainers, marketers, stylists and p.r. experts" ("Big Poppa's Bubble Gum Machine," *Time,* February 1, 1999). Pearlman's biggest successes so far are 'N Sync and Backstreet Boys. By 1999, Backstreet Boys had grossed over $900 million in sales; Pearlman spent about $3 million to bring them to the top.

Faith Hill: "This Kiss"
Courtesy: Warner Brothers Nashville

LESSON 11: FROM RAP TO RACHMANINOFF 113

Break It Down

The first activity is a media deconstruction. The Faith Hill song (**Audio CD Track #6**) and video excerpt (**Video Clip #26**) are benign as music videos go, but some students may feel uncomfortable with the kiss between the girl and boy. Invite a discussion: Is this an innocent depiction of "puppy love," or is it inappropriate? How do students feel about Hill's expressions and poses? What film techniques are used to create the product? The **Deconstructing the Media: Analyzing Music, Lyrics, and Music Videos** worksheet will help students with the process of analyzing the song and video. Many students will have seen the video in its entirety and may discuss other aspects of the video. The lyrics are available on the R&R disk in the file *Thiskiss*.

The Deconstructing the Media: Music Survey worksheet allows students to explore their own preferences as well as the two popular, but very different music genres explored in the rest of this section. Ask if thinking about these questions taught students something new about themselves. They may find, for example, that they love certain songs and even sing along with them, but they do not like the lyrics or they find the lyrics objectionable. Many chart-topping recordings discuss suicide, illegal drug use, and drinking binges; still others have male recording stars singing about the domination of females. Students may not have consciously considered the images that they sing about through the course of a day. The questions are not designed to have right and wrong answers, but rather to get students thinking about just what they are listening to and how it might affect their opinions and values.

The articles "Big Poppa's Bubble Gum Machine" (*Time,* 2/1/99) and "Hip Hop Nation" (*Time,* 1/7/99) are highly recommended resources. They could not be reprinted in this text, but you should be able to find copies in a well-stocked library. Both articles reflect on the big business side of the music industry. "Big Poppa" especially exposes the artificiality of some groups, destroying the fantasy image some students may have of local bands making it big. It will be interesting to note whether or not this knowledge affects their opinions of the bands.

How would you define bubble gum music? Do you like these groups? What subjects do you find in their lyrics? Have you previously thought of the groups themselves, and not just the songs, as media constructions? Does this knowledge alter your opinion of the bands themselves or the producers?

Rap/Hip-Hop

No longer just the music of the urban streets, rap has flown to the top of the charts in the 1990s. The numbers speak for themselves: "In 1998, for the first time ever, rap outsold what previously had been America's top-selling format, country music. Rap sold more than 81 million CDs, tapes and albums last year, compared with 72 million for country. Rap sales increased a stunning 31% from 1997 to 1998, in contrast to 2% gains for country" ("Hip-Hop Nation," *Time,* January 7, 1999).

Though deeply rooted in the African-American community, over 70 percent of rap is now purchased by whites. Rap's roots began back in 1971 with Kool Herc, and the genre has progressed to a point that there are rap/hip-hop subdivisions: gangsta rap, white rap, suburban rap, Christian rap. Consumers will hear it on Top 40 radio stations, in TV commercials, and in blockbuster movies. They will find it in respected American novelist Tom Wolfe's best-selling 1998 novel *A Man in Full.* Teens wear rapper superstar Lauryn Hill, Puffy Combs, and Will Smith tee-shirts to school. The culture of hip-hop includes artistic collages (graffiti) and oversized jeans. Additionally, minor hip-hop groups are discovering a new method of marketing their music: Instead of hoping to be signed by a recording company, many are going directly to their audience via the World Wide Web.

How does hip-hop influence your culture and daily life? Do you listen to the music? Is it played on radio stations to which you listen? Are there versions that reflect your own values or beliefs?

Sum It Up

Do any patterns emerge in your analyses of the music and videos? Can you agree on aspects of the music and video interpretations, or do you discover that your music analyses are highly individualized?

For fun, on a scale of one to five (with one being unappealing and five being highly appealing), rate how well you like the following types of music:

- top 40.
- country/western.
- blues.
- rap/hip hop.
- heavy metal.
- alternative.
- ethnic/folk.
- classical.
- show tunes (musicals).
- other (specify).

"I've always felt rock and roll was very, very wholesome music."

Aretha Franklin

Tally the results on the board. What favorites and least favorites emerge, if any? Try to articulate why you make the choices that you make. Complete the worksheet **Deconstructing the Media: Music Survey** (p. 119).

THEN AND NOW

Songs of Social Protest—the 60s and 70s

The 1960s and 1970s were decades of great social and political upheaval. The early 1960s saw the height of the Civil Rights movement, when "freedom riders" tried to end segregation in bus terminals and Martin Luther King, Jr., led thousands to believe in a vision of racial equality. The Vietnam War and the military draft caused young people across the country to protest government policies. Male students burned their draft cards; some fled to Canada to avoid military duty in Southeast Asia.

The countermessage of many of these students was one of love, peace, and "flower power." Over a million hippies descended on the Yasgur Farm in Bethel, New York, for "Woodstock," a three-day rock concert of the best the decade had to offer in rock groups, including many who wrote civil rights and antiwar songs. Among them were Joan Baez; Arlo Guthrie; Country Joe and the Fish; and Crosby, Stills, Nash, and Young.

Music was a major symbol for this generation, and the lyrics conveyed their ideals, concerns, and hopes. Dion's "Abraham, Martin, and John" conveys sadness at the passing of great leaders; Edwin Starr's "War" blares an angry message about the futility of war. See what other groups and music you can find that display the social messages and inspirations of this time period. Interview a parent or other adult who was a teenager or young adult during the 1960s or early 1970s. How do they compare the music of their youth to today's contemporary hits?

What inspires your generation's music? What are its political and social themes? Is music an appropriate vehicle for protest messages? Why or why not?

Sum It Up

Music, like art, is a subjective medium, and value judgments are largely a matter of individual taste. Conclusions can be made in terms of the messages contained in lyrics and videos, and studies have determined that certain kinds of music tend to have predictable effects on people. But it is not logical to argue that, for instance, "Oldies are *better than* today's top 40" or "Beethoven sounds better than Bach." These are matters of personal preference. See if your class can figure this out, and understand that some things can be argued logically, while others cannot. It will also be fun to see if any patterns emerge in terms of students' preferences.

Songs of Social Protest - the 60s and 70s. This feature box introduces students to an important era in which popular music was a vehicle for social and political protest. There are several good Web sites that give details on the incident at Kent State, on Woodstock, and music from the time period. The site http://www.rockinwoman.com/oldies28.html includes the full version of many of these songs that students can download for listening. Have them transcribe some of the lyrics and discuss them. Ask: What songs today are critical of social and political actions? Are they effective in inspiring young people to agitate for reform?

Web sources:

- on Woodstock: http://www.publiccom.com/14850/9407/coverstory.html
- on anti-war protests and the Democratic National Convention of 1968: http://www.pbs.org/wgbh/pages/amex/1968/68antiwar.html
- on Vietnam and the music of the period: http://www.imsa.edu/edu/socsci/jvictory/unit7_coldwar_vn/background/base_background.html
- on Kent State: http://www.emerson.edu/acadepts/cs/comm/preface.html
- on the Civil Rights Movement: http://www.midsouth.rr.com/civilrights/

Put It Together

It will be very difficult to have students actually create a video unless they are in an advanced film class. However, students can write a script for their music video, describing the scenes, actors and their costumes, lighting, close-ups, etc. Students who are musically inclined could even choose do a new interpretation of an already recorded song. Recording artists themselves have used this technique successfully. One example is Eric Clapton's "Layla," which was a hit both when he recorded it as a rock song in the 70s and when he remade it as a blues song in the 90s.

The idea of this activity is to get them thinking about the effort that goes into creating music and music videos as well as to have them create music messages.

Put It Together

Now that you've had a chance to think about positive and negative aspects of music, lyrics, and music videos, you will have the opportunity to build your own music creation.

Not everyone is comfortable creating a new musical composition, so if you are not, you can work with an existing piece of music. This activity will require you to:

1. Communicate a message by creating an original piece of music.

OR

2. Create a music video concept for an existing piece of music.

If you are creating an original musical composition, you may choose to work alone. Otherwise, you may opt to work with a partner and create a business proposal for your video ideas. Think carefully about your target audience, your message, and the music and actions that will best deliver your message. Music videos are very difficult to create because of the many quick cuts and different scenes found in most. However, you can create two or three storyboards to go with your written proposal, depicting the kinds of scenes you would include. Discuss the film techniques and camera angles you would use and the overall effect you want to create.

If you choose option 1, either play the piece live or tape record it to play in class. Discuss your goal and how you determined the lyrics and the music.

In all cases, take questions from students in class. Have answers ready about your purpose, your choices in music, instrumentation, lighting, camera angles, and other pertinent topics.

Take It Further

Choose a music video to deconstruct. Write about its message, point of view, and video techniques, as well as the feelings that it conjures in the listeners. Use specific examples to illustrate your opinions.

Spend several days listening to radio stations that play music you do not normally listen to. For instance, if you're a Top 40 listener, you might choose a classical, country, or rap station. Pay attention to how you feel about the music and why. Write a report about the experience.

Choose a song that has music and/or lyrics you like but a music video you dislike. Write a description and video directions for creating a better music video for the song.

WORLD VIEW

Music, the International Language

Although international citizens may not understand one another's verbal language, we all share a love of music, and the music of cultures has intermingled with other musical traditions to create even more pleasing compositions. The following discussions and exercises will help you to see the interconnectedness of nations, people, and music.

Worldwide, even though countries from other parts of the world have harmonic scales that are different from the western music scale, people are able to differentiate between music that sounds happy, sad, frightening, funny, and so forth. Studies have shown that music has a direct effect on people's moods, that people associate certain tones with certain emotions (although these may differ somewhat depending on the emotional makeup of the individual), and that background music can determine how people perceive other people and situations.

1. What do you think it is in music that causes diverse peoples to "feel" it in the same way? Why do you think that most people can "read" the language of music?
2. Much, if not most, of contemporary music is an amazing blend of musical traditions from many lands. Think of some popular songs, and talk about the traditions found in the music.
3. Using a globe, locate the countries from which your favorite groups have come.
4. Trace the history of a genre of music such as blues, gospel, rock, or jazz. Many genres that we may think of as American phenomena have their roots in other countries. Report what you find to the class.

Take It Further

The first exercise is a deconstruction similar to what students did together in **Break It Down.** Question #2 asks for more personal reflection and analysis, similar to the lab-type experience students did in part one of **Break It Down.** The third activity gives students another chance at constructing a more positive music video.

WORLD VIEW

Music, the International Language. Research studies on the effects of music can be found at http://musica.uci.edu. Specific articles of interest include:

- http://musica.uci.edu/mrn/V2I1S95.html#earliest (on infants' musical abilities)
- http://musica.uci.edu/mrn/V3I1S96.html#coloring http://musica.uci.edu/mrn/V2I2F95.html#elevator (on music and mood)
- http://musica.uci.edu/mrn/V5I2S98.html#understanding (music and its effects on emotions)

In their discussion, students may point out that some musical sounds mimic natural sounds that also evoke emotions in us. For example, loud, explosive music sounds may remind us of lightning, a gun firing, or a large object dropping. Gentle sounds may remind us of waves, the breeze, or birdsong.

Analyzing Music, Lyrics, and Music Videos

1. Students may answer rock, light rock, pop, country, or cross-over of rock and country. Indications are the beat of the music, the lyrics, the slight twang in the guitar and Hill's voice, etc.
2. The music is upbeat and light. It is uncomplicated, 4/4 time, and somewhat repetitive.
3. The lyrics proclaim the joy of a kiss and love. Opinions about them will vary.
4. Happiness, young love, and innocence are depicted in Faith Hill's smiles and expressions, the young people kissing, butterflies, flowers, and play. Some will also see images as sexual and stereotypical.
5. Answers will vary, but the images do reflect a feeling of joy that is conveyed by the lyrics. Look for students to explain their answers.

WORKSHEET

Deconstructing the Media

Analyzing Music, Lyrics, and Music Videos

File: Music

Answer the following questions about the Faith Hill song, lyrics, and video that accompany this chapter. You can also use this worksheet to deconstruct other music and videos.

1. What genre of music is the song: blues, swing, rock, jazz, rap, or other? How can you tell?

2. What mood does the music itself convey? How?

3. What are the lyrics about? Do you like them? Agree with them? Why or why not? Is there anything you would change? If yes, what?

4. What is depicted in the music video of the song?

5. Do the scenes make sense for this song? Do they help to convey the message and mood of the song? Why or why not? What changes, if any, would you make?

WORKSHEET

Deconstructing the Media

Music Survey

File: Survey

You've heard the expression "You are what you eat." Are you also what you listen to? What do your music preferences reveal about you? Answer the following questions as you consider how your music preferences may or may not reflect your personality.

1. What is your favorite kind of music? What is your least favorite kind of music? Why?

2. What draws you to music more: the tune or the lyrics? If it is the music itself, do you usually know the lyrics? Like the lyrics? Sing along?

3. What subjects do your favorite groups tend to sing about? Do you usually agree with the messages of their lyrics?

4. How many hours per week would you guess that you spend listening to music? Do you study with music in the background?

Music Survey

All of the answers to these questions will be highly individual, as this worksheet asks students to explore their own taste in music.

Lesson 12 Pages of our Lives: *The Magazine Industry*

What's Ahead?

Goals: This lesson will help students to understand that magazines are carefully constructed with editorial and design tools to reach specific audiences. While many of the articles contain easily accessible and quick information that meets readers' needs and interests, some of the messages and ideals put forth (particularly by advertising, which comprises nearly one-half of the content) are counter-productive and can create unhealthy ideals for unsuspecting readers.

Disciplines: This lesson can be used in association with language arts, health, and other disciplines if the magazines examined fall under the subject area (for instance, geography or history instructors could use examples from *National Geographic* or *Smithsonian*; science instructors could use *Discovery* or *Popular Science*, etc.).

Objectives: After completing this lesson, students will be able to:

- Define key terms related to publishing.
- Determine target audience by deconstructing magazine covers and tables of contents.
- Evaluate the effectiveness of a magazine in reaching its target audience.
- Understand the deceptiveness of computer-manipulated fashion models and the effect they can have on a reader's self-concept.

LESSON 12

Pages of Our Lives

What's Ahead?

In spite of competition from television, newspapers, radio, books, and the World Wide Web, the magazine industry continues to thrive, trying out an average of 15 new magazines each week. Do you read magazines? How often? Which ones? Do you subscribe to any? What do magazines tell us about ourselves and our society?

In this chapter, you will learn some history of magazines and how they have evolved as society has changed. Today's successful magazines carefully study their target audiences. You will learn about the composition of special-interest magazines and closely examine a cover, table of contents, and an article from a popular magazine targeted at teens.

Major Points to Ponder

- The target audience of a magazine, by its preferences and interests, helps to shape the contents and point of view of the publication.
- Because magazines have different points of view and readerships, they often cover the same events, personalities, or information differently.
- Advertisers influence the content of magazines. Additionally, advertisers shape the layout and contents of their ads to match the intended audience.

A magazine is best analyzed, of course, when a student can go through the entire publication to determine its effectiveness. As it is not practical or timely to reproduce a complete magazine for this lesson, instructors are encouraged to go beyond the examples in the lesson and have students bring in copies of magazine favorites to discuss and deconstruct. This will also help students realize the amazing variety of magazines available for the multitude of special interests in the country—sports, music, home decorating, fashion, beauty, health, science, mechanics, space flight, history, animals, etc. It is also valuable to bring in old issues of *Life, Look, The New Yorker, Harper's,* or *The Saturday Evening Post.* Compare an old issue to its modern counterpart, such as

Did You Know?

- Roughly 2,500 consumer magazines are available in the United States.
- The term "magazine" grew out of the military term for rifle ammunition storage. Magazines are storage places for ideas.
- In the 1800s, magazines were the publications of choice for serializing Harriet Beecher Stowe's *Uncle Tom's Cabin* and novels by Dickens.
- The first photographers of the Civil War, Alexander Gardner and Matthew Brady, rearranged bodies for more effective compositions in layouts.

Key Ideas

Box - a short feature that is related to the main article in which it is placed. Boxes are usually set off in a lined box, often with a different background color.

Circulation - distribution among readers; the average number of copies sold in a given time period.

Columns - regularly established feature of a magazine, usually written by the same writer each time, who becomes known and enjoyed for his or her particular style and opinions.

Features - often considered soft news, these stories provide readers with background on current issues, products, personalities, and trends.

Fonts - in printing, these are an assortment of type styles. Commonly used fonts include Times New Roman and Arial.

Layout - the way the words and images are arranged on the page. Photography and illustrations, type size and fonts, titles and box placements all determine the image of the magazine.

Mix - a predictable combination of feature stories, columns, and subject matter that readers come to expect in a given magazine. For example, in a women's magazine, readers expect a certain percentage of articles on health, beauty, fashion, dating, and women's issues. They will even expect a certain mix of advertising.

Tag Lines - Short phrases on a magazine cover that entice potential readers to purchase the publication.

a 1970s *Seventeen* to the one on today's shelves. Students will find amazing differences between what models looked like then and now. Ask students to compare the kinds of articles, the illustrations, lengths of articles. What do the differences say about the readers?

Did You Know?

This section includes some interesting trivia and alludes to just how big the magazine industry is. The last bullet acts as a prelude to design manipulation and image versus reality, topics to be discussed at more length in the **Ethics in Action** feature in this lesson.

Key Ideas

Be sure that students understand the vocabulary; use magazines brought into class to illustrate each term. Show them where they can find out the circulation numbers, the editors, and publishers. It is also interesting to point out current fads in magazine publishing. For instance, many magazines now spread out their table of contents over two or three pages, with numerous advertisements between the pages. Point out how many ads are in the opening pages. These opening pages cost advertisers the most, as they are most likely to be seen as readers are searching for the table of contents.

Materials

This lesson uses:

- The cover, table of contents, and article "A Reason to Live" from the November 1998 issue of *Teen People* (Text in file name *Reason* on R&R disk)
- Complete interview with magazine writer Barbara Forster (File name *Forster* on R&R disk)
- Magazine Covers and Contents Worksheet (File name *Magcov* on R&R disk)
- Magazine Articles Worksheet (File name *Magart* on R&R disk)

Get Started

If your students have not completed Lesson 7 on advertising, you might want to go over the concepts with them. Magazines are loaded with ads, and many readers actually buy the magazines primarily for their ads. They learn about the newest products in their sport, the latest computer equipment, cosmetics, fashions, and health products by skimming advertisements. Lesson Seven helps students realize that ads are often more persuasive about the product than they are informative.

While short information-bites are popular on the pages of today's magazines, people in the mid-1800s craved the next publication of their favorite magazines to read the next chapter of a serialized novel. The serialization of Charles Dickens' *The Old Curiosity Shop* is perhaps one of the most famous examples. Dickens' readers were so involved with the character Little Nell that they gathered at the docks in New York awaiting the arrival of the magazine issue that would reveal whether or not the character had died. As the ships approached from England, the crowds would shout out, "Is Little Nell dead?" When they finally received the affirmative answer, they quietly turned and walked slowly away, many in tears.

An interesting class conversation could involve a discussion about reading books versus magazines. In earlier decades, magazines were actually used to publish books, and now, many turn to magazines to avoid the lengthiness of books. Ask the class to speculate on why this is the trend and what it might say about us as a society. Have students consider why they buy magazines: for the subject matter, the promise of great articles found in the cover tags, the personalities featured on the cover, photos in the magazine?

Get Started

The modern American magazine was born in the late 1800s, the brainchild of Frank Munsey. Munsey determined that he could create a large circulation by publishing inexpensive periodicals. To keep down the price of the magazines, he let advertisers pay most of the costs by purchasing ad space. Today advertisements may take up half the pages in a magazine (publishers try to keep ads to under 45 percent of the content). While we enjoy the benefit of relatively inexpensive and timely reading materials, we pay the price of contents being affected by advertisers, just as television series are affected by advertisers.

General-interest magazines were more prevalent in the early part of the century, but some, such as *Reader's Digest,* are still quite successful. Most magazine publishers, however, have found that targeting a specific audience is more effective. Special interest magazines' content is determined by carefully analyzing demographics. Some such as *Sports Illustrated,* have broad coverage within a specific category; others focus more tightly, such as magazines that target one specific sport. Discuss the range of magazines that you read.

You can detect the carefully designed differences in mix, layouts, and advertisements by examining two magazines with similar, yet different target audiences. Look, for example, at recent issues of *Working Woman* and *Working Mother.* Both of these popular magazines target women who work. Yet, as you will see, the slight difference in emphasis influences the contents considerably. If you look for a car ad in each, you are likely to find a woman in a business suit next to a car in *Working Woman* and a woman with her children next to a mini-van in *Working Mother.*

Another major difference in today's magazines, as compared to those published in the earlier decades of this century, involves the length of articles. The faster pace of today's society has resulted in shorter magazine articles. The idea behind the shorter length is that people just don't have the time to read lengthy articles. They will read for a few minutes while commuting to work on a bus or subway, waiting for a professor to begin class, or trying to unwind for five minutes before turning off the lights to sleep. People even give the short length of magazine articles as a reason that they prefer periodicals to books.

Break It Down

teen market is a substantial one for magazine publishers. Teen maga-
es are often conceived based on similar publications. Such examples in-
de *Zillions* (in the image of *Consumer Reports*) and *Sports Illustrated for*
s. A Time/Warner magazine, *Teen People,* is based on their highly suc-
sful *People* magazine.

first thing that draws a reader to a magazine is its cover. Look carefully
the *Teen People* below. What conclusions can you draw about its target
ience? Explain. Answer the questions on your worksheet **Deconstructing**
Media: Magazine Covers and Contents (p. 127), and discuss them in
ss.

rinted from *Teen People* with permission.

SSON 12: PAGES OF OUR LIVES 123

Break It Down

If you are teaching a high school class, many of the magazines your students bring in will fall into the teen category. Discuss the ways in which the contents and concerns of these magazines differ from their counterparts in the adult world. Students are likely to find that many topics are similar in both teen and adult magazines, though the treatment of them will differ. (For example, teens will prefer certain actors and singers, while adults prefer others; teen magazines may contain articles on finding that first job, while adult ones may talk about asking for a raise, balancing work with family life, or changing careers.)

The questions on the worksheets can be easily adapted to refer to other magazines that your students may be more interested in deconstructing. While considering questions about design, layout, and copy content, students might notice the following elements:

- The black background color of the cover makes the white and red type stand out boldly.
- The stars chosen have wide appeal to teens.
- The main feature article is about celebrities. Some students may argue that this appeal is limited, especially since two other taglines are also about stars (Leo DiCaprio and the band 'N Sync). Male students may argue effectively that this cover would appeal more to female students with its emphasis on Hollywood stars, makeup, and the social concern of suicide. They might suggest improvements by adding a feature on a sports star or Tyree Coleman, the teenager who fights crime in his neighborhood.
- The Table of Contents is split into two pages (what they won't know that you can tell them is that, in order to arrive at the first page, the reader must leaf through 14 pages of advertisements for makeup, fragrance, and hair spritzer, and to find the second page they will pass three more pages of ads devoted to men's cologne and clothing). Three photos of stars and one of a girl working to lose weight add design elements to the Table of Contents. Subcategories are easy to find due to their larger blue font; they are "start here," "stars & entertainment," "looks & style," and "the real world." Titles are also easy to find in a capitalized red font.

- "A Reason to Live" is designed to inform readers about the seriousness of teen suicide (it is the "third highest cause of death among 15- to 24-year-olds"), including its signs and prevention.
- Design elements include photos of Kenny White (whose suicide story opens the article), his parents, sister, friends, and his grave. Most moving, probably, is Kenny's handwritten suicide note.

File: Reason

After you've determined that the cover and table of contents are worthy of your $3.95, the test of whether or not you will purchase the next issue is found in the editorial content.

Carefully read the handout "A Reason to Live," one of the feature articles in the November 1998 *Teen People*. Answer the questions on the worksheet **Deconstructing the Media: Magazine Articles** (p. 129), then evaluate the story with the class.

a reason to live

Eight teens from a small midwestern town have committed suicide over the last three years. Their loved ones are determined to stop the epidemic

Reprinted from *Teen People* with permission.

IN THE SPOTLIGHT

Barbara Forster, Freelance Magazine Writer

Barbara Forster, a freelance writer for ten years (and one of the writers of this text) tells what it takes to survive in this highly competitive profession. (The complete interview is on computer disk.)

How did you break into the business?

I answered an ad for "Freelance Writers" that appeared in a specialized community newspaper. The first piece I did was on "spec"—they didn't pay me—just to see if I could put a sentence together.

Do you ever write about topics for which you have no particular interest or background? How do you come up with contents for these kinds of articles?

Over the years I have been fortunate to have great people to interview when I'm in an area that doesn't appeal to me. They are usually excited about their work or the subject, and that enthusiasm is catching. Preparing for those articles, however, is tricky. Not only is my advance time limited, but becoming an overnight expert is impossible. On the other hand, knowing what to ask is essential.

How do you maintain enough clients to make this business full time?

Hustle is the short answer. The longer response is mastering a few tricks of the trade. I've learned to write relatively quickly, and that means turning short pieces of about 600 to 700 words around in two or three days, including interviews. Another part of the job is always looking for work; making cold calls to various publications, sending out queries—letters suggesting an article I'd like to write for a particular publication—and talking to people about writing possibilities. Juggling those tasks while working on the paying end is challenging.

File: Forster

IN THE SPOTLIGHT

The full-length interview is provided on the R&R disk (file name *Forster*). In addition to discussing Barbara Forster's career as a freelance writer, look at the masthead of some magazines to discover other jobs in the magazine field, such as editors, art directors, designers, researchers, sales representatives, and customer service personnel. If anyone in your class is interested in these careers, he or she could find out more by writing to some of the people listed in care of the magazine; by finding the magazine online and emailing people in the occupations that interest them; by contacting the offices of a local magazine; or by arranging an interview with a journalism professor at a nearby college or university.

Sum It Up

Discuss your answers to questions on **Deconstructing the Media: Magazine Covers and Contents** and **Magazine Articles.** On a scale of one to five, how do you rate:

- the quality of the magazine cover?
- the overall appeal to the target audience?
- the substance of "A Reason to Live"?
- the balance in "A Reason to Live"?
- the newsworthiness of "A Reason to Live"?
- the appeal of the article to the target audience?

Did you learn anything new about teen suicide from "A Reason to Live"? Did the article influence your opinions about the topic or encourage you to get involved in prevention?

Put It Together

What kind of magazine is still needed by American consumers? Do you have a special interest that isn't covered by today's publications?

Now is your chance to create it! For this exercise, you will develop your own magazine and present a business proposal for it. The class will be the board of directors that you must convince to support your new magazine.

Determine the target audience, point of view, mix, style, and advertisers for the product. Explain to the board why you think the publication can be successful. Include:

1. A sketch of the first cover (you can use illustrations, photography, or images cut from other magazines in creating your layout).
2. A layout of your table of contents.
3. A sample article with ideas for design.
4. A list of potential advertisers. Discuss how you will work with these advertisers to maintain the integrity of your editorial content.

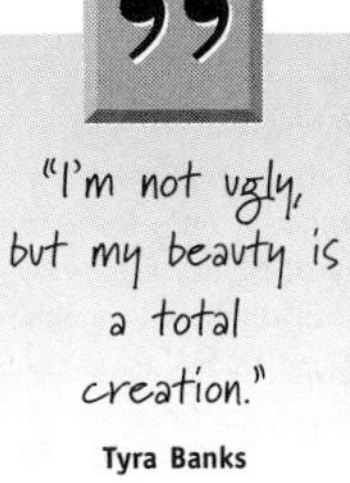

"I'm not ugly, but my beauty is a total creation."
Tyra Banks

Sum It Up

Answers will vary according to students' preferences and beliefs about the target audience. They should, however, tend to agree that "A Reason to Live" is newsworthy.

Put It Together

In this exercise students must conceptualize a magazine and demonstrate its viability. They will learn that new magazines don't appear simply because someone thinks they're a good idea; they need to be financed as well. Magazines are sold not only to a potential audience, but also to potential investors and advertisers. Additionally, students need to think about how to maintain editorial control over content that advertisers may not like.

Brainstorm with your students about potential problems with major advertisers and supporters. For instance, a cosmetic advertiser would not like an article in someone's new fashion magazine that revealed the company's policy of testing on animals. While students may not come up with completely satisfactory answers to these dilemmas, they will get practice in problem solving and thinking about real-world business problems and solutions.

This activity may be done individually or in pairs. Students fearful of their artistic ability should be encouraged to do their best with sketches and photos and illustrations pulled from other sources. In fact, this is what frequently occurs in the early planning steps in the business world, though a final presentation would be polished, and illustrations and photos would be created by professionals in those fields.

Take It Further

Numbers 1 and 2 are deconstruction activities. The first is similar to the **Break It Down** work presented earlier in the lesson, except that it allows students to work with their choice of magazine and to treat the entirety of the magazine. The second is an interesting exercise in discovering the difference in purpose and point of view. If students are stuck thinking about subjects that could be found in two different magazines, you could suggest the following ideas to start them thinking:

- A health issue featured in a teen magazine and a parent magazine.
- A national news item treated by a conservative and a liberal news magazine.
- A computer issue discussed in a Macintosh magazine and a PC magazine.
- A sports star featured in a children's sports magazine and an adult one.

Take It Further

1. Deconstruct and evaluate an issue of your favorite magazine in terms of contents, layout, mix, style, and audience appeal. Why do you think that the magazine is successful?

2. Find the same topic treated in two different magazines, and compare and contrast the contents and layout. You can easily find examples in different news magazines. What is included and excluded from one article to the next? Why? How do the lengths compare? Discuss the effectiveness of each article as pertains to its purpose.

ETHICS IN ACTION

Manipulation of Photos

The cover girl photo you see today on a current fashion magazine probably cost thousands of dollars and was three to four months in the making. Since every model's body is different, clothes are tied, pinned, taped, and clipped in the back; models are wrapped to squeeze their figures or padded to fill them out. From the photo shoot, the photos are then manipulated on computers—lips are made fuller; flesh tones are evened out; teeth are whitened; and legs, arms, necks, and chins are reshaped to create the ideal figure. Even models' already thin thighs are regenerated by computer to be inches thinner.

"That's what a fashion picture is all about," says Sandra de Nicholais, fashion designer for *Cosmopolitan* magazine. "It has to look perfect on the page so that every girl that sees that outfit will want to go out and buy it." Designers justify the images because having one's fashion on the cover of a magazine can increase its sales by as much as 60 percent.

Unfortunately, when glamour, success, and happiness are associated with abnormally thin and flawless people, it is no wonder that people will go to unhealthy lengths to try to conform to this image. According to the National Eating Disorder Organization, "North American models [already] weigh 23 percent less today than the average female weighs. To try to conform to this unrealistic level of thinness, research has found that by the age of 18, 80 percent of females are or have been actively dieting." Dissatisfaction with body image affects males as well, and 10 percent of those afflicted by eating disorders are male.

How do these images affect you, and what can you do about it? Recognizing that the body images you see in print are not the real thing is a positive first step. You can also actively let publishers know when you think their practices are unethical. In the November 1998 issue of *Teen People,* managing editor Christina Ferrari writes, ". . . we're using regular teens instead of ultra-skinny models in our fashion stories. We're committed to showing a wide range of body types, because we believe there's no such thing as an 'ideal' physique." Look at a recent issue to see if the magazine is adhering to that commitment, and write a letter to the editor, stating whether or not the commitment has been kept. Analyze your favorite magazines for the models they use in their stories, and write to these editors as well. Companies want to please their buyers, and they are interested in their readers' opinions. *(Source: http://www.laureate.com/whwhocau.html#eating)*

ETHICS IN ACTION

The depiction of super-thin, beautiful, flawless young women as popular and successful is a serious concern to parents and health professionals. Adolescent girls (though boys are also affected) already have insecurities about their body image, their chances of dating the guys they like, and measuring up to their peers. Constantly inundated with media messages of perfect, though truly unreal, bodies and faces, they can easily be discouraged. Of course, this is one ploy that companies hope to achieve, and they use it on women and men of all ages. The message, "So you don't look this gorgeous? Buy our product, and you too will be beautiful" is what increases the sales of cosmetics, hair products, and clothing every year. For most, this message has annoying, but manageable consequences. For others, however, there are health implications, including depression and eating disorders.

WORKSHEET

Deconstructing the Media

Magazine Covers and Contents

File: MagCov

Most people will look at a magazine cover and its Table of Contents to determine whether or not they will purchase the issue. Analyze the ones in this chapter to determine their effectiveness:

1. Examine the layout of the *Teen People* cover. Why would a designer choose the elements found there? What would his or her purpose be in including nine photos of stars?

____

____

____

2. What is effective or ineffective about the color scheme on the cover? What changes might you make to improve it? Explain your choices.

____

____

____

3. Consider the tag lines and type fonts. Are they appealing to you? To whom might they appeal? Why? Based on the tag lines and style of this cover, what do you anticipate you will find inside this magazine, generally and specifically?

____

____

____

4. Is the Table of Contents easy to follow? If yes, what devices are used to increase ease of use? Can you easily find the stories that have tag lines on the cover? Why or why not?

____

____

____

SSON 12: PAGES OF OUR LIVES 127

Magazine Covers and Contents

1. The celebrities chosen have particular appeal to teens. There is an attempt to be multicultural in the selection, and both men and women are included. Some students may not think that the layout, in which words take precedence over images, is effective.
2. Some students may like the black background because it allows the images and graphics to stand out. Some may not like the use of so many colors in the words and may find that distracting.
3. The tag lines will appeal to readers who like to learn about stars and popular music groups. It may appeal more to young women than men with the tag lines about Leo DiCaprio and makeup. The cover indicates that the contents will be about mainstream entertainers and fashion, with at least a small portion of the magazine pertaining to a serious topic (suicide).
4. The Table of Contents is easy to follow, as it uses easy-to-find categories and red lettering for titles of articles.

5. While there are some features for males, the contents tend toward an appeal to females. The photos draw attention to teen girls' idols, weight issues, and fashion. "Dreamy bed linens" are not likely to interest male readers. Some of the real-world articles, however, will appeal to teen boys, and they may be interested in some of the features on stars.
6. Answers will vary according to personal taste.
7. The appeal is to a teen market likely to be in a middle-class mainstream demographic. Readers will be interested in the lives of celebrities and are likely to be fashion conscious. They will also be interested in some real-world issues facing teens, such as friendships, safety, appearance, and teen tragedies.

5. *Teen People* is intended to attract both male and female readers. What elements in the Table of Contents work to achieve this purpose? Do you think that the magazine holds enough appeal for both young women and men? Why or why not?

6. Are there particular articles in the Table of Contents that you want to read? How do the tags under the article titles contribute to their appeal?

7. Based on the cover and the Table of Contents, would you purchase this magazine? Why or why not? What demographics might readers of this magazine share, in terms of interests, finances, social groups, and other factors?

128 MEDIA MATTE

WORKSHEET

Deconstructing the Media

Magazine Articles

File: MagArt

Once you buy a magazine, the factor that determines whether or not you will buy the next issue is the appeal of the articles. After reading "A Reason to Live," intended for both male and female young readers, consider the effectiveness of the article for that audience.

1. What is the purpose of the article "A Reason to Live"?

____

____

____

2. What is its main argument and point of view?

____

____

____

3. Is its argument supported, balanced, and effective? Explain.

____

____

____

4. Aside from the target audience, what other readers might be interested in this story, and why?

____

____

____

5. Did this article appeal to you? Why or why not? Would you buy another issue of this magazine, knowing that it will contain articles of this quality and layout? Why or why not?

____

____

____

Magazine Articles

1. The purpose is to inform readers about the tragedy of teen suicides.
2. The article has an indirect argument that tries to convince readers to help anyone they think may commit suicide and to convince readers that the action is a tragic waste of life.
3. The argument is mainly supported by one in-depth investigation of an unexpected suicide. The use of reactions by family and friends is effective in conveying the tragedy of this suicide, which represents teen suicide in general. Balance is tough to determine, as most readers would not be able to imagine an argument in favor of teen suicide. But there is balance in that the article explains reactions from many members of the community.
4. Parents and other concerned adults would be interested in the article.
5. Answers will vary, according to personal interests and taste.

Lesson 13 Surfing That Web: *The Internet and World Wide Web*

What's Ahead?

Goal: This lesson introduces students to the complex and controversial nature of the World Wide Web. Students will learn the importance of carefully analyzing their online sources and will be asked to evaluate several Web sites by looking specifically at the source, content, and design of the sites.

Disciplines: This lesson includes information on language arts, technology, and current events. Depending on what subjects and sites students choose for their projects, it can also be applied to any of the other subject disciplines.

Objective: After completing this lesson students will be able to:

- Define new terms specific to the Internet.
- Understand the disadvantages and advantages of doing online research.
- Analyze and evaluate the quality of several Web sites by looking at their source, content, and design.
- Design an effective Web page that incorporates the characteristics of quality presented in this lesson.

Ask students to visit several Web sites and report back to the class on what they like and don't like. Have them consider what separates the good sites from the poor ones.

LESSON 13

Surfing That Web

What's Ahead?

Just a few years ago, hardly anyone had heard of the Internet. Then, while we were marveling at the amazing things we could do with word processing on our computers, along came the modem and the creation of an entirely new realm, Cyberspace. Today the World Wide Web is rapidly changing the ways we run businesses, conduct research, communicate, buy and sell products, and receive information. Nearly every aspect of our lives has been affected by the rapid growth of the Net.

Although the advantages of the Internet are many, it can also pose challenges and risks to its users. Users should approach this medium with both excitement and caution.

In this chapter you will learn how to evaluate Web sites. You will visit, analyze, and critique some Web sites based on three main criteria.

Main Points to Ponder

- To judge the quality of a Web site, you must know who created the site and for what purpose. It is important to know about the origins of the information on your computer screen.
- The contents of a Web site should be assessed for accuracy and validity. Much of what is online is not verified before it is published. This is especially true of personal sites and home pages.
- The design of a Web site is important. An easy to navigate, well-organized site will help users find the information they are seeking.

130 MEDIA MATTE

Ask students to rank newspapers, books, magazines, television, and the Internet (from best to worst) based on their: 1) ease of use, 2) accuracy, 3) trustworthiness, 4) fun, 5) value as a research tool, and 6) preference as a research tool. What do the results suggest about their preferred methods of research vs. their perceptions of that tool's credibility?

Did You Know?

- In spring of 1998, a Californian woman delivered a baby "online" while thousands of people watched.
- Traffic on the Internet has been doubling every 100 days.
- In 1996, Amazon.com, the first Internet bookstore, recorded sales of less than $16 million. In 1997, it sold $148 million worth of books to Internet customers. *(Source: http://www.ecommerce.gov)*

Key Ideas

Chatroom-a "virtual space" where you can talk to other users. Chatrooms occur in "real time": Messages you read in chats are being typed as you see them appear.

Cyberspace-name given to the realm of the Internet (or any network of computers); this is the "place" you are "in" as you navigate the virtual landscape of the Internet.

Internet (or Net)-literally, a network of computer networks.

Links-underlined, highlighted, or colored text, graphics, or other screen features that immediately connect you to another location on the World Wide Web.

Navigate-the process of working your way through sites and topics on the Internet.

Net Appeal-the aesthetics of a site; what makes it appealing or attractive; how it looks and sounds.

Search Engine-a tool that helps you navigate the Internet. Examples include Yahoo, Lycos, and Webcrawler.

World Wide Web (WWW or just the Web)-a hypermedia system that lets you browse the Internet. The WWW is the fastest way of accessing the Internet.

Key Ideas

Discuss terms with students, citing examples when possible. When discussing search engines, remind your students that not all search engines are alike. You may want to discuss which engines are better for which subjects (or searches). For a general search, try a directory like Yahoo; specific searches may work better on engines like HotBot or AltaVista that search an index of keywords. Search engines are constantly being created and combined. (MetaCrawler, for example, is a search engine of search engines.) Try http://www.searchenginewatch.com for current search engine monitoring.

Materials

This lesson uses:

- Clip from "America Links Up" (Video clip #27 - 2:16)
- Internet capability
- Various Web sites (to be chosen by you or by your students)
- Web Sites Worksheet (File name *Websites* on R&R disk)

Get Started

Ask students to discuss how gathering research has changed in that last 5–10 years. What are the advantages and disadvantages of entering the "Information Age"? How do they imagine things will change in the next decade?

Compare two sources on the same topic—one print based and one from the Internet. Discuss the ways that the coverage changes depending on the medium used. What are the strengths and weaknesses of each? Print sources are often more in-depth, while people often say that the Internet's audience prefers short bits of information. The Internet's strengths include its immediacy, graphics, and interactivity, such as the ability to directly email a writer or an expert on a given topic.

Get Started

The origins of the Internet began in the U. S. Defense Department in the early 1970s with a group called ARPA—the Advanced Research Projects Agency. The military needed to keep defense computers interconnected in case the country was attacked by nuclear weapons. They developed a system in which information was sent in packets along a complex network of electronic paths. If any one path or computer system was destroyed, information could still continue to travel along alternate paths. Since many universities were conducting research for the Defense Department at that time, they began to use this system for transferring information and messages.

Next came the idea for a system that would allow users to post information on a computer that others could visit—the first Internet sites. Instead of just transferring information along the network, users could now visit specific sites in order to retrieve the information they needed. In just a few years, the amazing potential of this system of interconnected networks was realized in the World Wide Web, transforming the ways we communicate and share information. The Internet now includes over 50 million users worldwide. It contains hundreds of thousands of Web sites, from major corporations and media outlets to second-grade classrooms and skateboarders' conventions.

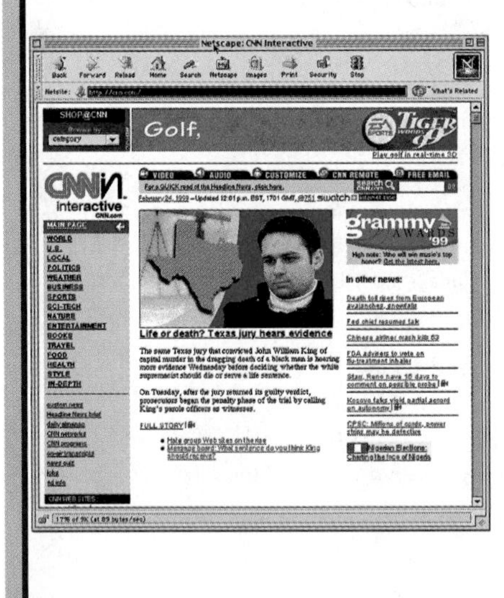

Despite the amazing benefits to online research, there are risks for online users to avoid. The Web may house thousands of valuable research and sales sites, but it is also home to a plethora of inaccurate information. In one of the most publicized mistakes, well-known journalist Pierre Salinger publicized the rumor that TWA flight 800 had been shot down by a Navy missile. Because of Salinger's reputation as an ethical journalist, many people believed his incredible accusations. However, his claims were quickly discredited. It turned out that the source of his information had been a Web site run by a man named Ian Godderd, an unreliable conspiracy monger whose Web site included information about alien abductions and JKF assassination plots, as well as the erroneous flight 800 information. In a statement to CNN, Godderd admitted that he had made up the information on his Web site about flight 800. In spite of this admission, the lies remained on his Web site for several more months.

It is a good idea to approach every site you visit with a healthy dose of skepticism. Some of the first questions to ask yourself when you begin to evaluate Web sites are the following:

- What is the purpose of this site?
- Whose interests does it serve?
- Who is its intended audience?
- What is the source of the information?

ETHICS IN ACTION

Censorship

A boy in Minnesota sent death threats to the president via e-mail. Students in California brought bomb recipes to school that they had found on the Internet. Hate groups and white supremacists recruit new members online. Con artists have created fake charity sites to swindle people out of thousands of dollars. Some criminals illicitly link their sites to popular children's sites. These are just a few examples of some of the dangers found on the Net.

Parents, teachers, and government officials are all concerned about what children and teens may encounter online. In response to this, in 1996 the United States Congress passed the Communications Decency Act, making it illegal to communicate "obscene or indecent" material to minors. However, some claimed that this law infringed on Americans' basic right to freedom of speech, and the courts declared it unconstitutional.

Several companies have developed software that will help keep children from accessing adult sites. But this software is also controversial. Many people worry that any kind of online censorship will damage the Internet's most valuable feature—the free flow of information. Others, however, worry that children will encounter violence, hate groups, pornography, drugs, and other dangers while innocently surfing for information on World War II, the White House, breast cancer, or chemotherapy, for example.

Video clip #27
Turner Learning:
"America Links Up"

Watch the *America Links Up* video clip on safe Web practices. Are these rules that you follow when online? How do you feel about software that is intended to block inappropriate material? Does your school have an Acceptable Usage Policy that you must follow? Discuss the issues that surround censorship and safety on the World Wide Web.

In a computer classroom, visit some sites with your students, pointing out their relative strengths and weaknesses. Try to visit a site like www.forces.org—a pro-tobacco site—that shows a merging of very good Internet-specific features (it's well designed, easy to navigate, well organized, and visually appealing) with poor quality content (unverifiable sources, blatant bias, and decontextualized evidence) and dubious sources (authors' credentials and their links to tobacco companies are never stated). Ask students to reflect on the ways that the high quality, Internet-specific features impact their overall perception of the site. In other words, if the site appears to be thorough and well organized, does that make them more willing to believe that its content is trustworthy and reliable?

ETHICS IN ACTION

ETHICS

Censorship. View **video clip #27** and discuss. Online censorship has been a major concern since the Web has been popularized for home and school use. While book shops put their "adult" materials behind the counters, anyone knowing how to type the word "sex" into a search engine can bring an amazing array of pornographic materials. Worse still are the hidden links that someone researching an innocent topic may come upon by simply clicking on a hyperlink.

How should a family, school, or library balance the interests of protecting children and avoiding censorship? Students are likely to have given this subject some thought. Discuss their views in class. You can also have them do research on this topic online by typing something like "internet censorship" or "web filters" into a search engine.

Break It Down

In Lessons 2, 5, and 12, students practiced evaluating print media. At this time you may want to review that material by discussing the biases and influences that different sources bring to their publications (i.e., the articles concerning Pakistan and India, Lesson 5).

Also discuss with students the editorial process. Reputable sites like CNN, *The New York Times*, American Cancer Society, Smithsonian, and others are carefully written, edited, and maintained by professional webmasters and staff. However, many other sites do not meet any editorial criteria due to the constantly changing nature of the Web.

Make sure students separate the content and evaluate it apart from the design. It can be so simple to fall prey to the fun graphics or activities of a site and miss the fact that the information presented is mediocre.

You may want to also discuss the nature of search engines. Different search engines will provide different results, and the first hits that the engine provides are often not the best ones! Students frequently resist digging through long lists of sites, but emphasize the importance of considering more that just the first few listed when doing a search.

You may let your students select a site as directed, or you may prefer to select a few specific sites for students to evaluate as a group. Ideally, you and your students can do this together in a computer class setting. If this option is not available, then ask students to visit the site on their own at a library or using their home computers. Discuss the students' findings, observations, and evaluations.

Break It Down

Before you actually start using the Internet to do research, you must know how to evaluate the sites you find. You evaluate newspapers and books and other media sources differently than you do Web sites. For example, nearly all printed materials—books, magazines, periodicals, and the like—go through an extensive editorial process before they are published. In contrast, online materials can be published by anyone, anywhere, anytime. They frequently are not checked for accuracy, truthfulness, or reliability. You may not know whether a seventh grader or a national expert has written the site you visit. Consequently, you must learn to assess any source you find. Internet sites can also be evaluated in terms of technological features such as design, speed, net appeal, graphics, visuals, multimedia, and ease of navigation. Sometimes these latter criteria can even give you clues about the site's professionalism.

"With so much information now online, it is exceptionally easy to simply dive in and drown."
Alfred Glossbrenner

Your worksheet **Deconstructing the Media: Web Sites** (p. 139) includes important questions to ask when evaluating Web sites. Read it carefully and discuss any questions you have about it in class. You may think of other important questions to ask when evaluating a site.

Working with a partner, use the questions on your worksheet to evaluate a particular Web site. You may use this activity in conjunction with a project in another class. For example, if you are writing an English essay on Charles Dickens, a history paper on the conflict in Kosovo, or a science report on nuclear fusion, use a search engine to find a site on the subject, then evaluate the site before using its information for your other project. Explain your answers with details and examples from the site. In class, share your team's findings with the rest of the class.

Sum It Up

Once you have analyzed the sample Web sites, evaluate and compare them:

- Which sites had the most reputable sources?
- Which sites seemed the least biased in presentation of information? Give examples of places where you found biased information.
- Which sites presented the most comprehensive information? Point out important information or perspectives that were missing from sites.
- Which sites were the easiest to navigate? What features made them user friendly?
- Which sites were visually appealing? Did the visual features enhance the sites' information or were they just decorations? Give examples.
- Which sites had the best links? What characterizes a good link?

Briefly compare using online versus print sources for research. What are the differences? What are the advantages and disadvantages of each? Are there topics that would be better covered online? Is print more important for others?

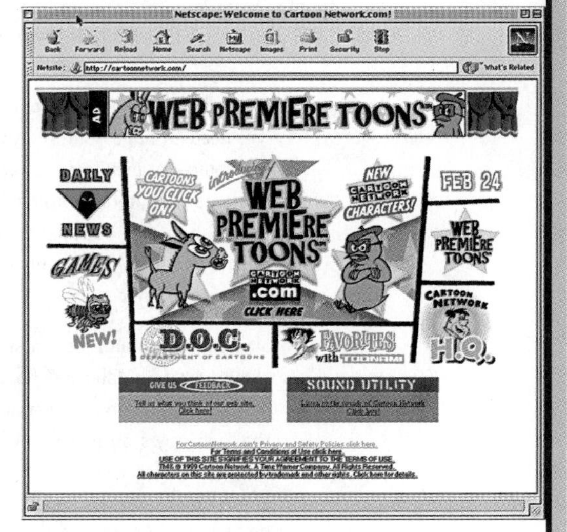

Cartoon Network Web Site

Courtesy: Cartoon Network, Inc.

Sum It Up

Students now have a list of criteria for evaluating Web sites that they can apply to any site they encounter. Initially they may want to take their new evaluation tools to their favorite entertainment sites. Remind them to keep asking themselves: What is the purpose of this graphic, audio, information, link, etc? How does it improve the quality of the site? Otherwise it is too easy to be swayed by the quality of the visuals rather than the quality of the overall site.

Put It Together

Having your students create a "dummy" on paper has a two-fold purpose:

1. Students will realize the importance of organization, source information, and good writing skills as well as be able to see what a site looks like.
2. Students without sufficient Web service in school can still create the project on paper, mapping out the site while indicating internal and external links and interactive portions. Students would still need to research what they need to know to make the site a reality. (HTML, HTML editor, Web server, etc.)

Put It Together

Build Your Own Web Page

Home Page ("index.htm")
My Page

My favorite Sports & Hobbies
My favorite Web Sites
Favorite Vacation Sites

May include links to sites about your favorite sports & hobbies
links to favorite sites
www.yahoo.com
www.cnn.com
www.amazon.com
may include links to your favorite vacation spots

In small groups select a topic for a small Web site (four pages). While you will need to build your site using the evaluative criteria discussed earlier, the topic you pick is a matter of personal choice. Anyone can have a home page. (Literally, a home page is the first page that appears when you go to a Web document. But most people refer to a site built by an individual as his or her "home page.") Build your site with a particular audience in mind.

Just as you would create a storyboard for a video or live presentation, you should create a "dummy" for your Web site. Use graphics (pictures from magazines, artwork, animation, etc.) as well as text for the layout. Sketch the Web pages on paper.

Components of Your Web Page

Divide your Web team into four groups, each with its own focus. While all members contribute to each focus, one member of the team should be the "editor" of each section. The sections include:

1. **The "front door":** What will the audience see first? What types of graphics will you include? What colors? What fonts? What information?

2. **General information:** What is the actual information you wish to convey to your audience?
3. **Resources:** What will you use to find your information? How will you document these resources on your site? With links? Through bibliographic credit?
4. **Special features:** After viewing other sites using the evaluative criteria on the **Deconstructing the Media: Web Sites** worksheet, what special features were of interest to your group? Graphics? Animated features? Images? Colors? You will need to work closely with the "front door" editor for consistency.

Designing Your Web Page

Use the questions on the **Deconstructing the Media: Web Sites** worksheet to help you design and evaluate your work. Don't forget the importance of clear organization, reliable source information, and good writing skills as well as the Net appeal of your site. Remember to address the important evaluative criteria for each of the three main elements of a site:

1. **Source:** What is your intended purpose? Have you used correct information from reliable sources? How can you show that you are a reputable source?
2. **Content:** Is the information accurate and valid? Have you checked and re-checked the information?
3. **Design:** Is the page easy to navigate and well organized? Are the graphics and audio helpful, fast, and easy to use?

If you have the capabilities, put the site (or at least the home page) online. If you do not already have a Web page at your school to link to, you may have to contact your school or home Internet service provider (ISP) to set up your Web page. Remember that a site is never a finished project; you must maintain and update the site to keep it current and attractive for your audience.

Evaluate each other's Web pages using the criteria on the **Deconstructing the Media: Web Sites** worksheet.

In the past, any novice Web designer had to learn HTML (HyperText Markup Language) to create a Web page. While HTML is relatively easy to learn, it can take up time and energy. To address this problem, a host of HTML software has been created that makes Web design fast, fun, and fairly easy. Two of the more popular tools are Adobe PageMill and Claris Home Page. This software makes it easy to create frames and tables, include audio, video, text documents (original and imported), add animation, add links, and more. You will also find helpful suggestions on the Internet itself. Try going through a search engine's "Computers and Internet" section. Many sites exist on the Web to help you design Web pages, including lessons in HTML and software downloads.

Take It Further

1. If your school does not have an Acceptable Use Policy, help students find another school or library that does. Suggest that they interview the people who designed that policy in order to provide them with some models. Remind students that the AUP should cover a variety of Internet uses including Web sites, research, chatrooms, email, etc. Be sure that students include persuasive explanations for why they are suggesting each feature of this AUP.
2. While this lesson has concentrated on using the Internet for research, there are other useful and entertaining purposes for the Web. Students could consider setting up a business, creating a game, or designing an entertainment trivia site, to name a few examples. Features they should consider would make use of the unique features of the Web: links, interactivity, automated graphics, audio, video, forms, etc. Unless this is an activity for an advanced Internet class, they should not be expected to create or even know all the technical terms for some of these devices (such as JavaScript, C++, Perl, etc.).
3. After students have found and reviewed a site that they believe needs improvement, discuss with them the conventions of a letter (or email) of complaint. The tone should be helpful and polite. The writer should describe specific, concrete problems and offer specific, realistic solutions to them in a helpful way.

Take It Further

1. Does your school have an Acceptable Use Policy (AUP)? Review the policy and find out how it is implemented. Write an essay supporting or opposing the policy. If your school does not have an AUP, write one for it.
2. Map out a Web site that makes use of the unique features of Web technology for entertainment, business, or research. Explain what content and Web features you would include to make your site engaging and useful.
3. Find a Web site that you think is particularly unhelpful or poorly designed. Write a letter or e-mail message to the site's moderator, politely offering specific suggestions for improvement.

PRODUCTION NOTES

"Besides the Internet . . ."

While the Internet is dominating the computer world, other dynamic functions of the personal computer should not be overlooked. Software is no longer expensive, nor is it difficult to learn to use. A wide variety of programs are available, ranging from educational software to games to landscaping programs. The Internet provides some shareware that you can download and use for a limited time and freeware that you can download for free. With the incorporation of the CD-ROM (Compact Disc/ Read Only Memory) in 1991 into multimedia personal computers, companies are able to store massive amounts of information on one disk. Electronic encyclopedias with multimedia capabilities, dictionaries, extensive databases, and other reference materials are readily available to consumers.

Hardware, too, has become more affordable. Many personal computer users now own scanners, color printers, and digital cameras.

As always, you need to evaluate each product to determine whether it will be beneficial to you, whether the cost is worth the benefit, and whether the company producing it has a good reputation for quality and endurance in the market. It is often worth waiting for a time after a new product comes out to see how users like it. Sometimes problems arise in a "1.0" first edition that are corrected in a revised version. Additionally, if you buy the hottest, latest software and need or want to share what you create with others, they may not be able to access your data files if they do not also possess that new software. Many new products are introduced with lots of advertising hype. Be sure the bells and whistles will benefit you in the long run.

Evaluate a software product that you use at school or at home, such as an educational program, a word processing application, or a game. Try to find out its purchase price. Look at the graphics, content, and ease of use. Is it something that will be quickly outdated? Is it engaging? Easy to understand? Is it worth the price?

PRODUCTION NOTES

Besides the Internet . . . This feature recognizes another vast source of media available to computer users: software on computer disks and CD-ROMs. While most do not connect to the Internet (though this is a new feature on some software), these products include many features available on the Web, such as moving graphics, video, and navigation. As these are mass-produced for consumers, most go through an intensive editing process that tends to catch errors in spelling, syntax, and informational accuracy. Still, the elements need to be evaluated, as they do in any medium, for quality.

WORKSHEET

Deconstructing the Media

Web Sites

File: WebSites

Source

1. Who is the creator of this site? What are the writer's credentials? Can these credentials be checked? Who is funding the site?

____
____
____

2. What makes this a credible source?

____
____
____

3. Does this source have a bias? (For example, what would you expect the Marlboro site would say about the health risks of cigarettes versus what the American Cancer Society site would say?)

____
____
____

4. Is the site affiliated with a reputable organization? Have other reliable sources referred to or linked you to this site?

____
____
____

Content

1. Is the information accurate? How do you know?

____
____
____

Web Sites

Source

1. Students can often find the site developer at the bottom of the home page. There may be hyperlinks to learn more about the Web developer and/or the authors of the site.
2. Students can look for the information to be verified on other sites or sources. The site may be by an organization or person that they respect.
3. Students should look for balance and for language as clues about site biases.
4. Answers will vary depending on the site being analyzed.

Content

1. Students can compare information they find against other sources to determine accuracy.

2. Sites usually give update information near the bottom of the page.
3. Students should look to see whether more than one argument is presented or whether a site is completely in favor of or against a topic discussed.
4. Sources will vary, depending on the site being examined. Students can see whether information includes links to other sites where it can be verified.
5. Answers will depend on the site being examined.
6. Again, answers will vary, depending on the site chosen.

Design

1. Use of clear organizing principles, such as sidebars, a site map, and links at the top and/or bottom of pages determine the ease of use.
2. Sometimes graphics are used to create hyperlinks. Sometimes they compliment the text. They may be used to create breaks in the text, but they should be purposeful, as they do add to download time.

2. When was the site last updated? Is this information current?

3. Are there multiple perspectives for the topic? What are they? What bias is shown, if any?

4. What sources—experts, scientific studies, statistics, etc.—does the site use? Can any of this be verified? Does the site credit its sources or list where it obtained its information?

5. Is information professionally and accurately written, with few grammar and spelling errors?

6. Are there a variety of external links that supplement the information given in the site? Are these links well maintained, and are they helpful and insightful?

Design

1. Is the site easy to navigate? How easy is it to see all the elements of the site and to understand its organization quickly?

2. What purpose do the graphics serve? What makes this site visually appealing or unappealing?

3. What does the site do that takes it beyond a print source? What does this site give you that a book or newspaper could not?

____

____

____

4. Does the site have "Net" appeal—is it interesting, unique, or fun? What makes this site different from others you have visited?

____

____

____

5. Is it organized in a logical fashion? Can users easily find the information they need?

____

____

____

6. Is there a working search engine on the site? How efficient is it?

____

____

____

7. Where audio and/or video would be helpful or appropriate, does this site include those features? Or do audio/video clips just get in the way and slow things down?

____

____

____

8. Is it user-friendly? What options are available to help users with slower/older computers (for example, text only, no frames, etc.)?

____

____

____

3. Some sites use interactive elements to add value. They may allow a person to purchase materials without leaving his or her home. They often add value by including useful hyperlinks to other sites.
4. Answers will vary.
5. Answers will vary.
6. Some sites will have their own search engine. Students can test the engine to see whether it is helpful in fulfilling their request for information.
7. Audio and video do take additional time to download. Most sites make these elements optional. Sometimes they are very helpful in presenting information, though.
8. User-friendly sites do contain options for those working with older computers and browsers. Their designers have also created images in ways that take less time to download than less experienced designers may use.

Lesson 14 A Media-Literate Society: *Power and Responsibility of Media Literacy*

What's Ahead?

Goal: In this lesson students will expand and apply their knowledge of media methods and issues to their daily lives and to their role as citizens in a democratic society. The lesson activities will help them use their knowledge to empower themselves to make wise media choices.

Disciplines: The contents in this lesson pertain to language arts, history and social studies, psychology, business, sociology, and health.

Objectives: Upon completing this lesson, students will be able to:

- Apply their knowledge of media to the contemporary issues that arise in their lives.
- Express their views about media issues to an audience and consider ways to improve media messages.
- Analyze the effects of media in many areas of their lives.
- Create positive media messages.

LESSON 14

A Media-Literate Society

What's Ahead?

You now have the tools to analyze, evaluate, and create media messages. Instead of watching, reading, and listening inattentively, you understand how to analyze the messages that surround you. You also understand that media create their own reality, convey value systems, use identifiable techniques, and are frequently motivated by economic interests. In short, you are media literate. But what are you going to do with your knowledge? Will your media literacy change the way you interact with media?

Major Points to Ponder

- Media corporations are motivated to continue producing shows and films that receive the highest ratings, and therefore the most ad dollars, and those that make the most money at the box office. The public can influence the contents of these shows.
- By making conscious use of media tools, you can increase your enjoyment of media while lessening the influence of media on your life.
- A democratic society works only when its citizens are well informed and are active participants. Such citizens can make the media into creative and positive tools for information and entertainment.

In this lesson, students should be challenged to consider their own responsibility when faced with media messages that may be unfair or even dangerous to individuals and to society at large. They will discuss questions of ethics and responsibility, and they will consider how they can respond when they believe that a message should be challenged.

You might begin the discussion by asking if there is a school, community, national, or international news issue about which students feel strongly. Ask them what they could do to express their opinion. It is likely that many students will contend that they are helpless, that their voices don't matter. Challenge them to consider the many types of media available, and have them list all of the possible actions they could do using media. From there, they can discuss the feasibility of each idea, and why they think it might or might not work.

Did You Know?

In an average day there are 2,605 acts of violence on television, the majority occurring in the morning, when children are most likely to be watching.

The average studio-financed picture in 1997 cost $53 million dollars to produce. *(Source: Motion Picture Association of America)*

Americans spend $8 billion a year on cosmetics, $2 billion more than the estimated annual total needed to give a basic education to everyone in the world.

The average political sound bite in 1968 was 42.3 seconds. The average sound bite in 1988 was 9.8 seconds. *(Source: Cited at www.pbs.org/pov/ad/ads/ad.fact/html)*

Key Ideas

Censorship - the act of removing or forbidding anything that a controlling body deems to be offensive or objectionable in some way.

Conglomerate - a large corporation formed by the merger or acquisition of numerous companies that represent widely diversified, often unrelated industries.

Monopoly - ultimate control over a given product or service in a given market that makes price fixing possible or eliminates competition.

Propaganda - mass dissemination of ideas, beliefs, or practices in order to further a particular cause or to disparage another one. Propaganda is usually associated with spreading misleading, distorted, or false information.

PSAs - public service announcements. These are similar to commercials, but they do not attempt to sell a product. Instead, they are intended to deliver information to the public.

Did You Know?

This section presents facts on situations that students may delve into as they proceed in the lesson (political ads are covered on the Web site). As they consider the responsibilities of citizens in a democratic society, you can encourage students to think about the economics and effects of big media business (illustrated in bullet point #2), and the relationship of advertising and too much consumerism (bullet point #3). Certainly part of the discussion in many media literacy groups involves the relationship between commercialism and consumerism, as well as the problems involved with producing and buying too many goods, such as environmental pollution.

Key Ideas

Many are related to the second activity in the **Break It Down** section. It is always controversial to introduce sensitive political terms in education. The intent here is to make a distinction and clarification, not a value judgment.

Materials

This lesson uses:

- CNN Inside Politics: Oliver North/Jesse Jackson debate (Video clip #28 - 8:28)
- Student production, “Fences: Death of the Land,” Searider Productions (Video clip #29 - 10:03)
- The Influence of Media Messages Worksheet (File name *Influence* on R&R disk)
- Censorship vs. Personal Responsibility Worksheet (File name *Responsibility* on R&R disk)

Get Started

In this section, students are asked to reflect on their study of the media and their habits both before and after studying it. They should be able to speak more fluently about media messages now, and they should be able to articulate the specific tools and devices that make media successful. Though students may disagree on what makes for "positive" and "negative" media, they should be able to defend their positions using specific examples and the language of media literacy.

Students may not have a hard time telling you what they consider to be positive or negative media messages. They may have more difficulty, however, if you introduce the terms "high" and "low quality" media messages. Are positive messages necessarily high quality, and vice versa? Is quality determined by popularity? If so, then are shows such as World Championship Wrestling "high quality"? And if students answer "No," then ask them why these shows are so popular, in their opinion.

Companies have no motivation to change programming that is followed by a large audience. It is also no simple task to change huge corporations, and it is rare that a single individual can make this kind of difference. Groups of people, though, can bring about change by working together to make their needs known. Change begins first with awareness, and this is largely what media literacy is all about. The ongoing active campaign demanding that tobacco companies take responsibility for their ads and their products is one dramatic example of citizens fighting to make a difference in their society. If you have a student who is particularly interested in this subject, he or she could do research on the history of tobacco ads, regulations, and restrictions: lost privilege of TV advertising, addition of the Surgeon General's warnings to ads and cigarette packs, law suits against tobacco companies for encouraging an unhealthy addiction.

Get Started

Think about how you viewed television shows, magazines, newspapers, movies, radio stations, and other forms of mass media prior to your study of the media. Look back on the lists you made for earlier chapters: what you watched, listened to, and read and why you made the choices that you made. Have any of your opinions or choices changed since you began studying the media? If yes, in what ways? If no, how has your understanding of these media choices changed?

Brainstorm a list of positive media messages that you have encountered in the recent past. Now create a similar list of media messages that you consider negative or propagandistic. Answer the following questions about your lists:

1. What makes the messages in the first list positive?
2. Why do you believe that the others are negative or misleading?
3. How could you turn these messages into positive ones?
4. Do you consciously choose to watch, read, or listen to any of the media messages that you consider negative or misleading? Why or why not?

"The freedom of the press works in such a way that there is not much freedom from it."
Grace Kelly

You have also studied messages that cause many adults to be concerned for children, such as those containing violence and those that equate products with success and beauty. Of particular concern in the latter category are ads that promote tobacco and alcohol consumption through the use of beautiful models, exciting settings, and romantic situations. Because of medical information that has shown negative health effects of tobacco and alcohol, concerned citizens and lawmakers have made a difference in the media presentations of these products. Tobacco can no longer be advertised on television. PSAs have increased in frequency and tone to inform people about effects of alcohol, tobacco, and drugs. As an informed citizen, do you think that more should be done? How would you use and/or restrict the media to protect children?

Break It Down

Exercise 1

Media expert David Considine, from Appalachian State University in North Carolina, suggests that media messages affect consumers in many ways. Referring to advertising, he asserts that the influence of ads can be felt in the following areas:

1. Psychological
2. Physical
3. Ecological/Environmental
4. Financial
5. Spiritual/personal
6. Intellectual
7. Cultural
8. Global

Discuss how ads affect these areas of consumers' lives.

Considine's thinking can be applied to other forms of media too. Working with a partner, brainstorm how other media have implications in each of these categories. Record your ideas on your worksheet **Deconstructing the Media: The Influence of Media Messages** (p. 150). When all pairs have finished with the brainstorming, discuss your answers in class.

Consider these areas when you go through the rest of this chapter, thinking of the ways media culture influences the broad areas of our lives and the lives of those around us.

Exercise 2:

The taped interview you will watch is taken from CNN's *Inside Politics,* and it is a debate about the effects of "hate talk" filling the airwaves. Specifically, the topic is the Oklahoma bombing of 1995, and the question is whether or not some radio talk show hosts were stirring up violent opinions and responses in the listening public enough to manifest the tragic bombing, which killed 168 people.

Video clip #28
CNN's *Inside Politics*

Break It Down

Exercise 1: This exercise asks students to consider media messages in a broader context, in the many ways in which they may affect their opinions and actions. As is the case with most of the exercises in this book, there are no right or wrong answers. The goal is to get students thinking about influences in their lives so that they can effect changes.

Exercise 2: You will need to show the Jackson/North debate (**video clip #28**) two or three times, as it is fast-paced, and students may have a hard time following it the first time through. They may want to discuss the credibility of the men involved in the debate as well—how much do they feel they need to know about either guest in order to evaluate their arguments? Do they feel that the arguments stand by themselves, in spite of the person delivering them?

One trait that Jackson has going for him is his demeanor. He is calm and appears to speak with the voice of reason. It is difficult to disagree with him. North, on the other hand, appears brazen and defensive. Such a demeanor can cause people to feel distrust, whether or not the argument he presents is a valid one.

North contends that President Clinton wants to curb the rights of some talk show hosts. Jackson is arguing that hosts who are guilty of raising the public's ire and mob-like feelings of hatred ought to curb themselves out of a sense of moral decency. This whole issue is one that your class may argue passionately: does free speech mean that people can say anything they want, even though it may cause others to become frenzied and act out their hostilities? If the answer is yes, how much responsibility should people take in deciding what they ought to say or refrain from saying? These questions can also be considered as one thinks about violent and sexual television, movie, and music productions.

The two debaters represent each end of the spectrum and are themselv colorful and famous past presidential candidates. Oliver North is a radi talk show host who was tried in the Iran/Contra affair, in which high-ranking officials of the Reagan Administration were found guilty of ille-gally providing military assistance to Nicaraguan rebels from 1984 to 1 by illegally selling arms to Iran. Reverend Jesse Jackson is an outspoke political figure and the founder of the Rainbow Coalition, a group advo cating civil liberties and racial equality.

As you watch the debate, consider the many techniques the debaters u to support their arguments. What do you find effective and ineffective the methods? Now think about the larger questions raised by this deba Should media be censored from content that is potentially dangerous t the public? Answer the questions on your worksheet **Deconstructing th Media: Censorship versus Personal Responsibility** (p. 151).

Oliver North and Jesse Jackson

Courtesy: CNN

Sum It Up

How effective is Oliver North? How effective is Jesse Jackson? Do you think one or the other is "right"? If yes, does the man that you think is right "win" the debate? Does he win because he is right, or because he is effective in his use of the media? Defend your answers.

THEN AND NOW

Fifty Years of Television

The 1998 Emmy Awards honored television's fiftieth anniversary by choosing a "Top Ten" list of television moments, chosen by 200 journalists. They were:

10. The Beatles' 1964 performance on the *Ed Sullivan Show*
9. Johnny Carson's departure from *The Tonight Show*
8. Lucy has a baby on *I Love Lucy* in 1953
7. The final episode of *M.A.S.H.* in 1983
6. The 1980 "Who Shot J.R.?" episode of *Dallas*
5. The 1986 explosion of the space shuttle Challenger
4. The assassination of President John F. Kennedy in 1963
3. The premier of *Hill Street Blues* in 1981
2. The broadcast of *Roots* in 1977
1. The Apollo 11 mission: Neil Armstrong steps onto the moon, 1969

Would you have watched if you had been in high school in 1969?

Courtesy: CORBIS/Bettmann

In groups of two or three students, research one of these events. Answer as many of the following questions as you can:

1. What genre of TV show is it?
2. What is its purpose?
3. Who is the target audience?
4. What makes this TV moment significant?
5. Would you nominate this TV event as one of the top ten? Why or why not?

As a class, come up with your own "Top Ten Moments in Media" in your own lifetime. Be able to say why your choices are significant.

THEN AND NOW

Fifty Years of Television. Assign each group one of the ten top TV moments. They can probably get most of their answers by consulting their parents and older adults. Here are some quick answers to the questions:

10. (Beatles): 1) variety show; 2) entertainment; 3) families; in particular, teens; 4) beginning of "Beatle-mania."
9. (Carson): 1) celebrity talk show; 2) entertainment; 3) adults enjoying light comedy and celebrity interviews; 4) end of his 30 years as most popular late night host.
8. (Lucy): 1) situation comedy; 2) entertainment; 3) families; 4) introduction of taboo topics, pregnancy and childbirth.
7. (*M*A*S*H*): 1) situation comedy; 2) entertainment; 3) families; 4) end to one of the longest running situation comedies.
6. ("Who Shot J.R.?") 1) dramatic series; 2) entertainment; 3) older teens and adults; 4) it seemed the nation was glued to the TV the night the attacker was disclosed.
5. (Challenger): 1) live news coverage; 2) information; 3) the world, of school age and older; 4) the deaths of the astronauts in this mission was more poignant because the shuttle held the first of what NASA hoped would be many "Teachers in Space," Christa McAuliffe.
4. (JFK): 1) news; 2) information; 3) ultimately, the world; 4) this was the first time such an event could be covered on television.
3. (*Hill Street Blues*): 1) dramatic series; 2) entertainment; 3) adults; 4) highly controversial because it advertised itself to contain adult situations and profanity, a first on a network station.
2. (*Roots*): 1) mini-series docudrama; 2) entertainment (and information); 3) older teens and adults; 4) Alex Haley's search for his own roots turned into this 12-hour top rated mini-series about the plight and history of American slaves.
1. (Moon landing): 1) live TV news coverage; 2) information; 3) the world; 4) there probably isn't anything that could top TV coverage of a human walking on the moon!

Students' answers to four and five will vary.

Put It Together

This construction activity can serve as a review of most of the media literacy concepts covered in this curriculum. Students need to consider their purpose, their audience, and their message, and they need to use appropriate production tools to create their own positive message. In this case, they will be encouraging people to become media literate and/or they will actually be teaching one or more media literacy concepts, using the media to do so.

Depending on the target audience they choose, students could present their media construction to an elementary class, a group of instructors, parents, a special interest group, or another appropriate group. Students should summarize for you an evaluation of their presentation, either in writing or orally. The in-class presentation can be more of a critique of their creation, with the other students deconstructing and questioning it.

"A people which is able to say everything becomes able to do everything."
Napoleon Bonaparte

Put It Together

Some media critics fear that the acquisition of smaller media companies by large media conglomerates could result in too much control of information, resulting in propaganda. For instance, when a corporation owns TV stations, radio stations, magazines, book publishing companies, and newspapers, it can advertise and recommend its own media products.

As a class, brainstorm the implications of media monopolies. In groups, consider solutions to the potential problems. Script a public service announcement in which you inform the public about ways to be media literate so that they, too, will look critically at the messages they see, hear, and read through the media. Choose a particular medium for your message—television, radio, song, newspaper, magazine, or Web and create the message using the appropriate tools for a target audience.

WORLD VIEW

Freedom and Responsibility

We do not live in a society in which we are forced to listen to propaganda or negative information. Our only glimpses into that kind of oppressive society are found in fiction, such as George Orwell's *1984*, a novel in which citizens' thoughts and beliefs are controlled by misleading language and mass media.

Other societies have not been so fortunate. Nien Cheng's autobiography, *Life and Death in Shanghai*, shows Orwell's fiction come to life. During Mao Tse-Tung's Cultural Revolution in China, beginning in 1966, slogan-like quotations from "Mao's Little Red Book" (titled *Quotations from Chairman Mao Tse-Tung*) were blared from loudspeakers in town squares. Schools were closed, and students became units of the Red Guard, empowered by the government to ransack citizens' homes looking for outlawed materials and proof of capitalistic connections. People were frightened into believing falsehoods about their neighbors, their relatives, and even themselves. For refusing to "admit" that she was a criminal, for example, Nien Cheng was imprisoned and tortured.

With freedom and knowledge comes responsibility. Citizens in a free democratic society have many avenues to ensure that their governments and institutions remain free, honest, and available to serve their constituents. Discuss the ways in which the many forms of media can be used to promote responsible citizenship.

WORLD VIEW

See if any of your students have read *1984*. You may want to bring a copy and read portions to the class that demonstrate the "doublespeak" put out by the fictional government in the book. Ask them to consider historical examples in which propaganda has been effective in getting people to believe lies (e.g., Nazi Germany, Stalin's Cult of Personality, Mao's Cultural Revolution, U.S. government—see "Duck and Cover" in Lesson 5).

You can use this section as a lead to many possible interesting and controversial discussions:

- Can students think of any current uses of propaganda?
- Do they believe they are misinformed about important topics? Do they believe that the misinformation is intentional? To what purpose?
- How much do students think they need to know about the organizations that produce media? In what instances do they "trust" the media?

Take It Further

1. You have been elected by the American public to develop a system of controls for television programming—both content and advertisements. What changes will you make? Describe your system of controls. Remember that your constituency is the entire American public. What do they want? What do they need to be effective citizens in this democracy?

2. A not-for-profit organization called TV-Free America, founded in 1994, sponsors "TV Turnoff Week" in April. More than eight million people have taken part in the event worldwide. Now it's your turn! Don't watch television for an entire week. (You don't have to wait until April to try this experiment!) Keep a daily journal about the experience. Does it get easier or harder with each day? Are you angry that you are missing your favorite shows? What important and/or educational shows do you miss out on that you would have watched? With what activities do you replace your viewing hours? After this week, do you think that you will make any permanent changes in the way that you use the television? If yes, what? If no, why not?

Video clip # 29
Fences, Death of the Land

3. Create a PSA or short documentary to inform a target audience about a subject for which you feel they need more information. Watch the award-winning student production *Fences: Death of the Land,* created by high school students in Hawaii, for an example. Remember to make use of good media techniques—clear purpose, careful construction using media tools, techniques that keep your audience interested, and so forth.

Take It Further

The first activity is one that places the student in a position of great power. How they will use that power is what makes this exercise so interesting, as well as how they problem solve just how to make their decisions stand.

Activity 2 asks students to exercise some willpower in finding alternatives to television for a week. It is not intended to cause students to abandon the TV forever, but a break from it can help them re-evaluate just how and why they use television and, perhaps, come up with more thoughtful television viewing practices.

Activity 3 is a construction activity that challenges students to use their previously learned knowledge to create a PSA or short documentary. The video example, **video clip #29**, "Fences: Death of the Land," is highly recommended for classroom viewing, even if students will not be working with this activity. It is an excellent example of a top quality student production. As always, look for the components of good media construction, but realize your students' limitations in equipment, sets, time, editing, etc.

The Influence of Media Messages

Possible answers:

1. Media can make consumers feel good or bad about their lives. Media depicting violent actions could give some people ideas that may result in real-life violence.
2. Media may influence people's contentment with their bodies, their homes, their schools, and their material possessions.
3. Some media messages can inform consumers about needed steps for helping the environment. On the other hand, media consume materials, such as paper, energy, etc.
4. Some messages may help people learn to save. Other messages can make them want more material objects they cannot afford.
5. People can learn lessons about friendships, relationships, etc. by watching, reading, and listening to some media messages. Other messages contain harsh and violent messages that may adversely affect one's values or beliefs.
6. Many media messages serve to inform consumers. Others contain propaganda or misleading information.
7. Through the media, consumers can learn about other cultures and countries they may never have a chance to visit. Some media messages, though, contain racist and prejudiced messages that affect people's beliefs and actions.

WORKSHEET

Deconstructing the Media

The Influence of Media Messages

File: Influence

Although consumers tend to first associate media with entertainment (and possibly news), there are many other ways that media influence us. Consider the many types of media. What are their implications in the following areas of your life?

1. Psychological

____

____

2. Physical

____

____

3. Ecological/environmental

____

____

4. Financial

____

____

5. Spiritual/personal

____

____

6. Intellectual

____

____

7. Cultural/Global

____

____

WORKSHEET

Deconstructing the Media

Censorship versus Personal Responsibility

File: Responsibility

We live in a country that prizes its freedoms, among which are free speech and freedom of the press. But just what do, or should, those terms mean? Should people be allowed to say absolutely anything that they want, even if it is untrue, unjust, and potentially dangerous? And if such freedom must be allowed, can people be convinced to exercise personal responsibility in producing media messages that are not harmful to the public? Consider these questions as you answer the following questions on the Jackson/North debate.

1. What is "hate talk"? What examples of this rhetoric can you find in the video clip?

____

____

____

2. How do you feel about the atmosphere between the debaters and the host in the video clip? Is the debate easy to follow? If it is difficult, what could have been done to make this talk show more accessible to an audience?

____

____

____

3. State your opinions about Jesse Jackson, Oliver North, and the moderator after viewing the video clip. On what do you base these opinions?

____

____

____

4. How do you feel about the quality of the debate, and why?

____

____

____

Censorship versus Personal Responsibility

1. Hate talk is the use of words that are prejudiced, racist, or inflammatory. Jackson talks about many examples, such as how to shoot at government agents, "environmental whackos," women as "maggots," blacks as "savages," etc.
2. There is certainly tension between the debaters, and North feels himself put on the defensive. It is difficult to follow when the men interrupt each other and talk at the same time. The moderator might have tried to lessen this problem, but he contributes to it.
3. Opinions will vary, depending on students' reactions to the men and their opinions about what should be allowed on the talk shows.
4. Students may choose to determine the quality based on the structure of the debate, their feelings about the men on camera, their opinions about the topic, etc.

5. Answers will vary, depending somewhat on the side that each student takes about the issue.
6. Look for students to support either side they take with specific examples, details, etc. Implementation of a policy is perhaps the most difficult piece of this short essay, as it deals with freedom of speech. Students might consider making modifications to systems already in place, such as the voluntary ratings systems, parental guidance, education, or separate places for the distribution of controversial content.

5. Write down effective and ineffective moments in the clip.

6. Write a short essay in which you defend or oppose the censoring of controversial and potentially dangerous content in the media. Be sure to support your argument with specific examples and suggestions for implementing your media policy.

Glossary

a

Aesthetics The study of art, its creative sources, its forms, and its effects.

Agent A person who has been authorized to act for another person or group of people. In the music industry, an agent is one who books appearances and negotiates contracts for musicians.

b

Balanced coverage Intended to provide the many perspectives of a given event; more than one side of the story. (For instance, a balanced news story about a murder suspect would include not only the facts of the crime and the suspect's apprehension, but also information about the victim and statements by the suspect's friends or family.)

Box A short feature that is related to the main article in which it is placed. Boxes are usually set off in a lined box, often with a different background color.

Browser A program used to view, download, upload, or surf documents (pages) on the World Wide Web. Most browsers these days can decode both text and graphics. Browsers interpret coding, such as HTML, into what we see as a language-based Web page. Netscape Navigator and Microsoft Internet Explorer are examples of Web browsers.

Bubble gum In the music industry, this term refers to light, noncontroversial bands that usually appeal to young adolescents. They share characteristics that appeal to this age group, and their music and lyrics are not usually offensive to the mainstream public.

c

Censorship The act of removing or forbidding anything that a controlling body deems to be offensive or objectionable in some way.

Chatroom A "virtual place" on a site in which you can enter discussions with other site users. Chatrooms occur in "real time": messages you read in chats are being typed just before you see them appear.

Choreography The carefully arranged or detailed movements of a dance.

Circulation Distribution among readers; the average number of copies sold in a given time period.

Classified information A label used to restrict access to controversial information that might be detrimental to the provider, creator, consumer, or collector of the information.

Codes and conventions Familiar techniques used by media to convey certain ideas or a particular impression. Symbolic codes include lighting, sound, dress, etc.

Column A regularly established feature of a magazine, often written by the same writer each time, who becomes known and enjoyed for his or her particular style and opinions. These writers are called "columnists."

Conglomerate A large corporation formed by the merger or acquisition of numerous companies that represent widely diversified, often unrelated industries.

Consumer A person who buys or uses goods or services for personal needs; in relation to media literacy, one who buys or devotes time to various media products.

Context The complete situation or background of a particular event or production.

Correspondent A reporter who supplies news articles or newscast segments from a distant place.

Corroborate To support or confirm by new evidence; attest to the truth or accuracy of a statement or report.

Cropping The technique used to cut away the surroundings of photos in order to give greater prominence to a specific person, idea, or object.

Crossover In music, a product that is a blend of two music genres; for example, a song that combines country/western with pop.

Cyberspace Name given to the realm of the Internet (or any network of computers); this is the "place" you are when you are navigating the virtual landscape of the Internet.

d

Deconstruction In media literacy, recognizing or revealing the parts and techniques that make up the media product. An example might be to notice that a shot in a movie was a special effect rather than a "natural" shot or to notice that there is a cut in a chase scene just before the hero jumps off the cliff into a chasm of raging water.

Demographics The statistical characteristics of human populations, such as classifying by age, gender, race, income, health, education, etc. These figures are widely used in market research.

Docudrama A feature movie presentation that is based on real historical events and people. Fictional elements are added to preserve the dramatic integrity of the production.

Documentary A film that uses interviews, newsreels, and video footage of real events or people to inform viewers about events, people, science, history, and other nonfiction topics.

Drama A story presented through action and dialogue that deals with complex human emotions and life situations.

Dramatic conventions Techniques that are used as substitutions for reality. An audience accepts them as real, even though they know them to be fictional. Examples include actors impersonating characters, scenes and props taking the place of real places, and dream sequences or foreshadowing that the audience accepts as real within the fictional context.

e

Editing The art of splicing or putting together film clips in a sequential order to tell a story. Today most films are edited on computer.

Emotional argument Persuasion that appeals to an audience's feelings, beliefs, and respect for the writer/speaker of the opinion. Figurative language, repetition, and rhythm of words are frequently employed conventions.

Entertainment Something that holds one's attention and gives pleasure, diverts, or amuses (*Webster's New World Dictionary*).

Escapism Flight from the responsibilities and routines of real life, often through imaginative activities.

Ethics The study of standards of conduct and moral judgment. One displays ethical behavior by acting according to socially acceptable and moral standards.

f

FAQ (Frequently Asked Questions) Found on most sites/Web pages. A great help, these pages list questions and answers that seem to be the most helpful for the site's users.

Features Generally considered soft news, these stories provide readers with background on current issues, products, personalities, and trends.

Figurative language Words used not in their usual or literal sense; words used symbolically to go beyond literal meaning, such as "The tired tree dropped its leaves." Similes and metaphors are examples of figurative language.

Film score Background music for a movie. Often it includes a theme song.

Flaming Sending a strongly negative e-mail to someone (such messages can also be posted to an Internet bulletin board or chatroom). Because people on the Internet rarely meet face to face, they are sometimes more willing to be harshly critical of others.

Focus groups A small number of people, usually 10 to 20, gathered together by a company to express their opinions and make suggestions about a specified topic or product.

Foley artist A technician who creates the sounds that cannot properly be recorded during the shoot.

Fonts In printing, these are an assortment of type styles. Commonly used fonts include Times New Roman and Arial.

Foreshadowing Something that indicates an event that will occur in the future; looking back on the scene, you would view it as a hint.

Format The overall focus of a station. Radio stations today air programming that targets specific markets based on various demographics, including music preferences and other interests such as sports, news, and conservative and liberal talk shows.

Framing Using borders to limit the background of a photograph.

g

Genre The French word for *kind* or *type*; it refers to the category of the medium, e.g., the medium of television contains the genres of advertising, news, sports, soap operas, etc., and the medium of film contains the genres of romance, comedy, adventure, drama, etc.

h

Hard news Reporting on significant state, national, and world events, such as elections, weather disasters, peace negotiations, and major crime.

Hip hop The music that accompanies rap; the culture of rap, including clothing and art.

Historical fiction A dramatic film that uses real historical events as a backdrop to a fictional plot and characters.

Home page The first page of a Web site. It usually includes an introduction to the site and navigational tools to bring users to other pages in the site.

HTML (Hyper Text Markup Language) A collection of symbols indicated by markup tags (< >) that define the various components and functions of a World Wide Web document. For instance, <p> is an HTML tag that indicates the start of a new paragraph. These tags are read by the browser to create the words and organization on a Web page.

HTTP (Hyper Text Transfer Protocol) A protocol used to perform functions on the Internet, such as bringing to the computer screen a particular Web address requested by an Internet user.

i

Internet (or **Net)** Literally, a network of computer networks that are linked to provide a system of data transfer and communications.

j

Jingle A simple, catchy arrangement of words or light verse, usually put to music, used in advertising to help consumers remember the product.

l

Layout The way the words and images are arranged on the page. Photography and illustrations, type size and fonts, titles and box placements all determine the image of the magazine.

Links Underlined, highlighted, or colored text, graphics, or other screen features that immediately connect you to another location on the WWW.

Listserv A software program that automates and maintains electronic mailing lists. You can send messages to other members on the list. They often have a moderator who monitors the system.

Logical argument Persuasion that uses facts, statistics, expert opinions, and research to give credence to the opinion presented.

Lyrics Words put to music.

m

Mass media Communications media capable of reaching a large number of people at the same time, such as newspapers, radio, television, advertisements, or the Internet.

Materialism A philosophy suggesting that matter is the only reality; even thought and feelings are explained in terms of matter. Materialism also refers to the pursuit of material things rather than intellectual or spiritual goals. Comforts, pleasures, and wealth become the highest goals in life.

Media literacy The ability to access, analyze, interpret, evaluate, and create many kinds of media.

Medium (plural, **media**) The mode by which something is communicated, for example, radio, television, the Internet.

Mix A predictable combination of feature stories, regular columns, and subject matter that readers come to expect in a given magazine. For example, in a specific women's magazine, readers expect a certain percentage of articles on health, beauty, fashion, dating, and women's issues. They will even expect to find a certain mix of advertising.

Monopoly Ultimate control over a given product or service in a given market that makes price fixing possible or eliminates competition.

Multimedia (also known as **"mixed media"**) Integration of text, graphics, animation, audio, and video within a given product.

Music video A multimedia genre of film that combines songs with videos. Sometimes the video tries to depict the words of the song or shows an artistic or symbolic representation of it. Sometimes the video has little to do with the lyrics, but joins together a song with something desirable to the viewer, such as fantasies of popularity, success, or love. Most videos also include clips of the artists singing and playing the song.

n

Narrowcasting Segmenting the audience based on their radio interests.

National Public Radio (NPR) The only major noncommercial radio network in the United States.

Navigate (also called **"surfing"**) The process of working your way through sites and topics on the Internet.

Net appeal The aesthetics of a site; what makes it appealing or attractive, how it looks and sounds.

News Reports of recent happenings and previously unreported information, locally, nationally, and internationally. Topics range from local charity auctions to a Hollywood actor's recent wedding to the bombing of an embassy.

Newsgroup A part of the Internet that allows users to "post" and "reply to" messages from other users. Newsgroups are usually subject specific, and users can sign up to be members of those in which they have an interest.

News media All the means of communication that provide the public with news: radio, television, newspapers, magazines, the Internet.

Nielsen ratings Ratings of television shows by the Nielsen Media Research Company. The process it uses to determine a program's ratings is explained in Lesson 8.

o

Objective coverage Intended to be factual, without bias.

p

Pan To rotate a camera from side to side to create the impression of a continuous view, or to follow an object with the camera.

Photojournalist A news reporter whose primary job is to photograph news events.

Press The business of creating newspapers, news magazines, news programs, or the people who write for them; journalists.

Product crossover When two or more otherwise unrelated companies join together to market items that benefit both businesses (also called **"cross-merchandising"**).

Propaganda Mass dissemination of information, beliefs, or practices in order to further a particular cause, institution, or person or to disparage another one. Propaganda is usually associated with spreading misleading, distorted, or false information.

Psychographics The study of a target audience's emotional make-up, insecurities, desires, and wants.

Public service announcement (PSA) A message, similar to an ad but not selling a product, created to inform or alert the public. PSAs may promote positive actions and behaviors.

q

Quick cuts A series of very quick shots from many angles that follow the action in a scene. Quick cuts are often used in chase or high-action sequences.

r

Rap The rhythmical pattern of rhyming words used by some musicians, usually accompanied by hip hop background music.

RealAudio Software that allows Internet users to listen to and/or record over 100 radio stations from several countries.

Reliable sources Sources that can be depended upon to make accurate reports or to corroborate statements of fact.

s

Search engine a tool that helps you navigate the Internet. Examples include Yahoo, Lycos, and Webcrawler.

Share The percentage of television sets in use that are tuned to a network during a specific time period.

Shareholder A person who holds stock in a company or corporation.

Sitcom A television comedy series.

Soft news Reporting on human interest stories, such as new information on music groups, beauty pageant queens, and citizens rescuing kittens stuck in trees.

Sound bite A short audio message that encapsulates a key point or main idea.

Spamming Electronically sending inappropriate or unwanted news or mail (**"junk mail"**).

Stereotype An idea or belief held about a person, group, place, etc. that allows for no individuality or differentiation.

Still Either a photograph blown up from a frame of a motion picture film or a photograph taken by a photographer of the production set and used for promotional purposes.

Subjective coverage Opinionated reporting of an event, with a definite bias. Editorials and commentaries fall into this category.

Syndicates Organizations that supply television stations around the country with programming—some of it first-run, some of it rerun.

t

Tag lines Short phrases on a magazine cover that entice potential readers to purchase the publication to read the complete article.

Target audience The audience that the writers and producers have in mind when creating and distributing media messages.

Television market Any geographic area receiving programming from a television program provider.

Theater of the Mind Refers to visual images people create in their minds "to fill in the blanks" between the words and sounds they hear on radio. The effect is similar to the one that occurs when people attend live theater.

u

URL (Uniform Resource Locator) The "address" of a Web site. It begins with http:// All Web sites have a unique URL, just as all phones have a unique phone number and homes have an individual address.

Uses and gratifications research Research conducted by communication scholars that attempts to answer these questions: Why do people select particular media and programming options? What needs are being satisfied through their use of these media and these programs?

v

Viewership The audience (or sometimes the size of that audience) for a television program.

Voice-over A voice that comments or narrates off-camera. For instance, when you do not see the person who is saying the words of a commercial, you are hearing a voice-over.

Voice-over/cutaway During the editing phase, one can add narration over existing visuals on film (the voice-over) or add more visuals to go along with existing sound (a cutaway). This usually occurs when editing film shot from more than one camera.

w

Webmaster The person who maintains a Web site.

World Wide Web (WWW or just **the Web)** When people talk about the Internet, what they are often really referring to is the Web. The WWW is not a network, but rather a hypermedia system that lets you browse the Internet. You navigate by clicking hyperlinks, which display other documents also containing hyperlinks. Web technology lets you access not only text, but also graphics, video, sound, and animations. The next document you see could be housed on a computer next door or half-way around the world.

z

Zoom-in/Zoom-out Zooming refers to changing the framing of a shot. Zooming in moves from a wide-angle shot to a telephoto, or close-up, shot. The effect is to draw attention to the person or object receiving the close-up. Zooming out is the reverse technique, used to place the person or object in a larger context.

Index

t

u

v

w

z